I0888756

Transforming Business Finance in the Digital Era

21st Century Business Management

Transforming Business Finance in the Digital Era

Sanjay Taneja, PhD
Mohammad Kashif, PhD
Ercan Özen, PhD
Luan Vardari, PhD
Editors

APPLE ACADEMIC PRESS

First edition published 2026

Apple Academic Press Inc.
1265 Goldenrod Circle, NE,
Palm Bay, FL 32905 USA

760 Laurentian Drive, Unit 19,
Burlington, ON L7N 0A4, Canada

CRC Press
2385 NW Executive Center Drive,
Suite 320, Boca Raton FL 33431

4 Park Square, Milton Park,
Abingdon, Oxon, OX14 4RN, UK

© 2026 by Apple Academic Press, Inc.

Apple Academic Press exclusively co-publishes with CRC Press, an imprint of Taylor & Francis Group, LLC

Reasonable efforts have been made to publish reliable data and information, but the authors, editors, and publisher cannot assume responsibility for the validity of all materials or the consequences of their use. The authors, editors, and publishers have attempted to trace the copyright holders of all material reproduced in this publication and apologize to copyright holders if permission to publish in this form has not been obtained. If any copyright material has not been acknowledged, please write and let us know so we may rectify in any future reprint.

Except as permitted under U.S. Copyright Law, no part of this book may be reprinted, reproduced, transmitted, or utilized in any form by any electronic, mechanical, or other means, now known or hereafter invented, including photocopying, microfilming, and recording, or in any information storage or retrieval system, without written permission from the publishers.

For permission to photocopy or use material electronically from this work, access www.copyright.com or contact the Copyright Clearance Center, Inc. (CCC), 222 Rosewood Drive, Danvers, MA 01923, 978-750-8400. For works that are not available on CCC please contact mpkbookspermissions@tandf.co.uk

Trademark notice: Product or corporate names may be trademarks or registered trademarks and are used only for identification and explanation without intent to infringe.

For Product Safety Concerns and Information please contact our EU representative GPSR@taylorandfrancis.com Taylor & Francis Verlag GmbH, Kaufingerstraße 24, 80331 München, Germany

Library and Archives Canada Cataloguing in Publication

CIP data on file with Canada Library and Archives

Library of Congress Cataloging-in-Publication Data

CIP data on file with US Library of Congress

ISBN: 978-1-99851-122-8 (hbk)
ISBN: 978-1-99851-123-5 (ebk)

Online: ISSN 2997-8742
Print: ISSN 2997-8734

DOI: 10.1201/9781998511235

21st Century Business Management

BOOK SERIES EDITORS:

Arvind K. Birdie, PhD
Associate Professor, School of Humanities, Social Sciences and Education, G. D Goenka University, Sohna, Gurgaon, India

This book series focuses on the emerging trends and revolution in technology and knowledge in business management. The series presents rich insight and analyses from a diverse range of research and explores new concepts, theories, and implications in the area of contemporary business management.

In the recent years, business management has emerged in a big way and is evolving in new dimensions. With the advancement of technology, globalization, and liberalization, new markets have grown, and businesses have crossed borders and are poised to offer new challenges and opportunities for leaders and organizations. Culture, demography, and new factors, such as increasing sedentary lifestyles, are impacting the development and management of business for entrepreneurs. These impacts can be seen by business organizations becoming more service oriented in reaction to consumers demand for 24/7 service.

With the external and internal business environments changing at such a fast pace, management of business has become an art and science for managers, leaders, and entrepreneurs. More entrepreneurs are launching startups, and employees are opting for protean careers. New technology is being introduced into business management on an almost daily basis. This series explores the exciting myriad aspects of today's business management challenges.

Current Books In The Series:

Employees and Employers in Service Organizations: Emerging Challenges and Opportunities
Editor: Arvind K. Birdie, PhD

The Future of Organizations: Workplace Issues and Practices
Editor: Arvind K. Birdie, PhD

Cross-Cultural Exposure and Connections: Intercultural Learning for Global Citizenship
Editor: Arvind K. Birdie, PhD

Artificial Intelligence Techniques in Human Resource Management
Editors: Soumi Ghosh, PhD, Soumi Majumder, and Santosh Kumar Das, PhD

Reshaping the Business World Post-COVID-19
Editors: Arvind K. Birdie, PhD, and Ruchi Joshi, PhD

Pharma Marketing and Pharmacoeconomics: Opportunities, Challenges, and the Way Forward
Editors: Rishabha Malviya, PhD, Pramod Kumar Srivastava, PhD, Swati Verma, MPharm, and Shashikant Srivastava, PhD

Transforming Business Finance in the Digital Era
Editors: Sanjay Taneja, PhD, Mohammad Kashif, PhD, Ercan Özen, PhD, and Luan Vardari, PhD

Other topics/volumes are planned on these topics:

1. Globalization and Emerging Leadership
2. Positive Psychology and Today's Organizations
3. Changing Consumer Behavior and Organizations
4. The Impact of Technological Advancement on Organizations
5. Emerging Employer and Employee Relations
6. Designing Future Organizations and Emerging Sectors
7. Aging in South Asia and the Impact on Emerging Businesses
8. Issues in Intercultural Management
9. The Role of Spirituality in Management
10. Increasing Workforce Diversity in Organizations
11. Creating Innovation in Organizations
12. Purchasing Power and Happiness in Customers

ABOUT THE BOOK SERIES EDITOR

Arvind K. Birdie, PhD
Visiting Professor, School of Humanities, Social Sciences and Education, G. D. Goenka University, Sohna, Gurgaon, India

Arvind K. Birdie, PhD, has been with various organizations in different roles and has more than eighteen years of experience in higher education. Presently she is a Visiting Professor, School of Humanities, Social Sciences and Education, G. D. Goenka University, Sohna, Gurgaon, India. She was formerly Assistant Director of International Affairs at Amity University, Gurgaon. As an avid reader, she has expertise in teaching various interdisciplinary subjects with equal ease. In addition to academic teaching and training, Dr. Birdie organizes management development programs for corporate and academicians. She is a regular presenter at international and national conferences, and she has published papers in refereed journals. Her areas of interest include leadership, work-life balance, virtual work, and positive psychology. Dr. Birdie has been honored with the Prof. Mrs. Manju Thakur Memorial Award 2016 for Innovative Contributions in Research/Test Construction/Book Publication for her book *Organizational Behavior and Virtual Work: Concepts and Analytical Approaches,* presented at the 52nd National and 21st International Conference of the Indian Academy of Applied Psychology. She is also editor-in-chief of the book series 21st Business Management, published by Apple Academic Press.

About the Editors

Sanjay Taneja, PhD
Associate Professor (Research), Graphic Era University in Dehradun, India; Affiliate Professor, Usak University, Türkiye

Sanjay Taneja, PhD, is an Associate Professor in Research at Graphic Era University in Dehradun, India, and an Affiliate Professor at Usak University in Turkey. He has published extensively in SCOPUS/Web of Science/SCI/ABDC/UGC Care journals, with over 50 publications to date, including research papers, e-books, textbooks, and edited books. He has also published cases in Case Centre, ABDC-B, and Scopus journals, and holds several patents. Dr. Taneja has a strong academic record, with citations on Google Scholar and Scopus, and a history of participation in conferences and faculty development programs. He is frequently invited as a speaker and has served as a session chair, resource person, and judge at various conferences. He is known for his dynamic and positive approach, with a commitment to personal and professional growth. With a focus on areas such as banking regulations, fintech, sustainable finance, and environmental finance, he holds a double master's degree in management with a specialization in Green Finance and Marketing. He completed his PhD in Banking and Finance, and his post-doctoral degree on the impact of the European Green Deal on Carbon Emission in Turkey.

Mohammad Kashif, PhD
Assistant Professor, Department of Management Studies, Graphic Era Deemed to be University, Dehradun, India

Mohammad Kashif, PhD, is an Assistant Professor in the Department of Management Studies at Graphic Era Deemed to be University, Dehradun, India. He is an esteemed academic and researcher specializing in Management, Finance, Financial Economics, and International Business at Graphic Era (Deemed to be University), Dehradun, India. He holds a PhD from Pondicherry Central University and an MCom from Aligarh Muslim

University, having earned his BCom (Hons.) from MJP Rohilkhand University, Bareilly. Recognized with awards such as the Research Excellence Award from IIMT University, Meerut, and the Global Faculty Award 2021 from Aks Education Society, he has received both Senior and Junior Research Fellowships from the University Grants Commission. With publications in WoS, Scopus, and ABDC journals, he has authored textbooks and mentors PhD scholars. Additionally, he actively participates in academic events, delivering keynote lectures and organizing national-level conferences.

Ercan Özen, PhD

Professor (Finance), Department of Finance and Banking, Faculty of Applied Sciences, University of Uşak, Türkiye

Ercan Özen, PhD, is currently a Professor of Finance in the Department of Finance and Banking, Faculty of Applied Sciences at the University of Uşak, Türkiye (Turkey). His current research interests include different aspects of finance. He served as co-editor for books by eminent international publishing houses and has more than 100 publications to his credit. He has also participated in many international conferences. He is board member of five international conferences and workshops. In addition, he is Chair of the International Applied Social Sciences Congress, co-editor of two international journals (*Journal of Corporate Governance, Insurance and Risk Management and Opportunities and Challenges in Sustainability*. Dr. Özen is also a certificated accountant, member of the Agean Finance Association, and member of TEMA (Turkey Combating Soil Erosion, for Reforestation and the Protection of Natural Resources Foundation). He earned his BSc in Public Finance (1994), MSc in Business Accounting (1997), and PhD in Business Finance (2008) from University of Afyon Kocatepe, Turkey.

Luan Vardari, PhD

Assistant Professor of Finance, Faculty of Economics at University, UKSHIN HOTI, Prizren, Kosovo

Luan Vardari, PhD, is an Assistant Professor of Finance in the Faculty of Economics at University "Ukshin Hoti," Prizren, Kosovo. He teaches finance courses at graduate and undergraduate levels. His research interests include financial markets and institutions, portfolio optimizations, and international finance. Dr. Vardari is the founder and editor-in-chief of *Prizren Social Science Journal*. He is also an editor for book chapters and articles in national and international journals. He received his master's degree (MA) in Finance (Balkan Countries Stock Markets) in 2012 from Trakya University and finished his PhD in Business Administration at Trakya University in 2019.

Contents

Contributors

Mohd. Atif Afzal
Center for Distance and Online Education, Aligarh Muslim University, Aligarh, Uttar Pradesh, India

Priyanka Agarwal
Graphic Era (Deemed to be University), Dehradun, Uttarakhand, India

Kapil Kumar Aggarwal
University School of Business, Chandigarh University, Punjab, India

Shahid Alam
Department of Business Administration, College of Administrative and Financial Services, Saudi Electronic University, Kingdom of Saudi Arabia

Nilesh Arora
Chandigarh University, Mohali, Punjab, India

Manju Babu
School of Business, Bahrain Polytechnic, Isa Town, Bahrain

Rubeena Bajwa
Sri Guru Granth Sahib World University, Fatehgarh, Punjab, India

Gunjan Bhatia
Berlin School of Business and Innovation, Berlin, Germany

Karim Darban
University Hassan II Casablanca, Morocco

Harshi Garg
School of Commerce and Management, IIMT University, Meerut, Uttar Pradesh, India

Divya Goel
Jaypee Business School, Jaypee Institute of Information Technology, Noida, Uttar Pradesh, India

Abhay Grover
Chandigarh University, Mohali, Punjab, India

Medha Gupta
University School of Business, Chandigarh University, Mohali, Punjab, India

Neema Gupta
University School of Business, Chandigarh University, Mohali, Punjab, India

Swati Gupta
Chitkara Business School, Chitkara University, Punjab, India

Mostafa El Jai
University Hassan II Casablanca, Morocco

Smail Kabbaj
University Hassan II Casablanca, Morocco

Dixit Kalra
University School of Business, Chandigarh University, Mohali, Punjab, India

Shivani Kapoor
Jaypee Business School, Jaypee Institute of Information Technology, Noida, Uttar Pradesh, India

Mohammad Kashif
Department of Management Studies, Graphic Era (Deemed to be University), Dehradun, Uttarakhand, India

Jaspreet Kaur
University School of Business, Chandigarh University, Mohali, Punjab, India

Deepak Kaushal
Department of Management Studies, Graphic Era (Deemed to be University), Dehradun, Uttarakhand, India

Rizwan Khan
University School of Business, Chandigarh University, Mohali, Punjab, India

Pawan Kumar
University School of Business, Chandigarh University, Punjab, India

Puneet Kumar
School of Commerce and Management, IIMT University, Meerut, Uttar Pradesh, India

K. K. Mishra
University School of Business, Chandigarh University, Mohali, Punjab, India

Ercan Ozen
Department of Banking and Finance, University of Uşak, Türkiye

R. V. Palanivel
Berlin School of Business and Innovation, Berlin, Germany

Poonam
University School of Business, Chandigarh University, Punjab, India

Reepu
University School of Business, Chandigarh University, Mohali, Punjab, India

Shikha Saloni
University School of Business, Chandigarh University, Mohali, Punjab, India

Kapil Sharma
University School of Business, Chandigarh University, Mohali, Punjab, India

Rajat Sharma
Department of Management Studies (DOMS), Graphic Era (Deemed to be University), Dehradun, Uttarakhand, India

Vikas Sharma
University School of Business (Commerce), Chandigarh University, Mohali, Punjab, India

Harpreet Singh
School of Management Studies, Punjabi University, Patiala, Punjab, India

Mandeep Singh
AIT-APEX, Chandigarh University, Mohali, Punjab, India

Mitushi Singh
Jaypee Business School, Jaypee Institute of Information Technology, Noida, Uttar Pradesh, India

Muskan Singh
Department of Management Studies, Graphic Era (Deemed to be University), Dehradun, Uttarakhand, India

Praveen Singh
Department of Management Studies, Graphic Era (Deemed to be University), Dehradun, Uttarakhand, India

Sneha Singh
Department of Management Studies, Graphic Era (Deemed to be University), Dehradun, Uttarakhand, India

Tejinder Singh
University School of Business (Commerce), Chandigarh University, Mohali, Punjab, India

Sanjay Taneja
Department of Management, Graphic Era (Deemed to be University), Dehradun, Uttarakhand, India

Mohd. Taqi
School of Business, Bahrain Polytechnic, Isa Town, Bahrain

Luan Vardari
University "Ukshin Hoti" Prizren, Kosovo

Vivek Verma
Department of Management Studies, Graphic Era (Deemed to be University), Dehradun, Uttarakhand, India

Renu Vij
Department of AIT Management, Chandigarh University, Mohali, Punjab, India

Abbreviations

AC	acceptance criteria
AI	artificial intelligence
AML	Anti-Money Laundering
API	application programming integration
ATMs	automated teller machines
BDA	big data analytics
CCP	customer churn prediction
CCPA	California Consumer Privacy Act
CI	computational intelligence
COIN	contract intelligence
CPC	cost-per-click
CPM	cost-per-thousand impressions
DApps	decentralized applications
DeFi	decentralized finance
ER	eligibility restrictions
ESG	Environmental, Social, and Governance
FP RATE	false positive rates
GDP	Gross Domestic Product
GDPR	General Data Protection Regulation
GRISIL	Green Rating and Information Services of India Ltd.
GTB	gradient tree boosting
HFT	high-frequency trading
IMF	International Monetary Fund
IoT	Internet of Things
kNN	k-nearest neighbors
KYC	Know-Your-Customer

LLMs	large language models
LR	logistic regression
ML	machine learning
NFTs	non-fungible tokens
NLP	natural language processing
NLU	Natural Language Understanding
NSE	National Stock Exchange
PNB	Punjab National Bank
POS	part-of-speech
PSD2	Payment Services Directive 2
RegTech	regulatory technology
RF	random forest
RL	reinforcement learning
ROC	receiver operating characteristics
SERP	search engine results page
SMOTE	synthetic minority oversampling technique
SqLL	squared logistics loss
SVC	support vector classifier
TP RATE	true positive rates
TPB	Theory of Planned Behavior
WCB	workplace cyberbullying
XAI	explainable AI

Preface

The ways in which the operations of various firms are conducted have greatly changed, especially in the context of the currently evolving digital environment, where some sectors, such as banking, operate within this framework. The identified areas and their development also influence the financial industry's speed of transition and the adoption of innovative technologies, including machine learning and artificial intelligence (AI and ML). The goal of this book, *Transforming Business Finance in the Digital Era*, is to analyze these developments through a definitive assessment of how AI and ML have influenced today's business finance processes.

This book is the result of collaboration among a team of authors, complemented by the involvement of specialists from other disciplines. Each chapter explores an important area in finance, such as the opportunities and risks that may arise from fintech or the ethical issues connected with artificial intelligence. Key contributors are leaders in their fields, bringing extensive experience and diverse perspectives for readers.

This work will be beneficial for specialists, scientists, and learners engaged in studying the shift in finance within the digital environment. It is our desire to equip our readers with the knowledge needed to thrive in this ever-evolving landscape by shedding light on current issues and establishing future trends.

—Sanjay Taneja
Graphic Era (Deemed to be University),
Dehradun, Uttarakhand, India

Introduction

A modern-day impressive formation embraced by the finance industry is the inclusion of artificial intelligence (AI) and machine learning (ML). These technologies are changing the manner in which financial services are delivered, investment schemes are structured, and consumers are managed. To deconstruct this transition, *Transforming Business Finance in the Digital Era* provides a conceptual analysis of AI and ML uses and their impact on business finance.

The authors introduce the fundamental concepts of machine learning in finance in Chapter 1, titled *"Unlocking Financial Intelligence: Navigating the Machine Learning Landscape in Finance."* This chapter lays the groundwork for understanding the intersection of machine learning and financial intelligence, setting the stage for subsequent discussions in the book.

Chapter 2, *"AI Ethics: From Search Engines to AI Assistants, Analyzing the Transformation of Internet Browsing and Its Consequences for Content Websites and Online Advertising,"* explores the ethical considerations surrounding artificial intelligence (AI), particularly in relation to internet browsing, content websites, and online advertising. This chapter examines how AI has transformed digital interactions and the ethical challenges that arise from these advancements.

As the book progresses, it explores the opportunities and challenges that modern investors face while delving deeper into the ever-changing world of investments. The survey of the literature on workplace cyberbullying offers a critical examination of this expanding problem in the digital workplace and emphasizes the necessity of a methodical approach.

Fintech innovations are thoroughly examined, highlighting both the fascinating advancements and the challenges that remain to be solved. The book also explores the nexus between machine learning and social commerce, providing insights into how these domains are transforming finance.

While practical applications of AI and ML in financial services are comprehensively addressed, readers are given a thorough glimpse of the academic scene through a bibliometric tour of machine learning research.

In Indian finance, the conversation surrounding AI and ML offers a regional perspective, emphasizing the current landscape and future trajectory.

Another important area of emphasis is sustainable financing, with a dedicated chapter evaluating client understanding and involvement in green banking. A thorough examination of predictive analytics is provided, emphasizing its potential for use in market risk management, which is one of the most promising applications of AI in finance.

The last few chapters offer useful insights into machine learning applications, ranging from anticipating consumer buying intents to forecasting client turnover in the motor insurance sector. A provocative analysis of gender bias in investing behavior and how machine learning might assist in overcoming these biases is included in the book's conclusion.

Transforming Business Finance in the Digital Era offers a comprehensive understanding of how AI and ML are influencing the future of finance through these varied topics. By embracing new tools and utilizing them to spur innovation and expansion in their financial practices, we hope that this book will inspire readers.

CHAPTER 1

Unlocking Financial Intelligence: Navigating the Machine Learning Landscape in Finance

MOHAMMAD KASHIF,[1] SHAHID ALAM,[2] PUNEET KUMAR,[3] and HARSHI GARG[3,*]

[1]*Department of Management Studies, Graphic Era (Deemed to be University), Dehradun, Uttarakhand, India*

[2]*Department of Business Administration, College of Administrative and Financial Services, Saudi Electronic University, Kingdom of Saudi Arabia*

[3]*School of Commerce and Management, IIMT University, Meerut, Uttar Pradesh, India*

**Corresponding author.*

ABSTRACT

Financial intelligence is defined as the capacity to comprehend and manage one's financial affairs successfully. It involves a combination of perception, expertise, and knowledge that enables individuals to make economically prudent financial decisions. On the other hand, artificial intelligence (AI) in computing refers to the creation of algorithms that allow computers to perform functions typically requiring human cognitive abilities. These functions include reasoning, analysis, problem-solving, perception, language processing, and, in specific instances, decision-making. Intelligent technology aims to develop programs or devices that can mimic brain functions and adapt to various scenarios, becoming increasingly beneficial to the world of finance over time. Data mining, a component of AI, relies

Transforming Business Finance in the Digital Era.
Sanjay Taneja, Mohammad Kashif, Ercan Özen, and Luan Vardari (Eds.)
© 2026 Apple Academic Press, Inc. Co-published with CRC Press (Taylor & Francis)

DOI: 10.1201/9781998511235-1

on mathematical models and algorithms that enable systems to extract information from data and make decisions or predictions without explicit programming. This chapter outlines how machine learning is playing a significant role in the finance sector. The fundamental concepts and positive impacts of predictive modeling for businesses are also addressed.

1.1 INTRODUCTION

Financial intelligence entails a combination of attitudes, abilities, and knowledge that empower individuals to make wise financial decisions (Serov and Vasiliev, 2023). It is the capacity to comprehend and successfully manage one's financial affairs. Financial literacy, budgeting, investing, risk management, debt management, economic awareness, and financial planning are essential components of financial intelligence (Ch et al., 2020). Developing financial literacy is a lifelong process that often requires education, experience, and a commitment to continuous learning about personal finance (Januszewski and Kujawski, 2021). Individuals with high financial intelligence are better equipped to make decisions that support their financial well-being and navigate the complexities of the financial world (Doguc, 2021; Malhotra, 2015).

The application of machine learning (ML) and neural networks in economic forecasting represents a significant breakthrough in the field of finance, with profound implications for the financial well-being of Americans, merchants, and banking institutions. The traditional landscape of financial forecasting, previously dominated by classical statistical methods, has been transformed by the emergence of advanced ML and artificial intelligence (AI) techniques that offer superior accuracy and efficiency in predicting market fluctuations and asset valuations.

Machine learning, particularly advanced forms such as neural networks, has revolutionized the capabilities of financial market analysts. These methods are now widely used for various purposes, including assessing asset values, analyzing market conditions, identifying potential investments, and optimizing portfolios (Doguc, 2021; Malhotra, 2015).

1.1.1 THE THEORY OF EVOLUTION: FROM CONVENTIONAL TO AI INTEGRATION

The transformation of financial forecasting in the United States markets for financial products has been marked by a significant shift from conventional methods to the integration of AI and ML (Ch et al., 2020). This transition reflects a broader trend of technological and digital advancement in financial services, fundamentally altering the landscape of financial decision-making and evaluation.

Traditionally, financial predictions and subsequent evaluations were primarily quantitative, relying on limited datasets and human expertise (Trapletti and Hornik, 2017). Methods based largely on fundamental and technical analysis required financial assessment reports and market trend evaluations to predict expected market activity. However, the advent of AI and ML has introduced an era characterized by sophisticated software analysis, enabling deeper insights and enhanced predictive capabilities (in 't Hout et al., 2018; Mathis and Almarzoqi, 2022).

Despite these advancements, the transition from conventional forecasting to AI-driven prediction has not been without challenges (Schwartz et al., 2013; Ziritt Trejo et al., 2018). Issues related to data performance, model interpretability, and regulatory concerns remain key obstacles. Updating the skill sets of financial professionals and establishing standardized guidelines for AI-driven algorithms in the industry are critical priorities (Catania, 2021). Ultimately, the shift from traditional modeling to AI in stock markets represents an evolution into a new era of financial analysis and decision-making (Januszewski and Kujawski, 2021; Figure 1.1).

1.1.2 REVOLUTIONARY EFFECT ON THE FINANCIAL SECTOR

The banking and insurance industry is experiencing a significant turning point. The business sector has undergone major modifications in recent years, primarily due to the rapid growth and adoption of new technologies, including artificial intelligence (AI), such as large language models (LLMs) (Kashif, Thiyagarajan et al., 2017). Emerging technologies and public opinion have facilitated the adoption of novel technologies in commercial banking, with the COVID-19 pandemic further accelerating these changes (Doguc, 2021; Januszewski and Kujawski, 2021; Thekkethil et al., 2021; Vedder et al., 2016).

Building on this upward trend, the development of computer vision in the financial sector provides companies with opportunities to significantly increase efficiency while reducing operational expenses by engaging with and serving individuals in entirely new ways. AI has proven to be profitable in banking and securities, enabling enterprises to streamline tasks, enhance client interactions, and identify potential risks (Kashif et al., 2023).

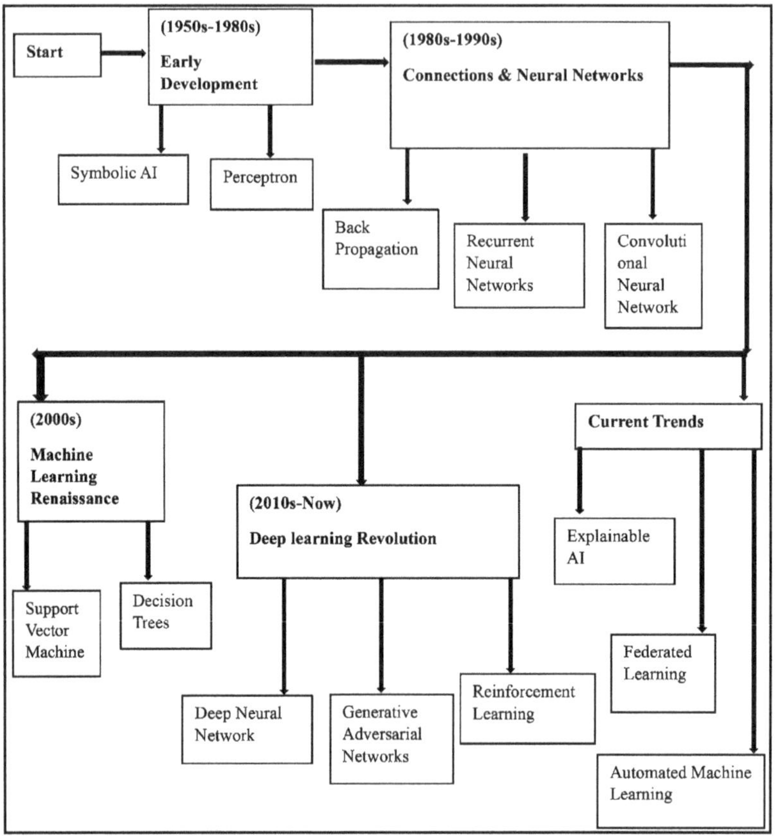

FIGURE 1.1 Significant milestone in the evolution of machine learning.

Source: Author's compilation.

TABLE 1.1 Advancements in Machine Learning

Years	Description
1950s	Early statistical methods
1980s	Algorithmic trading
1990s	Neural networks
2000s	Growing adoption of ML
2008	Financial crisis
2010s	Rise of robotics
2018	AML and compliance
2020s	Continued advancements in ML

Source: Authors' compilation.

This chapter summarizes the significant achievements on the path we anticipate will lead the finance and banking industry toward improved consumer interactions, greater market dominance, and enhanced economic growth by leveraging the limitless possibilities of AI (Vedder et al., 2016). Data mining has driven major advancements in finance and banking, disrupting conventional workflows and decision-making processes. The following list of events highlights key inflection points and innovations in the application of machine learning to economics.

The use of data mining in accounting has progressed beyond basic mathematical methods to advanced techniques capable of processing vast databases in real time. Applications include the digitalization of spending approaches, fraud detection, risk management, and enhanced client service. Ongoing technological advancements and the increasing use of deep learning across various financial transactions will continue to shape the banking sector.

1.1.3 OBJECTIVES OF THE STUDY

The primary objective of this study is to thoroughly investigate the combined use of ML and AI in financial prediction, examining technological innovations, identifying challenges, and assessing the broader implications for consumers in the finance sector. The chapter's specific aims are:

- To understand and compare the most innovative ML algorithms available today.
- To examine the progression of ML in financial prediction.
- To assess the challenges of AI in automated economic forecasting.

1.2 LITERATURE REVIEW

1.2.1 FUNDAMENTAL PRINCIPLES OF ML

The application of ML in economics is becoming increasingly prevalent due to the demand for more advanced and efficient analytical methods in a complex and rapidly evolving business environment. The key concepts of deep learning in economics involve using computational algorithms to analyze vast datasets, identify patterns, and predict market dynamics and activities (Januszewski and Kujawski, 2021).

Another fundamental aspect of AI in banking is the classification and organization of financial information using both fundamental and technical indicators. Fundamental indicators assess a business's financial condition, competitive advantage, and economic factors, while technical metrics analyze statistical trends based on market behavior and price fluctuations. Doguc (2021) and Malhotra (2015) discuss the application of data mining models in categorizing financial indexes.

1.2.2 OVERVIEW OF MACHINE LEARNING (ML) METHODS

ML methods have become essential in economic forecasting, enabling sophisticated tools to analyze market trends and assess stock values (Schwartz et al., 2013; Ziritt Trejo et al., 2018). The application of various ML techniques has transformed the way economic data is structured and interpreted, providing analysts and investors with more precise and efficient methods for predicting market movements (Ch et al., 2020).

Evaluating different ML methods in economic forecasting is crucial for determining which models are most effective. Studies such as those conducted by Ch et al. (2020), Doguc (2021), and Malhotra (2015) provide substantial insights into the advantages and limitations of various ML algorithms, helping traders and investors select the most suitable models for their specific needs.

Ultimately, an overview of ML methods in economic forecasting reveals a comprehensive range of tools for market assessment. From predictive models to advanced AI-driven programs, ML offers a robust foundation for analyzing and forecasting market dynamics. As the field continues to evolve, the application of these methods is likely to become even more widespread, enhancing the accuracy and efficiency of economic forecasting.

1.3 RESEARCH METHOD

The subsections outline the approaches used to conduct a comprehensive literature review and content analysis on the subject. This methodology is designed to facilitate an in-depth and systematic examination of relevant research, adhering to established criteria for selection, evaluation, and analysis.

1.3.1 DATA SOURCES

The primary sources of information for this study include academic databases, research papers, and conference proceedings that have made significant contributions to the fields of finance, robotics, and neural networks. Key sources such as IEEE Xplore, ScienceDirect, and the Web of Science were extensively reviewed.

1.3.2 SEARCH STRATEGY

A thorough retrieval approach has been developed for finding documents on AI and ML in economic modeling. To ensure a comprehensive collection of relevant literature, the search method included terms such as "machine learning" and "artificial intelligence." To focus on recent advancements and trends, the search was limited to English-language publications from 2012 to 2024.

1.3.3 SELECTION CRITERIA

The decision-making approach comprised a two-phase assessment. Initially, abstracts and titles were reviewed using the inclusion and exclusion criteria to identify potentially relevant research. Full-text articles were then obtained and examined for eligibility. Conflicts in the process were resolved through discussion or consultation with an additional reviewer to ensure impartiality and consistency in selecting studies for review.

1.4 DATA ANALYSIS

Metadata was examined through qualitative methods, focusing on identifying, categorizing, and summarizing issues related to the advancements, challenges, and implications of AI-powered economic forecasting. This involved an in-depth analysis of findings from relevant literature, emphasizing insights into the application, effectiveness, and regulatory implications of AI and ML in the financial industry. The research process also included a statistical assessment of the literature, such as generating time-based statistics and analyzing the distribution of research findings across various focus areas. The conclusions from the data analysis have been synthesized to provide a comprehensive overview of the current state of AI and ML in financial forecasting, highlighting key trends, challenges, and potential future directions.

1.4.1 ESSENTIAL APPLICATION OF DEEP LEARNING IN FINANCE

Machine learning systems enable humans to analyze vast amounts of data while identifying critical trends within it. Such insights can be used to enhance business operations, make more informed decisions, and contribute to forecasting opportunities. The financial services industry utilizes these tools to optimize rates, reduce the potential for human error, eliminate tedious processes, and more effectively assess customer behavior.

1.4.2 ALGORITHMIC TRADING

Algorithmic trading refers to the use of analytics to improve trading decisions. Typically, investors employ statistical frameworks that monitor market trends and trade activity in real-time to identify patterns that could cause security prices to rise or fall. These frameworks consist of structured guidelines based on various factors, such as timing, costs, volume, and other variables, to execute trades without direct broker involvement. Unlike individual traders, automated algorithmic trading systems can analyze vast amounts of data and execute thousands of trades per day. Machine learning facilitates lightning-fast trading decisions, providing traders with a competitive advantage over traditional methods.

1.4.3 FRAUD DETECTION

Fraud is a massive challenge for institutions and financial/banking services entities, resulting in thousands of dollars in costs annually. Typically, insurance companies uphold a significant portion of their client information globally, which leads to the probability of a security incident. Developments in technology have made forgery in the banking sector recognized as an imminent risk to critical data. Originally, systems to identify fraud evolved around a set of criteria that newer attackers could easily evade. As a consequence, numerous companies now deploy algorithms to identify and prevent illegitimate banking transactions. AI checks enormous data for specific anomalies or errors, which are generally flagged for further analysis by security analysts.

1.4.4 PORTFOLIO MANAGEMENT

AI-assisted web-based applications are designed using data mining to provide automated economic guidance to participants. These applications utilize technology to develop a portfolio of securities based on an investor's interests and risk tolerance. Automated advisors maintain modest account limits and are generally more cost-effective than conventional portfolio managers. When using automated advisors, users must input their financial details or investment goals into the system, which then selects the most suitable investment options with the highest potential return.

1.4.5 LOAN UNDERWRITING

Corporations in the financial sector possess vast amounts of customer data, which can be used to train machine learning models to automate the qualification process. Machine learning algorithms can make rapid decisions on underwriting and credit rating, saving companies both time and money that would otherwise be spent on manual processing. Data analysts can develop models to analyze billions of financial documents, identify correlations, detect anomalies, and determine whether an applicant qualifies for funding or insurance policies.

1.4.6 CREDIT SCORING

Credit scoring refers to a three-digit number, typically ranging from 300 to 850, that represents an individual's financial risk or likelihood of repaying debts on time. Employers and lenders assess credit scores as one of the key factors in deciding whether to approve a loan application. It is a statistical evaluation used by financial institutions and creditors to determine the financial standing of individuals or small businesses.

1.5 ADVANTAGES OF MACHINE LEARNING IN FINANCE

Machine learning is a branch of computer science that analyzes vast amounts of data to identify patterns, generate predictions and recommendations, and improve efficiency over time. The ability to enhance decision-making accuracy and speed while operating at scale has the potential to revolutionize the banking sector—and it is already doing so. Some of its key benefits are discussed in subsections.

1.5.1 REDUCING HUMAN ERRORS

Human errors are inevitable. However, in the banking industry, even minor mistakes can have severe consequences, resulting in billions in penalties. By integrating or enhancing machine learning approaches, manual errors can be significantly reduced, ensuring more accurate data analysis.

1.5.2 TIME EFFICIENCY

Machine learning requires less manual effort and delivers immediate results. It can accelerate traditional processes, facilitate complex decision-making, and enhance the accuracy of reliable predictions.

1.5.3 COST-EFFECTIVENESS

The fields of ML and AI continue to evolve over time. Apart from initial investments and operational costs, these technologies can prove to be cost-effective in the long run, offering significant financial benefits.

1.5.4 REDUCED WORKLOAD

Data mining can handle complex, repetitive, and time-consuming tasks, reducing the overall workload and minimizing tedious manual efforts.

1.5.5 FREE FROM DISCRIMINATION

Compared to human reasoning, neural network techniques are often more objective in processing information and making decisions. Therefore, AI-driven algorithms help ensure unbiased and accurate outcomes, which are crucial for the banking sector.

1.6 IMPORTANT IDEAS IN FINANCE-RELATED MACHINE LEARNING

The following are key concepts in machine learning for finance. Machine learning is a fascinating field that enables technology to extract insights and make data-driven decisions. In machine learning, there are three primary types of learning: supervised, unsupervised, and reinforcement learning. This chapter will explain these concepts in clear terms, using examples to illustrate their differences and advantages (Figure 1.2).

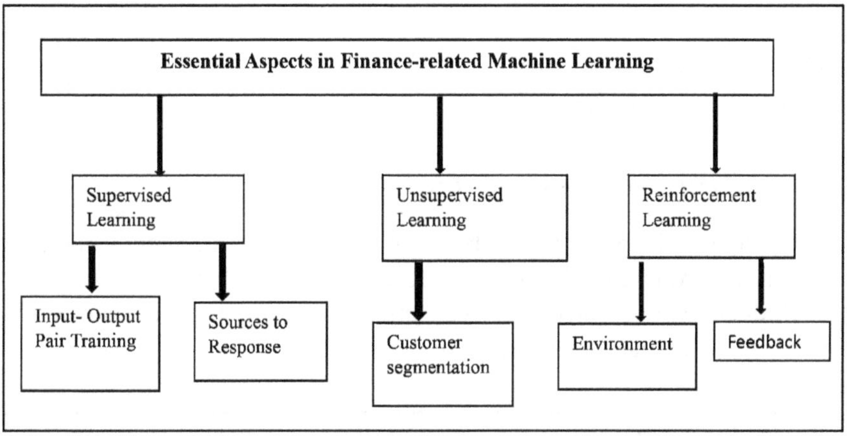

FIGURE 1.2 Key concepts in machine learning.

Source: Authors' compilation.

1.6.1 SUPERVISED LEARNING

Supervised learning is similar to an instructor guiding a student. In this approach, the model is trained using a labeled dataset, where each instance includes input features and corresponding target values. The goal of the model is to learn a mapping from inputs to outputs.

1.6.2 UNSUPERVISED LEARNING

Unsupervised learning is comparable to allowing a child to explore a room full of objects without instructions. In this method, the model is provided with an unlabeled dataset and tasked with identifying patterns, structures, or trends within the data on its own (Figure 1.3).

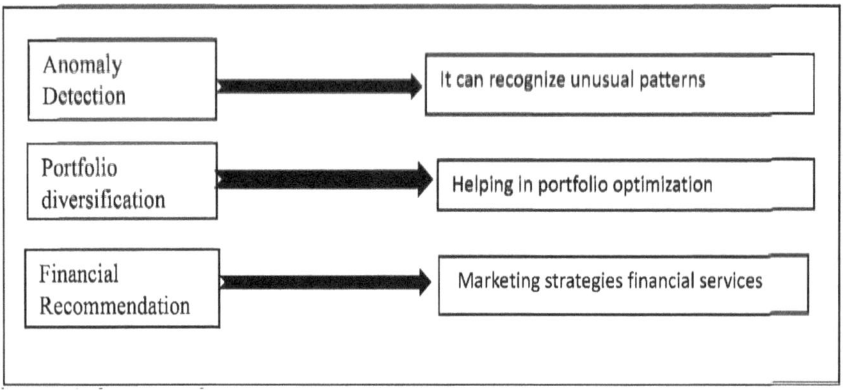

FIGURE 1.3 Unsupervised learning.

Source: Authors' compilation.

1.6.3 REINFORCEMENT LEARNING

Reinforcement learning is similar to training a pet. The model interacts with its environment and receives feedback in the form of rewards or penalties based on its actions. Over time, it learns to make decisions that maximize its overall benefit (Figure 1.4).

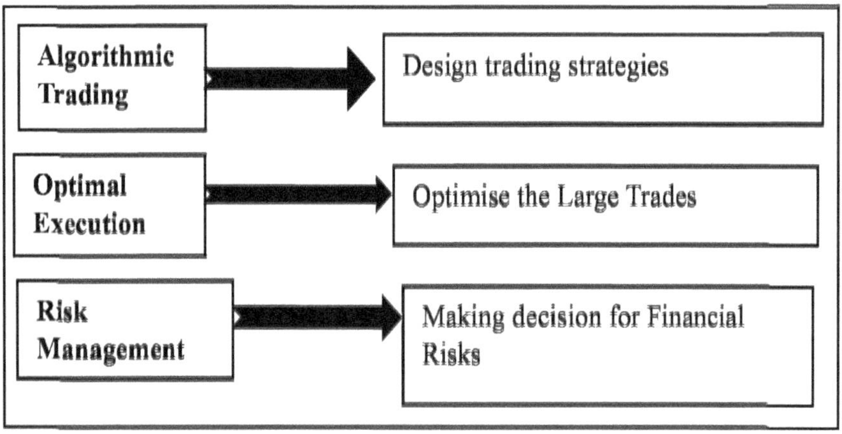

FIGURE 1.4 Reinforcement learning.

Source: Authors' compilation.

1.7 CONCLUSION

The field of machine learning, a branch of computer science, focuses on developing algorithms and techniques that enable machines to acquire knowledge from data and generate insights or predictions without requiring programming skills. The fundamental principle underlying artificial intelligence (AI) is its ability to identify patterns, develop new ideas, and improve efficiency as it processes and interprets increasing amounts of banking data. Machine learning techniques are widely applied across various industries, including sales, finance, and healthcare. Companies use these techniques to address challenges such as audio and image recognition, natural language processing, and autonomous decision-making. As technology evolves, predictive modeling will play an increasingly critical role in shaping automated developments and strategies across a broad spectrum of industries.

The potential applications range from enhanced risk management and fraud detection to robotic strategies and improved client interactions. The rising adoption of automated financial advisors—computerized, data-driven systems that provide financial advice based on client behavior and risk tolerance—is another example of deep learning's impact on the banking sector. Overall, AI is transforming the banking industry by increasing efficiency, reducing risks, and fostering innovation across various financial services.

Financial literacy refers to the ability to effectively recognize, manage, and understand one's financial situation. It encompasses knowledge of finance and banking, budgeting, fund allocation, risk management, debt handling, economic awareness, and financial strategy. Numerous applications of algorithmic learning have emerged in the banking industry, influencing how corporations manage risks, analyze data, and make decisions. Data mining plays a crucial role in various banking operations, including credit assessment, customer service, risk identification and management, automated investing, and anti-money laundering efforts. AI has significantly transformed the banking sector, ushering in a new era of transparency, efficiency, and innovation.

KEYWORDS

- **artificial intelligence**
- **data mining**
- **decision-making**
- **financial intelligence**
- **financial literacy**
- **machine learning**
- **neural networks**

REFERENCES

Catania, L. J. (2021). The evolution of artificial intelligence (AI). In *Foundations of Artificial Intelligence in Healthcare and Bioscience*. https://doi.org/10.1016/b978-0-12-824477-7.00002-x.

Ch, R., Gadekallu, T. R., Abidi, M. H., & Al-Ahmari, A. (2020). Computational system to classify cybercrime offenses using machine learning. *Sustainability (Switzerland)*, *12*(10). https://doi.org/10.3390/SU12104087.

Doguc, O. (2021). Applications of robotic process automation in finance and accounting. *Beykent Üniversitesi Fen ve Mühendislik Bilimleri Dergisi*, *14*(1). https://doi.org/10.20854/bujse.906795.

in 't Hout, K., Itkin, A., Sydow, L. von, & Toivanen, J. (2018). Special issue—Computational and algorithmic finance. *Journal of Computational Science*, *24*, 180–181. https://doi.org/10.1016/J.JOCS.2017.12.009.

Januszewski, A., & Kujawski, J. (2021). Best practices in robotic process automation in global business services. *27th Annual Americas Conference on Information Systems (AMCIS)*.

Kashif, M., Shajar, S. N., Singhal, N., & Kumar, P. (2023). Achieving sustainable investment practices through green finance: Challenges and opportunities. In *Sustainable Investments in Green Finance*. https://doi.org/10.4018/979-8-3693-1388-6.ch016.

Kashif, M., Sridharan, P., & Thiyagarajan, S. (2017). Factors affecting international reserves with special reference to India. *Vision: The Journal of Business Perspective*, *21*(4), 339–349. https://doi.org/10.1177/0972262917733157.

Kashif, M., Thiyagarajan, S., & Sridharan, P. (2017). Dynamics of Algeria's international reserves. *African Journal of Economic and Management Studies*, *8*(4). https://doi.org/10.1108/AJEMS-11-2016-0179.

Malhotra, Y. (2015). Cybersecurity & cyber-finance risk management: Strategies, tactics, operations, &, intelligence: Enterprise risk management to model risk management:

Understanding vulnerabilities, threats, & risk mitigation (Presentation slides). *SSRN Electronic Journal*. https://doi.org/10.2139/ssrn.2693886.

Mathis, F. J., & Almarzoqi, R. M. (2022). Global innovation, finance, and international commerce. In *Global Innovation, Finance, and International Commerce*. https://doi.org/10.4324/9781003024675.

Schwartz, R. A., Byrne, J. A., & Schnee, G. (2013). The quality of our financial markets: Taking stock of where we stand. In *The Quality of Our Financial Markets: Taking Stock of Where We Stand*. https://doi.org/10.1007/978-1-4614-5592-9.

Serov, E. R., & Vasiliev, S. A. (2023). Application of quantum technologies in banking. *Economics and Management, 29*(3). https://doi.org/10.35854/1998-1627-2023-3-248-255.

Thekkethil, M. S., Shukla, V. K., Beena, F., & Chopra, A. (2021). Robotic process automation in banking and finance sector for loan processing and fraud detection. *2021 9th International Conference on Reliability, Infocom Technologies and Optimization (Trends and Future Directions), ICRITO 2021*. https://doi.org/10.1109/ICRITO51393.2021.9596076.

Trapletti, A., & Hornik, K. (2017). tseries: Time series analysis and computational finance (*R Package Version 0.10-42*).

Vedder, R., Welters, M., Mints, A., & Ramkhelawan, A. (2016). Robotic process automation in the finance function of the future. *Ernst & Young*.

Ziritt Trejo, G., Taboada Hernandez, R., Moreno, Z., & Isabel Castellano, M. (2018). Public management and sustainable development: Expression of social responsibility. *Innovation Management and Education Excellence Through Vision 2020, Vols. I–XI.*

CHAPTER 2

AI Ethics: From Search Engines to AI Assistants, Analyzing the Transformation of Internet Browsing and Its Consequences for Content Websites and Online Advertising

KARIM DARBAN,* SMAIL KABBAJ, and MOSTAFA EL JAI

University Hassan II Casablanca, Morocco

*Corresponding author.

ABSTRACT

The present chapter delves into the ethical implications of AI assistants on the online advertisement industry. It argues that the ascent of AI assistants fosters an unethical dismantling of classic content websites, resulting in diminished user traffic and engagement. Furthermore, it highlights the ethical concerns surrounding content ownership and attribution, as AI assistants bypass traditional channels and provide information without due recognition. The exploration of these issues seeks to shed light on the intricate relationship between AI assistants and the online advertisement industry, urging stakeholders to consider ethical frameworks that promote fairness, transparency, and sustainability within this evolving landscape.

2.1 INTRODUCTION

The online advertising industry has evolved into a substantial multi-billion-dollar sector, experiencing rapid growth in recent years. In 2022, the global market for online advertisements reached a value of $614 billion,

Transforming Business Finance in the Digital Era.
Sanjay Taneja, Mohammad Kashif, Ercan Özen, and Luan Vardari (Eds.)
© 2026 Apple Academic Press, Inc. Co-published with CRC Press (Taylor & Francis)

DOI: 10.1201/9781998511235-2

with experts projecting further expansion to $910 billion by 2027 (Statista Market Insights, 2023). At the core of this industry lies the principle of the "attention economy," whereby advertisers compensate websites to showcase their ads, aiming to capture users' attention and increase the likelihood of product or service consumption (Asdemir et al., 2012).

Conventionally, users access online content via search engines, which provide a list of relevant results based on search queries. Upon selecting a link, users are redirected to the original website hosting the desired content (Ledford, 2015). Simultaneously, search engines generate revenue by placing advertisements in search results, while websites generate revenue through web banners typically positioned in visible areas of the page (Kashif et al., 2017; Tavor, 2011).

The emergence of artificial intelligence (AI) has profoundly impacted various industries, including online advertising. AI-powered virtual assistants, such as ChatGPT, Bard, and Bing Chat, have gained popularity and transformed the landscape of online content consumption. Previously, users relied on search engines to locate and access content, leading them to original websites. Consequently, content creators could generate revenue through advertisements on their platforms. However, AI assistants now offer direct content delivery to users, eliminating the need for redirection to the original websites (Choi & Drumwright, 2021). While this shift enhances user convenience, it disrupts traditional exposure to advertisements and poses challenges for content creators seeking sustainable revenue generation.

The rise of AI assistants presents several implications for the online advertising industry that warrant further exploration. First, the increasing use of AI assistants contributes to a decline in traffic and user engagement on traditional content websites. Users now rely more on AI assistants for instant, curated information, reducing their interactions with traditional websites. This trend presents a significant challenge for content providers who depend on web traffic and user engagement for sustainability (Bauer & Dubljević, 2020; Kashif et al., 2023).

Second, the conventional revenue model—reliant on advertisements placed on content websites—faces disruption as AI assistants bypass traditional content delivery channels. Since users access information directly from AI assistants, exposure to advertisements diminishes, leading to decreased revenue for content creators. This financial strain may compromise the viability and quality of online content, as creators struggle to sustain their operations.

Third, the increasing reliance on AI assistants raises profound ethical concerns regarding content ownership and attribution. With AI assistants providing information directly to users, original content creators may receive inadequate recognition or compensation for their intellectual property. Issues of attribution and fair use become more complex as AI algorithms curate and deliver information without explicit consent or proper acknowledgment of the creators (Mishra & Kern-Stone, 2023).

This chapter explores the ethical implications of AI assistants on the online advertising industry. It argues that the rise of AI assistants fosters an unethical dismantling of classic content websites, resulting in diminished user traffic and engagement. Furthermore, it highlights ethical concerns surrounding content ownership and attribution, as AI assistants bypass traditional channels and provide information without due recognition. By examining these issues, this chapter aims to shed light on the intricate relationship between AI assistants and the online advertising industry, urging stakeholders to consider ethical frameworks that promote fairness, transparency, and sustainability within this evolving digital landscape.

2.2 THE RISE OF AI ASSISTANTS

2.2.1 OVERVIEW OF ARTIFICIAL INTELLIGENCE AND AI ASSISTANTS (E.G., CHATGPT, BARD, BING CHAT)

Recent advancements in AI have led to the development of AI assistants that have revolutionized how users interact with technology. AI assistants, such as Google Assistant, ChatGPT, Bard, and Bing Chat, are sophisticated software applications designed to simulate human-like conversations and provide intelligent responses to user queries. These AI assistants leverage natural language processing (NLP) and machine learning techniques to understand user inputs and generate contextually relevant outputs (Canbek & Mutlu, 2016).

The evolution of AI assistants can be traced back to early chatbots and virtual agents (Underwood, 2017). However, recent advancements in deep learning and neural network architectures have significantly enhanced AI assistants' capabilities. Large-scale pretraining techniques, such as transformer-based models like Generative Pretrained Transformer 3 (GPT-3), have dramatically improved AI assistants' ability to process and generate human-like text (Yuan et al., 2022).

AI assistants are typically deployed as web or mobile applications, allowing users to engage in interactive conversations through text-based interfaces. Users can pose questions, request information, or seek assistance on a wide range of topics, and AI assistants respond by generating coherent and contextually appropriate answers. These assistants can handle various conversational scenarios, including providing factual information, offering recommendations, assisting with tasks, and engaging in casual conversations.

The technology powering AI assistants relies on deep learning models trained on vast amounts of text data from diverse sources, including books, articles, websites, and other textual resources. Through extensive pretraining and fine-tuning processes, AI assistants acquire linguistic knowledge, semantic understanding, and even some degree of world knowledge, allowing them to generate relevant and coherent responses (Maedche et al., 2019).

AI assistants employ sophisticated natural language understanding (NLU) algorithms to parse and interpret user inputs. These algorithms break down user queries into constituent parts, extract important keywords, and analyze syntactic and semantic structures to determine the user's intent. Subsequently, AI assistants leverage learned knowledge and reasoning capabilities to generate appropriate responses (Danaher, 2018). This process includes considering context, disambiguating ambiguous terms, and providing accurate and informative answers.

A defining feature of AI assistants is their ability to continuously learn and adapt from user interactions. These assistants use reinforcement learning techniques, where user feedback refines future responses. By collecting vast amounts of conversational data and leveraging advanced machine learning algorithms, AI assistants continually improve their language models, enhancing their linguistic fluency, accuracy, and overall conversational performance (Choi & Drumwright, 2021).

Additionally, AI assistants integrate with various external services and application programming interfaces (APIs), enabling them to fetch real-time data, perform tasks, and provide comprehensive and personalized experiences. They can access information from online databases, weather services, news feeds, e-commerce platforms, and more, making them versatile tools for information retrieval and interaction (Uysal et al., 2022).

The growing adoption of AI assistants can be attributed to their convenience, efficiency, and adaptability. These assistants offer a more natural and intuitive way to access information, eliminating the need for traditional search queries and providing immediate responses within a conversational framework. Users can engage in back-and-forth exchanges, ask clarifications, and pose follow-up questions, creating a more interactive and personalized experience compared to traditional search engine interactions.

2.2.2 INCREASING POPULARITY AND USAGE

The proliferation of AI assistants, such as ChatGPT, Bard, and Bing Chat, has been accompanied by a substantial increase in their popularity and widespread usage. Several key factors have contributed to the appeal and utility of these AI-powered conversational agents:

1. **Enhanced User Experience:** AI assistants have transformed how users interact with technology by offering a more intuitive and seamless experience. Traditional search engines require users to formulate precise queries and sift through numerous search results to find relevant information. In contrast, AI assistants allow users to engage in natural language conversations, facilitating more flexible and context-aware interactions. This conversational interface simplifies information retrieval, making it more accessible and efficient (Lv et al., 2021).
2. **Improved Language Understanding and Generation:** One of the most significant advancements in AI assistant technology is the ability to understand and generate human-like language. Through sophisticated NLP algorithms and deep learning models, AI assistants can interpret complex sentence structures, handle ambiguous queries, and generate coherent and contextually relevant responses. Continuous training and fine-tuning of these language models have resulted in significant improvements in linguistic fluency, semantic understanding, and overall conversational accuracy (Gratch & Fast, 2022).
3. **Personalization and Contextualization:** AI assistants excel at delivering personalized experiences by leveraging user data and preferences. They learn from previous interactions, adapt to individual user needs, and tailor their responses accordingly. By capturing user context and history, AI assistants provide recommendations and information that align with the user's interests, enhancing engagement and satisfaction (Malodia et al., 2021).

4. **Multi-Modal Capabilities:** AI assistants have expanded their capabilities beyond text-based interactions to support multi-modal experiences. They now process and generate not only textual content but also images, videos, and audio. This evolution allows users to engage with AI assistants through voice commands, visual input, and interactive media, catering to diverse user preferences and providing a more immersive experience (Canbek & Mutlu, 2016).
5. **Integration with Smart Devices and Applications:** The seamless integration of AI assistants with smartphones, smart speakers, wearables, and other Internet of Things (IoT) devices has significantly contributed to their popularity. AI assistants also support third-party applications and services through APIs, enabling users to perform various tasks, such as ordering food, booking rides, managing calendars, and controlling smart home devices (Choi & Drumwright, 2021).
6. **Availability and Accessibility:** AI assistants are accessible across multiple platforms, including mobile apps, web interfaces, and embedded features within existing services. This ubiquity enables users to interact with AI assistants conveniently, regardless of their device or operating system. Moreover, advancements in NLP have made AI assistants accessible to users with varying levels of technological literacy, further fueling their widespread adoption (Darban et al., 2023).
7. **Prominent Industry Deployments:** Leading technology companies have integrated AI assistants into their flagship products, such as virtual voice assistants in smartphones and smart speakers. This widespread adoption has exposed a vast user base to AI assistants' capabilities, increasing awareness and usage. Additionally, their integration with messaging and communication platforms has further expanded their reach (Danaher, 2018).

The increasing popularity and usage of AI assistants stem from their ability to enhance user experience, improve language understanding and personalization, support multi-modal interactions, integrate with smart devices, ensure widespread availability, and benefit from strong industry backing. As AI assistants continue to evolve, their influence on various sectors, including online advertising, will expand, necessitating further exploration of their implications and ethical considerations.

2.2.3 POTENTIAL IMPACT ON CONTENT CONSUMPTION HABITS

The rise of AI assistants has the potential to significantly reshape content consumption habits. As these AI-powered conversational agents become primary sources of information, several key behavioral shifts can be anticipated:

1. **Shift from Traditional Search Engine Interactions:** AI assistants present an alternative to traditional search engines, where users enter specific queries and receive a list of results. Instead, AI assistants provide direct, conversational responses, reducing the need for users to browse multiple websites. This shift may lead to a decline in traditional search engine usage as users increasingly prefer AI-driven content delivery (Bresnahan, 2019).
2. **Preference for Conversational Content Delivery:** AI assistants deliver content in a conversational format, offering users concise and contextually relevant responses. Unlike traditional content websites that often present information in lengthy articles or blog posts, AI assistants distill information into digestible, easy-to-consume segments. This shift may encourage a preference for shorter, more direct content (Maedche et al., 2019).
3. **Decreased Direct Traffic to Classical Content Websites:** As users rely more on AI assistants for information, traditional content websites—such as blogs, online news sites, and magazines—may experience a decline in direct traffic. Since AI assistants provide answers within their platforms, users may no longer need to visit external websites, impacting website engagement and revenue (Bauer & Dubljević, 2020).
4. **Disruption of the "Search Engine-Web Banners" Model:** The conventional online advertising model, in which search engines direct users to content websites that display ads, may be significantly disrupted. Since AI assistants provide content directly within

their platforms, users may bypass traditional websites, leading to fewer ad impressions and decreased revenue for publishers (Cam et al., 2019).

5. **Exploration of In-Platform Advertising Opportunities**: As AI assistants become primary content delivery platforms, advertisers may shift their focus toward in-platform advertising opportunities. These opportunities could involve partnerships with AI assistant providers to integrate sponsored content or product recommendations within conversational interactions. By adapting their advertising strategies to align with AI assistant platforms, advertisers may seek to maintain visibility and engagement with users in this evolving landscape.
6. **Evolution of Sponsored Conversations and Native Advertising**: The rise of AI assistants may also spur the evolution of sponsored conversations and native advertising. With users engaging in natural language interactions with AI assistants, advertisers have the potential to integrate branded content seamlessly into the conversational experience. Native advertising techniques, such as personalized recommendations or informational responses tailored to user inquiries, may emerge as effective means of reaching audiences through AI assistant platforms.
7. **Importance of Attribution and Content Ownership:** As artificial intelligence (AI) assistants mine content from various sources to provide information, ensuring proper attribution and content ownership becomes crucial. The lack of automatic redirection to original content websites may raise concerns regarding the recognition and acknowledgment of content creators. Establishing mechanisms to preserve the integrity of content ownership and ensure that creators receive appropriate credit for their work within the AI assistant ecosystem will be essential (Qin and Jiang, 2019).
8. **User Privacy and Data Protection Considerations:** AI assistants rely on collecting and analyzing user data to provide personalized experiences and generate contextually relevant responses. The increasing reliance on AI assistants for content consumption raises concerns about user privacy and data protection. Addressing these

concerns requires implementing robust privacy measures and ensuring transparency in data handling to safeguard user information and maintain trust in the AI assistant ecosystem (Stucke and Ezrachi, 2017).

The growing prominence of artificial intelligence (AI) assistants has the potential to reshape content consumption habits, leading to a shift from traditional search engine interactions to a preference for conversational content delivery. This shift may result in decreased direct traffic to classical content websites, disruption of the "search engine–web banners" model, exploration of in-platform advertising opportunities, the evolution of sponsored conversations and native advertising, increased emphasis on attribution and content ownership, and a greater focus on addressing user privacy and data protection concerns. Understanding and adapting to these potential impacts will be crucial for stakeholders in the online advertising industry as they navigate the changing landscape driven by AI assistants.

2.3 THE SEARCH ENGINE MODEL

2.3.1 EXPLANATION OF THE SEARCH ENGINE MODEL

The traditional search engine model has played a pivotal role in shaping how users find and access information online. It involves search engines such as Google, Bing, and Yahoo acting as intermediaries between users and content websites. This section explores the inner workings of the traditional search engine model, explaining its key components and functionalities.

1. **Crawling and Indexing:** Search engines employ web crawlers, also known as spiders or bots, to systematically explore the internet and discover web pages. These crawlers follow hyperlinks and navigate interconnected web pages, creating an extensive index of web content. During the crawling process, search engine bots gather data from web pages, including text, HTML structure, metadata, and links to other pages. This data is then analyzed and stored in the search engine's index, forming the foundation for efficient information retrieval (Seymour et al., 2011).
2. **Query Processing:** When a user initiates a search query, the search engine processes it to understand the user's intent and

retrieve relevant results from its index. Query processing involves several stages, including query parsing, tokenization, and query expansion. The search engine breaks down the user's query into individual terms or keywords, which are then tokenized for efficient matching against indexed web pages. Query expansion techniques may be applied to broaden or refine the query based on contextual information or user preferences (Vise, 2007).

3. **Ranking and Relevance:** The search engine employs complex ranking algorithms to determine the relevance of web pages to the user's query. These algorithms consider various factors such as keyword relevance, page authority, backlink profiles, user engagement metrics, and other signals indicative of content quality and user satisfaction. The ranking process assigns a relevance score to each web page, enabling the search engine to present the most relevant and authoritative results to the user. The order in which search results are displayed reflects this ranking score (Volokh and Falk, 2011).

4. **Display of Search Results:** After the ranking process, the search engine presents the search results to the user in a user-friendly interface, usually as a list of clickable links known as the search engine results page (SERP). Each result on the SERP includes a title, snippet, and URL, providing users with an overview of the web page's content. Additionally, search engines may display rich snippets, featured snippets, images, videos, or other media formats to enhance the user experience and provide more context about the search results (Seymour et al., 2011).

5. **Redirecting Users to Content Websites:** In the traditional search engine model, when a user clicks on a search result, the search engine redirects them to the corresponding content website. This ensures that users consume the content on the original website where it is hosted. Content websites, such as blogs, online news sites, and magazines, typically monetize their platforms by displaying web banners and advertisements. Through this model, users have the opportunity to view and engage with advertisements while accessing the desired content (Joachims, 2002).

The traditional search engine model encompasses a series of steps that users go through, starting from their initial search query to visiting a content website and potentially interacting with web banners and advertisements. This section provides a detailed explanation of these steps and highlights how revenue is generated through the advertisement business model, as illustrated in Figure 2.1.

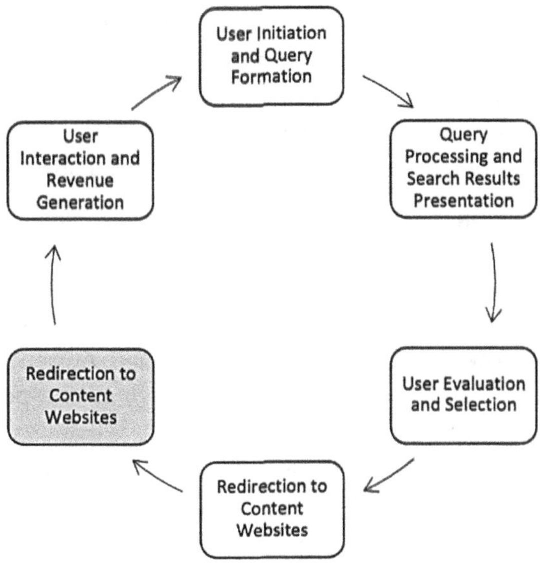

FIGURE 2.1 The search engine model.

Source: Authors.

1. **User Initiation and Query Formation:** The search engine model begins when a user initiates a search query by entering keywords or a specific question into the search engine's interface. This query formation represents the user's information needs or their quest for specific content.

2. **Query Processing and Search Results Presentation:** Upon receiving the user's query, the search engine employs advanced algorithms to process and understand the query's intent. It matches the query terms with indexed web pages and ranks them based on relevance. The search engine then presents the search results to the user in the form of a search engine results page (SERP).

3. **User Evaluation and Selection:** The user evaluates the search results presented on the SERP, considering factors such as snippet relevance, perceived source credibility, and other quality indicators. Based on this evaluation, the user selects one or more links to visit content websites that are expected to provide the desired information.
4. **Redirection to Content Websites:** When the user clicks on a search result, the search engine redirects them to the corresponding content website. This redirection is crucial for content websites, as it drives traffic to their platforms. Users can access the content directly on the original website, where they may also have the opportunity to interact with web banners and advertisements.
5. **Web Banners and Advertisements:** Content websites often generate revenue through web banners and advertisements. These ads are typically displayed alongside the website's content in various formats, such as banners or text ads. Advertisers pay content website owners to display their ads, and revenue is generated through different advertising models, such as cost-per-click (CPC) or cost-per-thousand impressions (CPM). When users visit content websites and engage with the displayed ads, content website owners earn revenue based on the agreed-upon advertising terms.
6. **User Interaction and Revenue Generation:** Upon visiting the content website, users may interact with web banners and advertisements in various ways. They might click on ads, leading to conversions, purchases, or further engagement with the advertiser's offerings. This interaction is tracked, and content website owners receive revenue based on the specific advertising model employed. The more users engage with the advertisements, the higher the potential revenue generated for the content website.

The search engine model, with its comprehensive process—from user initiation and query formation to the eventual visitation of content websites and interaction with web banners and advertisements—has been instrumental in generating revenue for content website owners. By providing a platform for users to discover and access content while incorporating targeted advertisements, search engines have facilitated the growth of the online advertising business model.

2.3.2 ROLE OF SEARCH ENGINES IN DIRECTING USERS TO CONTENT WEBSITES

One of the ethical aspects of search engines lies in their ability to create a fair revenue-sharing system between themselves and content creators. Content websites invest time, effort, and resources in producing valuable content that attracts users. Search engines act as intermediaries by directing traffic to these content websites through search results. In return, search engines generate revenue through advertising displayed alongside search results (Clarke and Willett, 1997).

Search engines such as Google have developed sophisticated advertising platforms, like Google AdSense, that allow content creators to monetize their websites. Through AdSense, content creators can display relevant advertisements on their pages and earn revenue based on user interactions with those ads, such as clicks or impressions. This model provides an opportunity for content creators to earn income while maintaining their focus on producing high-quality content (Gudivada et al., 2015).

Transparency and attribution are important principles upheld by search engines. Content websites are prominently displayed in search results through indexing, with their titles, snippets, and URLs provided to users. This visibility not only drives traffic to content websites but also ensures that users are aware of the original source of the content they are accessing. Search engines play a crucial role in attributing content to its rightful creators, maintaining integrity and ethical standards within the digital landscape (Ramos and Cota, 2008; Singh et al., 2023).

Search engines leverage advanced algorithms and user data to deliver targeted advertisements to users. By analyzing user search queries, browsing behavior, and demographic information, search engines can present ads that align with users' interests and preferences. This targeted approach benefits content creators by increasing the likelihood of ad engagement and conversion, thereby enhancing revenue potential.

To maintain user trust and ensure a positive user experience, search engines prioritize the quality and relevance of advertisements displayed on content websites. Ad quality guidelines are enforced to prevent deceptive or misleading advertising practices that could harm users or damage the reputation of content creators. By upholding these standards, search engines contribute to the ethical operation of the online advertising industry (Eliaz and Spiegler, 2011).

Search engines also employ algorithms and mechanisms to combat plagiarism and protect the intellectual property rights of content creators. These measures aim to prevent unauthorized copying or scraping of content from original sources. By penalizing websites that engage in copyright infringement or content theft, search engines foster an environment that encourages original content creation and rewards the efforts of content creators (Anagnostopoulos et al., 2006).

Revenue distribution is a crucial aspect of search engine ethics. Search engines typically have established systems for revenue distribution, ensuring that content creators receive their fair share of the advertising revenue generated through their platforms. Advertiser support services, such as customer assistance and dispute resolution, further contribute to the ethical functioning of the ecosystem. These measures promote fairness, accountability, and sustainability within the search engine advertising model.

2.4 THE AI ASSISTANT MODEL

2.4.1 DESCRIPTION OF THE NEW AI ASSISTANT MODEL

The AI assistant model, in contrast to the traditional search engine model, provides users with direct access to content within the assistant app or website, eliminating the need for redirection to external sources, even when crediting them. User interaction with the AI assistant model is facilitated through NLP and voice recognition technologies. Users can engage with the AI assistant by speaking voice commands or typing text queries within the assistant's interface. This intuitive and conversational approach enhances the user experience and enables seamless content retrieval.

Upon receiving a user query, the AI assistant employs sophisticated algorithms and extensive databases to retrieve and generate relevant content. These AI models are trained on large datasets, allowing them to understand user queries, grasp context, and provide accurate responses. The AI assistant utilizes machine learning techniques, including deep neural networks (DNNs), to process and analyze large amounts of textual data, ensuring the delivery of high-quality content (Felix et al., 2018).

A key advantage of AI assistants is their ability to comprehend user preferences and provide personalized responses. Through contextual understanding, some AI assistants consider the user's previous interactions, browsing history, and personal profile to deliver content tailored to their interests. This personalization enhances the relevance and utility of the content, resulting in a more customized content consumption experience (Yuan et al., 2022).

As illustrated in Figure 2.2, the AI assistant model presents content within the assistant's interface, enabling users to consume information directly within the app or website. The AI assistant employs various audio and visualization techniques, such as text summaries, bullet points, images, and videos, to effectively convey information. By providing a consolidated view of relevant content, the AI assistant streamlines the content consumption process, eliminating the need for users to navigate multiple external websites.

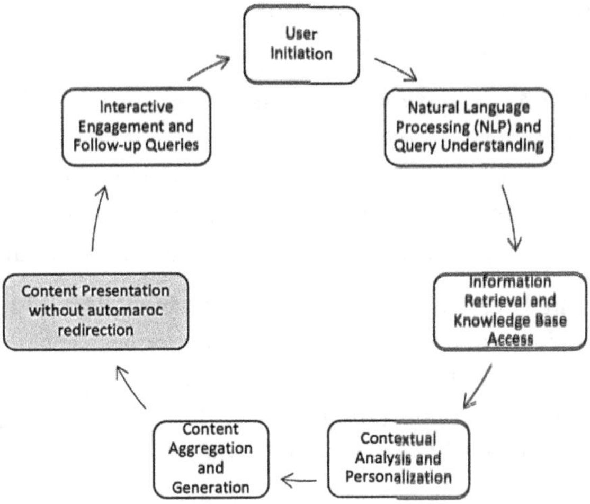

FIGURE 2.2 The AI assistant model.

Source: Authors.

1. **User Initiation:** The user initiates interaction with the AI assistant by activating the assistant app or website, typically through voice commands or by typing a query. This action prompts the AI assistant to listen to or receive the user's input.

2. **Natural Language Processing (NLP) and Query Understanding:** Using advanced NLP techniques, the AI assistant processes the user's query, extracting intent and understanding the request's context. NLP algorithms analyze the query's linguistic structure, semantics, and user preferences to generate a clear understanding of the user's information needs.

3. **Information Retrieval and Knowledge Base Access:** The AI assistant leverages its extensive knowledge base and access to vast repositories of information to retrieve relevant content. This process involves searching through various data sources, such as databases, web pages, articles, and other textual resources, to identify content that aligns with the user's query.
4. **Contextual Analysis and Personalization:** The AI assistant considers the user's profile, historical interactions, and contextual information to provide personalized responses. By factoring in the user's location, preferences, previous queries, and browsing behavior, the AI assistant tailors content recommendations to match the user's specific needs and interests.
5. **Content Aggregation and Generation:** Based on the user's query and retrieved information, the AI assistant aggregates and generates content to fulfill the user's request. This content may include text summaries, bullet points, images, videos, or other multimedia elements, depending on the query's nature and available resources.
6. **Content Presentation and User Interface:** The AI assistant presents content to the user within its own interface. The user can hear or view the content directly within the assistant app or website without being redirected to external sources. The assistant's user interface is designed to provide a user-friendly and intuitive experience, enabling easy consumption and navigation of the presented information.
7. **Interactive Engagement and Follow-Up Queries:** The AI assistant encourages interactive engagement by providing options for the user to ask follow-up questions or seek additional information related to the initial query. This iterative process allows users to explore specific topics further or refine their information needs, with the AI assistant delivering relevant content and responding to subsequent inquiries.

2.4.2 LACK OF REDIRECTION TO ORIGINAL CONTENT WEBSITES

A fundamental distinction between the AI assistant model and the traditional search engine model is the limited or absent redirection to external websites. AI assistants gather vast amounts of internet content through content mining, systematically scanning and indexing web pages, articles, blogs, and other textual resources to create a comprehensive knowledge base. Advanced web crawling algorithms traverse the web, discovering and collecting relevant content. Instead of providing links to external sources, the AI assistant delivers comprehensive information within its own interface. Users can access and consume content directly on the AI assistant platform without being redirected to the original content websites.

However, the AI assistant model poses challenges regarding content attribution and ownership. As users consume content within the AI assistant platform, original content websites may experience reduced direct traffic and user engagement. This raises concerns about proper content attribution and ensuring that content creators receive recognition for their work. Ethical considerations related to content ownership, copyright, and intellectual property rights must be addressed within the AI assistant model to ensure fair treatment of content creators.

Furthermore, the AI assistant model has significant implications for advertising and revenue generation. Since users consume content directly within the AI assistant interface, opportunities for traditional web banners and advertisements on content websites diminish. This shift presents challenges for advertisers and content creators who depend on the revenue mechanisms of the search engine model. To adapt to the evolving landscape of AI assistants, alternative advertising models and strategies must be explored.

2.5 IMPLICATIONS FOR CLASSIC CONTENT WEBSITES

In the AI assistant model, a significant departure from the traditional search engine model is the absence of web banners and advertisements on AI assistant platforms. This section explores the technical aspects of how this absence can potentially reshape the internet as a whole, challenging the existing business model of websites that heavily rely on internet advertising revenue.

2.5.1 DISRUPTION OF THE ADVERTISING ECOSYSTEM

Web banners and advertisements have played a vital role in the advertising ecosystem, serving as a primary source of revenue for content websites.

Through these advertisements, content creators have been able to monetize their offerings, fund their operations, and support the production of valuable content. However, with the emergence and growing popularity of AI assistants, the traditional advertising landscape is experiencing significant disruption. The shift toward content consumption directly within the AI assistant interface challenges the relevance and effectiveness of web banners and traditional advertisements, potentially altering the entire advertising ecosystem.

The disruption of the advertising ecosystem affects not only content websites and advertisers but also the internet as a whole. It challenges the sustainability of traditional content models, particularly those solely dependent on advertising revenue. The success and viability of content creators, journalists, and other information providers heavily rely on their ability to generate income through advertising. Without a steady flow of visitors and engagement on their platforms, content websites face a direct impact on revenue generation. The traditional revenue model, which depends on advertisers purchasing ad space on websites, becomes less viable in this new landscape. As a result, content creators and website owners must navigate this changing paradigm and explore alternative avenues for monetization.

2.5.2 SHIFT IN REVENUE GENERATION MODELS

Collaboration between content creators and AI assistant providers is essential in this evolving landscape. One potential avenue for revenue generation is through partnerships that enable sponsored content or native advertising within the AI assistant interface. By seamlessly integrating advertisements into the assistant's recommendations and responses, content creators can effectively reach their target audience while maintaining a cohesive user experience. These partnerships can be mutually beneficial, allowing advertisers to engage with users in a personalized and contextually relevant manner while content creators receive financial support for their offerings.

Another viable option is the implementation of subscription-based models or premium content offerings. As users increasingly rely on AI assistants for content consumption, content creators can leverage this trend by providing exclusive, high-value content accessible only through subscription plans or premium tiers. This approach enables content creators to directly monetize their offerings while providing added value to their most dedicated audience members.

Additionally, content creators and website owners can diversify their revenue streams by exploring partnerships with AI assistant providers.

This could involve revenue-sharing arrangements or licensing agreements, where content creators receive compensation for the use of their content within the AI assistant ecosystem. By capitalizing on the popularity and widespread usage of AI assistants, content creators can tap into new revenue opportunities and expand their reach to a broader audience.

However, it is crucial to strike a balance between revenue generation and user experience within the AI assistant model. As users turn to AI assistants for quick and convenient access to information, content creators and advertisers must ensure that any monetization efforts respect user preferences and do not compromise the assistant's primary function. Intrusive or disruptive advertising practices could lead to user dissatisfaction, potentially discouraging users from relying on AI assistants altogether.

Moreover, content creators should explore innovative ways to provide value beyond traditional advertising. This could include creating branded content, producing original audio or video content tailored for AI assistant platforms, or offering interactive experiences exclusive to the assistant interface. By embracing creativity and leveraging the unique capabilities of AI assistants, content creators can enhance user engagement and increase their revenue potential.

2.5.3 REIMAGINING USER ENGAGEMENT

Content creators must reimagine user engagement strategies to remain relevant in the AI assistant era. This may involve focusing on creating unique, valuable content that offers an immersive and interactive experience beyond what AI assistants can provide. Engaging users through personalized experiences, exclusive access to specialized knowledge, or fostering online communities can help content websites differentiate themselves and retain a loyal user base.

2.5.4 REDEFINING ADVERTISING APPROACHES

Advertisers must also adapt their strategies in response to the AI assistant model. Traditional web banners and advertisements may become less effective as user attention shifts to AI assistant interfaces. To stay relevant, advertisers may need to collaborate with AI assistant providers, leveraging data-driven targeting and native advertising opportunities within the assistant interface. They can also explore partnerships with content creators and websites to develop innovative advertising formats that seamlessly integrate with the AI assistant experience.

2.5.5 *IMPACT ON CONTENT DIVERSITY*

The absence of web banners and advertisements on AI assistant platforms raises concerns about its impact on content diversity. Advertising revenue has traditionally played a crucial role in supporting a wide range of content creators, enabling them to produce diverse and high-quality content. Without a sustainable revenue model, content websites may struggle to maintain their operations, potentially leading to a homogenization of content offerings. Efforts must be made to ensure that diverse content creation continues to thrive in this evolving landscape.

As the advertising ecosystem continues to adapt to the rise of AI assistants, it is crucial to navigate this disruption with careful consideration for the interests of all stakeholders. The absence of web banners and advertisements on AI assistant platforms represents a significant shift in the internet's business model. Content websites that rely solely on internet advertising revenue may face considerable challenges, necessitating innovation and adaptation to new revenue generation models. Collaboration among content creators, advertisers, and AI assistant providers is essential to reshaping the internet ecosystem, fostering sustainable monetization strategies, and maintaining content diversity in an AI-dominated era.

2.6 CONCLUSION

The emergence of AI assistants and their impact on content websites and the advertising ecosystem have presented both opportunities and challenges in the digital landscape. This chapter has examined the traditional role of search engines in directing users to content websites and compared it to the new AI assistant model, highlighting the implications for classic content websites and the potential disruption of the advertising ecosystem.

The traditional search engine model has played a crucial role in directing users to content websites by driving traffic through search results and providing revenue-sharing opportunities for content creators. Search engines have upheld principles of transparency, attribution, ad quality, and copyright protection, contributing to the ethical functioning of the online advertising industry. However, the AI assistant model, with its direct content access within the assistant interface, introduces a fundamental shift in content consumption and revenue generation dynamics.

The AI assistant model offers a user-friendly, fast, and personalized content consumption experience through natural language processing and contextual understanding. By presenting content directly within the assistant's interface, AI assistants streamline information retrieval, eliminating the need for users to navigate external websites. However, this lack of redirection raises concerns about content attribution and ownership, as well as its impact on advertising revenue for content creators.

In light of these findings, several recommendations can be made to address the challenges posed by the AI assistant model (Bhatnagar et al., 2024). Firstly, content creators and AI assistant providers should collaborate to establish clear mechanisms for content attribution, ensuring that original content websites receive recognition and credit for their work. This can be achieved through partnerships, licensing agreements, or other revenue-sharing models that compensate content creators for their contributions to the AI assistant ecosystem.

Alternative revenue generation models must be explored to adapt to the evolving landscape of AI assistants. Content creators should consider partnerships that allow sponsored content or native advertising within the AI assistant interface, providing advertisers with opportunities to reach their target audience in a contextually relevant manner. Additionally, content creators can explore subscription-based models or premium content offerings to directly monetize their work and provide added value to their most dedicated audience members.

It is essential to strike a balance between revenue generation and user experience within the AI assistant model. Intrusive or disruptive advertising practices should be avoided to maintain user satisfaction and ensure the assistant's primary function of providing valuable information. Advertisers should collaborate with AI assistant providers to develop innovative, non-intrusive advertising formats that seamlessly integrate with the assistant experience.

Furthermore, content creators and advertisers should focus on redefining their approaches to user engagement and advertising in the AI assistant era. Content websites can differentiate themselves by creating unique, immersive, and interactive experiences that go beyond what AI assistants can provide. Advertisers should leverage data-driven targeting and explore partnerships with content creators to develop innovative advertising formats that align with the AI assistant experience.

In terms of future research, further investigation is needed to assess the long-term implications of the AI assistant model on content diversity. The absence of web banners and advertisements on AI assistant platforms raises concerns about the sustainability of content creation and the potential homogenization of content offerings. Future studies could explore strategies to ensure diverse content creation thrives in this evolving landscape and identify ways to support content creators in the absence of traditional advertising revenue.

Additionally, research should focus on understanding user preferences and behaviors within the AI assistant model to enhance personalization and improve the relevance of content recommendations. By gaining insights into how users interact with AI assistants and consume information, AI algorithms can be further optimized to meet user expectations and deliver tailored content effectively.

The rise of AI assistants presents both challenges and opportunities for content websites and the advertising ecosystem. By embracing collaboration, exploring alternative revenue models, and redefining approaches to user engagement and advertising, content creators, advertisers, and AI assistant providers can navigate this evolving landscape and ensure a sustainable and diverse digital ecosystem. Future research should continue to explore these areas to better understand and adapt to the changing dynamics of content consumption in the AI assistant era.

KEYWORDS

- **artificial intelligence**
- **natural language processing**
- **information retrieval**
- **content attribution**
- **revenue-sharing models**
- **search engines**

REFERENCES

Anagnostopoulos, A., Broder, A. Z., & Punera, K. (2006). Effective and efficient classification on a search-engine model. In *Proceedings of the 15th ACM International Conference on Information and Knowledge Management* (pp. 208–217).

Anusha, G. (2016). Effectiveness of online advertising. *International Journal of Research–Granthaalayah, 4*(3), 14–21.

Asdemir, K., Kumar, N., & Jacob, V. S. (2012). Pricing models for online advertising: CPM vs. CPC. *Information Systems Research, 23*(3-part-1), 804–822.

Bauer, W. A., & Dubljević, V. (2020). AI assistants and the paradox of internal automaticity. *Neuroethics, 13*(3), 303–310.

Bayles, M. E. (2002). Designing online banner advertisements: Should we animate? In *Proceedings of the SIGCHI Conference on Human Factors in Computing Systems* (pp. 363–366).

Bhatnagar, M., Kumar, P., Taneja, S., Sood, K., & Grima, S. (2024). From digital overload to trading zen: The role of digital detox in enhancing intraday trading performance. In *Business Drivers in Promoting Digital Detoxification* (pp. 148–176). IGI Global.

Bresnahan, T. (2019). Artificial intelligence technologies and aggregate growth prospects.

Cam, A., Chui, M., & Hall, B. (2019). Global AI survey: AI proves its worth, but few scale impact.

Canbek, N. G., & Mutlu, M. E. (2016). On the track of artificial intelligence: Learning with intelligent personal assistants. *Journal of Human Sciences, 13*(1), 592–601.

Choi, T. R., & Drumwright, M. E. (2021). "OK, Google, why do I use you?" Motivations, post-consumption evaluations, and perceptions of voice AI assistants. *Telematics and Informatics, 62*, 101628.

Clarke, S. J., & Willett, P. (1997). Estimating the recall performance of web search engines. In *Aslib Proceedings* (*Vol. 49, No. 7*, pp. 184–189). MCB UP Ltd.

Danaher, J. (2018). Toward an ethics of AI assistants: An initial framework. *Philosophy & Technology, 31*(4), 629–653.

Danaher, P. J., & Mullarkey, G. W. (2003). Factors affecting online advertising recall: A study of students. *Journal of Advertising Research, 43*(3), 252–267.

Darban, K., & Kabbaj, S. (2021). Publicité digitale et achat de clics ciblés (CPC): Avantages et limites. *Revue Marocaine de la Prospective en Sciences de Gestion (4).*

Darban, K., Kabbaj, S., & Esmaoui, K. (2023). Crisis management, internet and AI: Information in the age of COVID-19, and future pandemics. In *Mathematical Modeling and Intelligent Control for Combating Pandemics*. Springer Optimization and Its Applications. ISBN: 978-3-031-33182-4.

Eliaz, K., & Spiegler, R. (2011). A simple model of search engine pricing. *The Economic Journal, 121*(556), F329–F339.

Felix, S. M., Kumar, S., & Veeramuthu, A. (2018). A smart personal AI assistant for visually impaired people. In *2018 2nd International Conference on Trends in Electronics and Informatics (ICOEI)* (pp. 1245–1250). IEEE.

George, A. S., & George, A. H. (2023). A review of ChatGPT AI's impact on several business sectors. *Partners Universal International Innovation Journal, 1*(1), 9–23.

Gratch, J., & Fast, N. J. (2022). The power to harm: AI assistants paves the way to unethical behavior. *Current Opinion in Psychology*, 101382.

Grewal, D., Guha, A., Schweiger, E., Ludwig, S., & Wetzels, M. (2022). How communications by AI-enabled voice assistants impact the customer journey. *Journal of Service Management* (ahead-of-print).

Gudivada, V. N., Rao, D., & Paris, J. (2015). Understanding search-engine optimization. *Computer, 48*(10), 43–52.

Joachims, T. (2002). Optimizing search engines using clickthrough data. In *Proceedings of the Eighth ACM SIGKDD International Conference on Knowledge Discovery and Data Mining* (pp. 133–142).

Karim, D. (2023). Uncovering the Facebook experience: Insights into users' behavior and motivations. *International Journal of Advanced Scientific Innovation, 5*(3).

Kashif, M., Shajar, S. N., Singhal, N., & Kumar, P. (2023). Achieving sustainable investment practices through green finance: Challenges and opportunities. In *Sustainable Investments in Green Finance* (pp. 234–244). IGI Global.

Kashif, M., Sridharan, P., & Thiyagarajan, S. (2017). Factors affecting international reserves with special reference to India. *Vision, 21*(4), 339–349.

Kashif, M., Thiyagarajan, S., & Sridharan, P. (2017). Dynamics of Algeria's international reserves. *African Journal of Economic and Management Studies, 8*(4). https://doi.org/10.1108/AJEMS-11-2016-0179.

Kim, G., & Moon, I. (2020). Online banner advertisement scheduling for advertising effectiveness. *Computers & Industrial Engineering, 140*, 106226.

Ledford, J. L. (2015). *Search Engine Optimization Bible* (Vol. 584). John Wiley & Sons.

Lv, X., Liu, Y., Luo, J., Liu, Y., & Li, C. (2021). Does a cute artificial intelligence assistant soften the blow? The impact of cuteness on customer tolerance of assistant service failure. *Annals of Tourism Research, 87*, 103114.

Ma, Y., & Siau, K. L. (2018). Artificial intelligence impacts on higher education.

Maedche, A., Legner, C., Benlian, A., Berger, B., Gimpel, H., Hess, T., & Söllner, M. (2019). AI-based digital assistants: Opportunities, threats, and research perspectives. *Business & Information Systems Engineering, 61*, 535–544.

Makridakis, S. (2017). The forthcoming artificial intelligence (AI) revolution: Its impact on society and firms. *Futures, 90*, 46–60.

Malodia, S., Islam, N., Kaur, P., & Dhir, A. (2021). Why do people use artificial intelligence (AI)-enabled voice assistants? *IEEE Transactions on Engineering Management.*

Marinchak, C. L. M., Forrest, E., & Hoanca, B. (2018). The impact of artificial intelligence and virtual personal assistants on marketing. In *Encyclopedia of Information Science and Technology, Fourth Edition* (pp. 5748–5756). IGI Global.

Mishra, S., & Kern-Stone, R. (2023). Smart assistants for smart living: Ideology and mythology in AI-powered smart speaker advertising. *Journal of Communication Inquiry.* https://doi.org/10.1177/01968599231155612.

Nasution, M. K. (2012). Simple search engine model: Adaptive properties. *arXiv preprint* arXiv:1212.3906.

Qin, X., & Jiang, Z. (2019). The impact of AI on the advertising process: The Chinese experience. *Journal of Advertising, 48*(4), 338–346.

Ramos, A., & Cota, S. (2008). *Search engine marketing.* McGraw-Hill, Inc.

Seymour, T., Frantsvog, D., & Kumar, S. (2011). History of search engines. *International Journal of Management & Information Systems (IJMIS, 15)* (4), 47–58.

Sharma, D., Shukla, R., Giri, A. K., & Kumar, S. (2019). A brief review on search engine optimization. In *2019 9th International Conference on Cloud Computing, Data Science & Engineering (Confluence)* (pp. 687–692). IEEE.

Singh, A., Taneja, S., & Kumar, P. (2023). Algorithmic approaches to financial technology: Forecasting, trading, and optimization. In *Algorithmic Approaches to Financial Technology: Forecasting, Trading, and Optimization.* https://doi.org/10.4018/9798369317464.

Stucke, M. E., & Ezrachi, A. (2017). How digital assistants can harm our economy, privacy, and democracy. *Berkeley Technology Law Journal, 32*(3), 1239–1300.

Tavor, T. (2011). Online advertising development and their economic effectiveness. *Australian Journal of Business and Management Research, 1*(6), 121.

Underwood, J. (2017). Exploring AI language assistants with primary EFL students. In *CALL in a Climate of Change: Adapting to Turbulent Global Conditions–Short Papers from EUROCALL, 2017* (pp. 317–321).

Uysal, E., Alavi, S., & Bezençon, V. (2022). Trojan horse or useful helper? A relationship perspective on artificial intelligence assistants with humanlike features. *Journal of the Academy of Marketing Science, 1–23.*

Vise, D. (2007). *The Google story. Strategic Direction, 23*(10).

Volokh, E., & Falk, D. M. (2011). Google: First amendment protection for search engine search results. *Journal of Law, Economics & Policy, 8*, 883.

Yuan, C., Zhang, C., & Wang, S. (2022). Social anxiety as a moderator in consumer willingness to accept AI assistants based on utilitarian and hedonic values. *Journal of Retailing and Consumer Services, 65*, 102878.

Zilincan, J. (2015). Search engine optimization. In *CBU International Conference Proceedings* (Vol. 3, pp. 506–510).

CHAPTER 3

Changing Landscape of Investments in Contemporary Times: Challenges and Opportunities

TEJINDER SINGH,[1] RUBEENA BAJWA,[2] VIKAS SHARMA,[1,*] and PRIYANKA AGARWAL[3]

[1]*University School of Business (Commerce), Chandigarh University, Mohali, Punjab, India*

[2]*Sri Guru Granth Sahib World University, Fatehgarh, Punjab, India*

[3]*Graphic Era (Deemed to be University), Dehradun, Uttarakhand, India*

**Corresponding author.*

ABSTRACT

The present study explores the changing dynamics of investments in contemporary times, shedding light on the challenges and opportunities posed by the cryptocurrency wave. Moreover, it delves into the role of robo-advisory services as a means to mitigate risks and empower investors with secure access to traditional securities markets. The study employed a stratified sampling design to select a representative sample of 30 stocks. This approach ensured that each market capitalization category (small-cap, mid-cap, and large-cap) was adequately represented in the analysis. In conclusion, our analysis has shed light on the dynamic relationship between option turnover, future prices, and the impact of automated investment platforms and fintech solutions.

Transforming Business Finance in the Digital Era.
Sanjay Taneja, Mohammad Kashif, Ercan Özen, and Luan Vardari (Eds.)
© 2026 Apple Academic Press, Inc. Co-published with CRC Press (Taylor & Francis)

DOI: 10.1201/9781998511235-3

3.1 INTRODUCTION

In the ever-evolving landscape of contemporary investments, the profound impact of technological advancements and innovative financial instruments cannot be ignored. One such phenomenon that has captured the imagination of investors worldwide is the rise of cryptocurrency trading (Chen, 2018; Wexler and Oberlander, 2020). The allure of quick and substantial returns has enticed many to this unregulated frontier, often driven by a potent mix of ambition and the desire for lucrative gains in a short span. Cryptocurrency markets, with their decentralized and often unregulated nature, present both challenges and opportunities. The promise of decentralized finance, rapid value appreciation, and financial autonomy has drawn investors from diverse backgrounds into this dynamic space (Fariya et al., 2024; Singh, 2020, 2022).

However, the uncharted territory of cryptocurrency markets is not without pitfalls. The lack of regulatory oversight opens the door to potential fraud, market manipulation, and extreme volatility, leaving investors vulnerable to significant financial risks. Amidst this landscape, the need for investor protection and prudent guidance becomes critical. In this context, robo-advisory services emerge as a technological solution with the potential to safeguard investors' interests. By providing automated, algorithm-driven financial planning services, robo-advisors offer a structured approach to navigating the complexities of financial markets (Chapman, 2021). Importantly, these platforms operate within regulatory frameworks, ensuring that investors gain access to securities markets through registered intermediaries overseen by market regulators (Roszkowska, 2021; Sharma et al., 2023a).

As we embark on this exploration, we will examine the challenges posed by the unpredictable nature of global markets, regulatory complexities, and the growing imperative to incorporate sustainable and ethical investment practices. At the same time, we will highlight the exciting prospects brought about by innovation, including enhanced portfolio diversification, access to previously untapped markets, and the democratization of investment through novel financial technologies.

This study explores the changing dynamics of contemporary investments, shedding light on the challenges and opportunities posed by the cryptocurrency wave. Additionally, it examines the role of robo-advisory services in mitigating risks and empowering investors with secure access to traditional securities markets. As we navigate this transformative period in the financial landscape, understanding the delicate balance between risk and opportunity becomes imperative for investors and stakeholders alike (Chopra and Gupta, 2023; Kashif et al., 2023a).

3.2 LITERATURE REVIEW

The contemporary investment landscape is a dynamic canvas shaped by numerous factors that have evolved over the years. As we examine the existing literature, it becomes evident that today's investment challenges and opportunities are deeply rooted in the complex interplay of economic, technological, and societal forces (Phillips, 2018).

One prominent theme that resonates across the literature is the impact of global events on financial markets. Scholars have extensively discussed the susceptibility of investments to geopolitical tensions, pandemics, and other unforeseen crises. These events, often beyond investors' control, underscore the importance of risk management strategies and the need for a resilient investment portfolio (Vatsa, 2004).

Simultaneously, the literature highlights the disruptive force of technology on traditional investment models. Studies explore the transformative power of artificial intelligence, blockchain, and data analytics in shaping the financial landscape (Sharma et al., 2023b). These technological advancements not only introduce novel investment opportunities but also raise critical concerns regarding privacy, security, and regulatory frameworks (Bhatnagar et al., 2022; Kashif et al., 2017b; Weber, 2010).

The regulatory environment also emerges as a pivotal area of discussion. Various authors shed light on the evolving regulatory landscape, emphasizing the challenges posed by increasing complexity and the need for adaptability among investors (Bhatnagar et al., 2024; Kashif et al., 2017a, 2023b; Sharma et al., 2023a). Compliance with changing regulations is crucial for navigating the intricate web of legal frameworks governing global financial markets (Alexander et al., 2005).

Ethical and sustainable investing is another key area of exploration. Researchers contribute to the discourse on the growing importance of environmental, social, and governance (ESG) considerations in investment decision-making. As societal awareness of sustainability issues rises, investors are increasingly compelled to integrate ethical considerations into their strategies, presenting both challenges and opportunities in aligning financial goals with social responsibility (Cohen, 1987; Kashif et al., 2024).

The literature also accentuates the transformative potential of financial technology in democratizing investment opportunities. Allen and Gale

(1995) discuss how innovations such as robo-advisors, crowdfunding, and digital platforms are reshaping access to financial markets, providing retail investors with tools and resources that were traditionally reserved for institutional players.

As we synthesize insights from the existing literature, it becomes evident that the evolving investment landscape is a multifaceted terrain marked by challenges that demand strategic acumen and opportunities that beckon those willing to embrace innovation. This chapter builds upon these foundations, offering a nuanced understanding of the challenges and opportunities that define the intricate tapestry of modern investments (John et al., 2023).

3.3 RESEARCH METHODOLOGY

1. **Rationale**: Studying robo-advisory services and other IT applications in modern investments is crucial due to their ability to provide efficient, accessible, and cost-effective investment management solutions. These platforms offer personalized advice, utilize data-driven decision-making, and employ advanced risk management techniques, ultimately enhancing transparency and continuously monitoring portfolios for optimal performance. Embracing these technologies empowers investors to achieve their financial goals more effectively while democratizing access to professional investment guidance and lowering overall costs.
2. **Sample Size and Selection**: The study employed a stratified sampling design to select a representative sample of 30 stocks. This approach ensured that each market capitalization category—small-cap, mid-cap, and large-cap—was adequately represented in the analysis. To achieve this, the top 10 stocks from each category were chosen based on their annual average market capitalization for the study period. This selection method aimed to balance the potential influence of different market segments while maintaining a manageable sample size.
3. **Data Collection**: Data for the study were primarily sourced from the National Stock Exchange (NSE) due to its dominance in equity derivatives turnover. The chosen variables included future

maturity prices (dependent variable) and option turnover (independent variable). The study period was divided into two phases: Phase 1 (2020–2021) and Phase 2 (2022–2023), allowing for an analysis of potential changes in the relationship between these variables over time, particularly in the context of evolving robo-advisory and information technology applications in portfolio management.

3.3.1 OBJECTIVES

- Analyze the impact of automated investment platforms and FinTech solutions on market depth;
- Examine the correlation between options turnover and future price movements.

3.3.2 MEASUREMENT

The EViews statistical package was used to perform ordinary least squares (OLS) regression along with generalized autoregressive conditional heteroskedasticity (GARCH) models to analyze volatility clustering and time series movements. These methods were applied for hypothesis testing and to achieve the study's objectives.

3.4 ANALYSIS AND FINDINGS

Below are the regression analysis results detailing the relationship between future prices and option turnover, as well as volatility patterns using the GARCH model.

In Table 3.1, the intercept (C) is estimated to be 4.291 with a standard error of 0.094. This indicates that when the option turnover is zero, the expected future price is 4.291. The coefficient for option turnover is 0.537, with a standard error of 0.023. This suggests that for every unit increase in option turnover, the future price is expected to increase by 0.537 units. The t-statistics for both the intercept and option turnover are highly significant (t-statistic > 2, p-value < 0.05), indicating a strong relationship between option turnover and future prices during Phase 1.

TABLE 3.1 Regression Analysis Results Between Future Prices and Option Turnover During Phase 1

Variable	Coefficient	Std. Error	t-Statistic	Prob.
C	4.291	0.094	45.343	0.00
Option turnover	0.537	0.023	22.977	0.00

Source: Author's computation/compilation (obtained from EViews).

This analysis suggests that during Phase 1, there is a statistically significant positive relationship between option turnover and future prices. Specifically, higher option turnover tends to be associated with higher future prices.

Figure 3.1 illustrates the volatility patterns observed in the regression equation incorporating future prices and turnover during Phase 1.

Future prices (dependent variable) – the GARCH equation's mean equation suggests a coefficient of 3.717 for the constant term, indicating the expected future price when the volatility components are zero. Table 3.2 presents the test results for GARCH(1,1) during Phase 1.

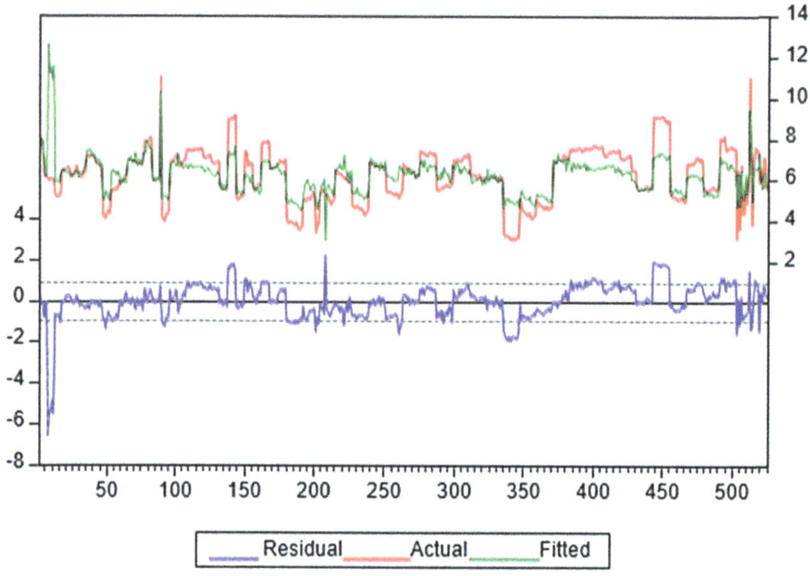

FIGURE 3.1 Volatility patterns of the regression equation with future prices and turnover during Phase 1.

Source: Author's computation/compilation (obtained from EViews).

In Table 3.2, the coefficient for option turnover is 0.740, implying that a one-unit increase in turnover leads to a 0.740-unit increase in the conditional mean of future prices.

Volatility components – the variance equation indicates a coefficient of 0.032 for the constant term, representing the long-run average volatility. The RESID(−1)^2 term has a coefficient of 0.173, indicating the persistence of past squared residuals in the volatility equation. The GARCH(−1) term has a coefficient of 0.758, indicating the persistence of past conditional variances in the volatility equation.

Overall, during Phase 1, the GARCH(1,1) model suggests that option turnover has a significant positive impact on future prices, while past volatility components contribute to the current volatility patterns observed.

GARCH model specification is given by:

$$\text{GARCH} = C(3) + C(4)^*\text{RESID}(-1)^2 + C(5)^*\text{GARCH}(-1)$$

TABLE 3.2 Test Results for GARCH(1,1) During Phase 1

Component	Variable	Coefficient	Std. Error	z-Statistic	Prob.	AIC	SIC
Mean EQ	C	3.717	0.044	83.161	0.00	2.070	2.110
	Option Turnover	0.740	0.012	61.574	0.00		
Variance EQ	C	0.032	0.005	6.262	0.00		
	RESID(−1)^2	0.173	0.031	5.513	0.00		
	GARCH(−1)	0.758	0.009	82.639	0.00		

Source: Author's computation/compilation (obtained from EViews).

In Table 3.3, the coefficient for option turnover is 0.839, with a standard error of 0.018. This suggests that for every unit increase in option turnover, the future price is expected to increase by 0.839 units. The t-statistic for both the intercept and option turnover is highly significant (t-statistic > 2, p-value < 0.05), indicating a strong relationship between option turnover and future prices during Phase 2.

This analysis suggests that during Phase 2, there was not only a statistically significant positive relationship between option turnover and future prices, but the relationship was also stronger compared to Phase 1, as indicated by the higher coefficient (0.839 in Phase 2 vs. 0.537 in Phase 1).

TABLE 3.3 Regression Analysis Results between Future Prices and Option Turnover During Phase 2

Variable	Coefficient	Std. Error	t-Statistic	Prob.
C	4.753	0.072	65.667	0.00
Option turnover	0.839	0.018	29.163	0.00

Source: Author's computation/compilation (obtained from EViews).

Figure 3.2 illustrates the volatility patterns observed in the regression equation incorporating future prices and turnover during Phase 2.

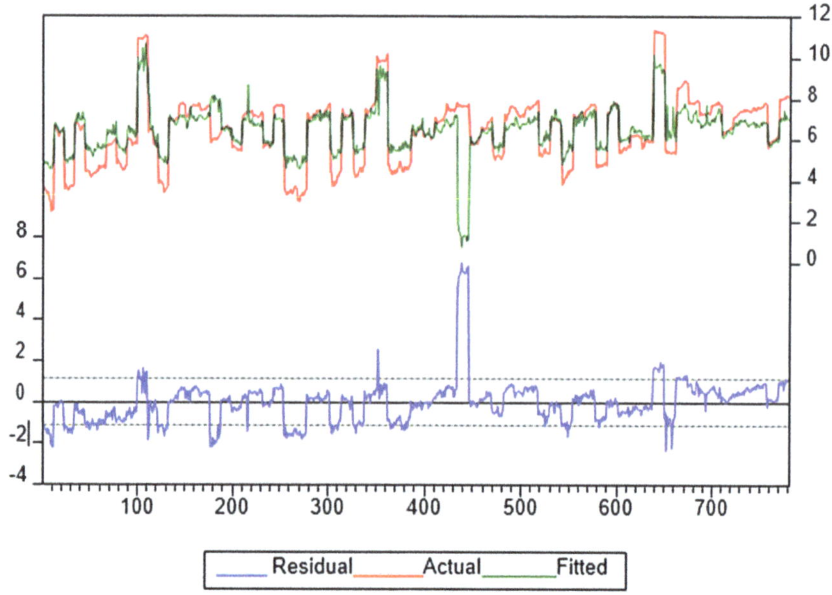

FIGURE 3.2 Volatility patterns of the regression equation between future prices and option turnover during the post-introduction phase of weekly expiry.

Source: Author's computation/compilation (obtained from EViews).

During Phase 2, the GARCH(1,1) model analysis in Table 3.4 reveals significant findings regarding the relationship between future prices and option turnover. The mean equation indicates that the expected future price, with zero volatility components, stands at 3.536 units.

Notably, a one-unit increase in option turnover correlates with a substantial 0.816-unit increase in the conditional mean of future prices.

Regarding volatility components, the variance equation highlights a constant term of 0.019, denoting the long-run average volatility. Additionally, the persistence of past squared residuals is evident, as indicated by the coefficient of 0.474 for the RESID(−1)^2 term. The GARCH(−1) term shows a coefficient of 0.628, suggesting the persistence of past conditional variances.

Overall, these findings underscore the enduring influence of option turnover on future prices, alongside the ongoing impact of past volatility components on current volatility patterns during Phase 2.

$$\text{GARCH} = \text{C}(3) + \text{C}(4)*\text{RESID}(-1)^2 + \text{C}(5)*\text{GARCH}(-1)$$

TABLE 3.4 Test Results for GARCH(1,1) During Phase 2

Future Prices		Variable	Coefficient	Std. Error	z-Statistic	Prob.	AIC	SIC
GARCH(1,1)	Mean EQ	C	3.536	0.030	117.847	0	1.91	1.94
		Option turnover	0.816	0.005	137.051	0		
	Variance EQ	C	0.019	0.004	4.272	0		
		RESID(−1)^2	0.474	0.068	6.944	0		
		GARCH(−1)	0.628	0.043	14.563	0		

Source: Author's computation/compilation (obtained from EViews).

3.4.1 DISCUSSION

Analysis indicates that during Phase 2, a statistically significant positive relationship between option turnover and future prices exists, with a coefficient of 0.839, surpassing Phase 1's 0.537 (Pathak and Rastogi, 2010; Usha et al., 2019). Automated investment platforms and FinTech solutions deepen market turnover and strengthen the correlation between option turnover and future prices (Mehrotra, 2019).

3.4.2 LIMITATIONS

The main limitation of the present study is its exclusive focus on option turnover and future prices without considering other indices.

Future studies could explore additional indices to provide a more comprehensive understanding of market dynamics. Additionally, conducting inter-country comparisons could offer valuable insights into how automated investment platforms and FinTech solutions impact market turnover and the correlation between option turnover and future prices across different global financial markets.

3.5 CONCLUSION

In conclusion, this analysis has shed light on the dynamic relationship between option turnover, future prices, and the impact of automated investment platforms and FinTech solutions. The primary objectives were twofold: first, to examine the correlation between option turnover and future prices, and second, to assess how automated investment platforms and FinTech solutions influence this relationship.

The findings reveal a statistically significant positive relationship between option turnover and future prices during both Phase 1 and Phase 2. Moreover, the coefficient representing this relationship was notably higher in Phase 2, suggesting a deepening correlation between the two variables. This underscores the growing influence of automated investment platforms and FinTech solutions in shaping market dynamics.

However, it is important to acknowledge the limitations of this analysis, particularly its exclusive focus on option turnover without considering other indices. Future research could address this limitation by incorporating additional indices to provide a more comprehensive understanding of market behavior. Furthermore, conducting inter-country comparisons could offer valuable insights into the global impact of automated investment platforms and FinTech solutions on market turnover and the correlation between option turnover and future prices.

In essence, this study highlights the significance of automated investment platforms and FinTech solutions in not only deepening market turnover but also strengthening the correlation between option turnover and future prices. These insights are crucial for investors, financial institutions, and policymakers in navigating the evolving financial markets and harnessing the potential benefits offered by technological advancements in investment management.

KEYWORDS

- **automated investment platforms**
- **cryptocurrency**
- **global financial markets**
- **market dynamics**
- **option turnover**
- **robo-advisory**

REFERENCES

Alexander, K., Dhumale, R., & Eatwell, J. (2005). *Global Governance of Financial Systems: The International Regulation of Systemic Risk.* Oxford University Press.

Allen, F., & Gale, D. (1995). A welfare comparison of intermediaries and financial markets in Germany and the US. *European Economic Review, 39*(2), 179–209.

Bhatnagar, M., Kumar, P., Taneja, S., Sood, K., & Grima, S. (2024). From digital overload to trading zen: The role of digital detox in enhancing intraday trading performance. In *Business Drivers in Promoting Digital Detoxification* (pp. 148–176). IGI Global.

Bhatnagar, M., Taneja, S., & Özen, E. (2022). A wave of green start-ups in India—The study of green finance as a support system for sustainable entrepreneurship. *Green Finance, 4*(2), 253–273.

Chapman, J. E. (2021). FinTech: Is the water fine? *Journal of International and Comparative Law, 8*(2), 435–458.

Chen, K. (2018). Financial innovation and technology firms: A smart new world with machines. In *International Symposia in Economic Theory and Econometrics (Vol. 25, pp. 279–292).* Emerald Group Publishing Ltd. https://doi.org/10.1108/S1571-038620180000025012.

Chopra, P., & Gupta, M. (2023). Fuzzy logic and ANN in an artificial intelligent cloud: A comparative study. In *Intelligent Communication Technologies and Virtual Mobile Networks* (pp. 559–570). Springer.

Cohen, A. M. (1987). *Contemporary Issues in Community Colleges: A Synopsis.*

Fariya, Saini, A., & Kashif, M. (2024). Exploring the influence of factors driving financial accessibility, financial activities, and financial education on sustainable development. In *Artificial Intelligence and Machine Learning-Powered Smart Finance* (pp. 23–49). IGI Global.

John, D., Hussin, N., Shahibi, M. S., Ahmad, M., Hashim, H., & Ametefe, D. S. (2023). A systematic review on the factors governing precision agriculture adoption among small-scale farmers. *Outlook on Agriculture, 52*(4), 469–485.

Kashif, M., David, A., Gupta, V. P., & Alam, S. (2024). Integration of artificial intelligence in the financial sector. In *Artificial Intelligence and Machine Learning-Powered Smart Finance* (pp. 96–108). IGI Global.

Kashif, M., Kumar, P., Ghai, S., & Kumar, S. (2023). Disruptive technologies in computational finance. In *Algorithmic Approaches to Financial Technology: Forecasting, Trading, and Optimization* (pp. 46–60). IGI Global.

Kashif, M., Shajar, S. N., Singhal, N., & Kumar, P. (2023). Achieving sustainable investment practices through green finance: Challenges and opportunities. In *Sustainable Investments in Green Finance* (pp. 234–244). IGI Global.

Kashif, M., Sridharan, P., & Thiyagarajan, S. (2017). Factors affecting international reserves with special reference to India. *Vision, 21*(4), 339–349.

Kashif, M., Thiyagarajan, S., & Sridharan, P. (2017). Dynamics of Algeria's international reserves. *African Journal of Economic and Management Studies, 8*(4), 410–419.

Mehrotra, A. (2019). Artificial intelligence in financial services – Need to blend automation with human touch. *2019 International Conference on Automation, Computational and Technology Management (ICACTM 2019)*, 342–347. https://doi.org/10.1109/ICACTM.2019.8776741.

Pathak, R., & Rastogi, N. (2010). Informational role of options open interests and volume in forecasting future prices: A study on Indian market. *The IUP Journal of Financial Economics, VIII*(3), 49–61.

Phillips, M. (2018). International data-sharing norms: From the OECD to the General Data Protection Regulation (GDPR). *Human Genetics, 137*, 575–582.

Roszkowska, P. (2021). FinTech in financial reporting and audit for fraud prevention and safeguarding equity investments. *Journal of Accounting and Organizational Change, 17*(2), 164–196. https://doi.org/10.1108/JAOC-09-2019-0098.

Sharma, V., Gupta, M., Jangir, K., Chopra, P., & Pathak, N. (2023a). The impact of post-use consumer satisfaction on smart wearables repurchase intention in the context of AI-based healthcare information. In *Enhancing Customer Engagement Through Location-Based Marketing* (pp. 77–101). IGI Global.

Sharma, V., Taneja, S., Gupta, M., & Özen, E. (2023b). Impact of service quality on behavioral intention to use FinTech payment services: An extension of SERVEQUAL model. *Asia Pacific Journal of Information Systems, 33*(4), 1093–1117.

Singh, T. (2020). FinTech adoption: A critical appraisal of the strategies of Paytm in India. *IUP Journal of Management Research, 19*(4), 7–17.

Singh, T. (2022). Artificial intelligence-application in the field of Indian banking sector. *AIP Conference Proceedings, 2555*(1).

Usha, B. A., Manjunath, T. N., & Mudunuri, T. (2019). Commodity and Forex trade automation using deep reinforcement learning. *1st International Conference on Advanced Technologies in Intelligent Control, Environment, Computing and Communication Engineering (ICATIECE 2019)*, 27–31. https://doi.org/10.1109/ICATIECE45860.2019.9063807.

Vatsa, K. S. (2004). Risk, vulnerability, and asset-based approach to disaster risk management. *International Journal of Sociology and Social Policy, 24*(10/11), 1–48.

Weber, R. H. (2010). Internet of Things—New security and privacy challenges. *Computer Law & Security Review, 26*(1), 23–30.

Wexler, M. N., & Oberlander, J. (2020). Robo-advisors (RAs): The programmed self-service market for professional advice. *Journal of Service Theory and Practice, 31*(3), 351–365. https://doi.org/10.1108/JSTP-07-2020-0153.

CHAPTER 4

Antecedents and Impact of Workplace Cyberbullying: A Systematic Literature Review

DIVYA GOEL, MITUSHI SINGH,* and SHIVANI KAPOOR

Jaypee Business School, Jaypee Institute Information Technology, Noida, Uttar Pradesh, India

*Corresponding author.

ABSTRACT

The style of the corporate world changed completely when the pandemic hit in December 2019. This shift forced businesses worldwide to adopt online working modes. While this transition has its advantages, it also has its drawbacks, one of which is cyberbullying. With the rise in remote work, incidents of cyberbullying have also increased. Over the past decade, cyberbullying has been a growing concern among school and college students, prompting extensive research to understand its causes and management strategies. More recently, it has become prevalent in the workplace, negatively affecting employees' mental health and organizational performance. Studies suggest that the consequences of workplace cyberbullying (WCB) are more severe than those of traditional workplace bullying. In this context, the present study systematically reviews existing literature to examine the impact of WCB on employees and organizations, as well as the factors contributing to cyberbullying behavior in the workplace. A systematic search was conducted across multiple databases, including Scopus, ProQuest, Web of Science, ScienceDirect, and Google Scholar. Inclusion and exclusion criteria were applied to shortlist relevant studies.

Transforming Business Finance in the Digital Era.
Sanjay Taneja, Mohammad Kashif, Ercan Özen, and Luan Vardari (Eds.)
© 2026 Apple Academic Press, Inc. Co-published with CRC Press (Taylor & Francis)

DOI: 10.1201/9781998511235-4

A total of 44 research papers published between 2002 and 2022 were reviewed, providing valuable insights into the effects of WCB on employee well-being and organizational performance.

4.1 INTRODUCTION

With the outbreak of the coronavirus, the economy has been severely impacted, and the working mechanism has undergone a complete transformation. The virus has affected numerous sectors, forcing individuals and organizations to adapt by maintaining social distancing and integrating virtual communication into daily operations. As a result, reliance on virtual communication has increased, with individuals prioritizing online interactions to minimize exposure to the virus. In this digital era, people are connected to the internet most of the time (WHO, 2020).

Internet-based communication has become an integral part of everyday life. Some people use online networks for social interactions, while others rely on them for work, studies, and daily routines. However, some individuals misuse the internet to bully others, a phenomenon known as cyberbullying. In recent years, as more companies have adopted internet-based workplace communication, workplace cyberbullying has become a growing concern. Vranjes et al. (2016) reported that 8 out of 10 people experienced cyberbullying in the workplace over the past six months, and 14%–20% felt they had been victims of cyberbullying in their workplace within the past few weeks. Workplace cyberbullying (WCB) is increasingly occurring across shared networks and has become a major issue for many organizations.

From an organizational perspective, WCB refers to situations and incidents where an employee is subjected to negative treatment regarding their work and tasks by internal members of the organization, such as peers or supervisors, or by external sources, such as customers or clients (D'Cruz and Noronha, 2013; Madden and Loh, 2020; Snyman and Loh, 2015).

Given the current business landscape, where organizations must compete on a global scale, companies are leveraging fast-paced information and communication technology to boost productivity, share knowledge, and facilitate communication. While these technologies are intended to enhance performance, they also have a downside—the growing prevalence of cyberbullying (Bhatnagar et al., 2024).

Workplace bullying has been the subject of extensive research. Traditional bullying is defined as a repetitive, intentional act of aggression involving one or more individuals, leading to a power imbalance. This undesirable behavior fosters a hostile work environment and causes significant stress among victims (Balducci et al., 2011).

Behaviors associated with WCB include intentionally withholding work-related information essential to an employee's job performance, as well as excluding colleagues from professional interactions (Brotheridge, 2013; Kashif et al., 2023a). Verbal aggression, such as spreading rumors and excessively criticizing work, is another common form of workplace bullying (Salin, 2008). Additionally, physical violence has been linked to traditional workplace bullying (Hershcovis, 2011).

Studies on cyberbullying among younger cohorts (Gradinger et al., 2009; Raskauskas and Stoltz, 2007; Smith et al., 2008) have revealed that most victims of traditional bullying are also victims of cyberbullying. This finding suggests a similarity between traditional and cyber forms of victimization. Other studies (D'Cruz and Noronha, 2013; Forssell, 2016; Privitera and Campbell, 2009) have also demonstrated a significant overlap between cyberbullying and traditional bullying. The similarities between traditional bullying and cyberbullying include the antecedents of bullying, the involvement of different organizational levels, associated behaviors, and outcomes.

4.2 METHODOLOGY

The present study aimed to review existing literature to understand the impact of workplace cyberbullying (WCB) on employees and organizations, as well as the factors contributing to cyberbullying behavior in the workplace. To conduct a systematic review of WCB and its associated factors, relevant studies were searched across multiple databases, including ProQuest, Scopus, Web of Science, and EBSCO. Google Scholar was also used as an additional source for identifying relevant studies.

The search was conducted using the following keyword combinations: "Workplace Cyberbullying AND Impact AND Antecedents;" "Cyberbullying AND Work AND Effects;" "Workplace Cyberbullying AND Outcomes;" "Workplace Cyberbullying AND Consequences AND Antecedents" for the period 2002–2022 (Kashif et al., 2023b).

This chapter included only those studies that highlighted the factors leading to cyberbullying incidents, as well as the consequences, impact, and outcomes of WCB. Studies that did not directly address the antecedents or impact of WCB and were either editorials, poster presentations, or case studies were excluded. After applying the inclusion and exclusion criteria and removing duplicate records, 44 relevant research studies were identified and analyzed.

The initial search across various databases yielded 562 studies, of which 283 were removed due to duplication. The remaining 279 studies were then screened based on their title, context, and findings, resulting in the exclusion of 217 studies that were either unrelated to the factors leading to WCB or did not provide findings on its impact on employees. Subsequently, the 62 shortlisted studies were distributed among the authors for a full-text review. The selected papers were critically analyzed and evaluated to assess their relevance based on the study's purpose, research methods, analysis, and implications.

Following a thorough evaluation, 44 studies were selected for a comprehensive review to examine the impact of WCB on employees and organizations, as well as the factors contributing to cyberbullying behavior in the workplace. The flow diagram (Figure 4.1) illustrates the search strategy used for selecting studies in this systematic review.

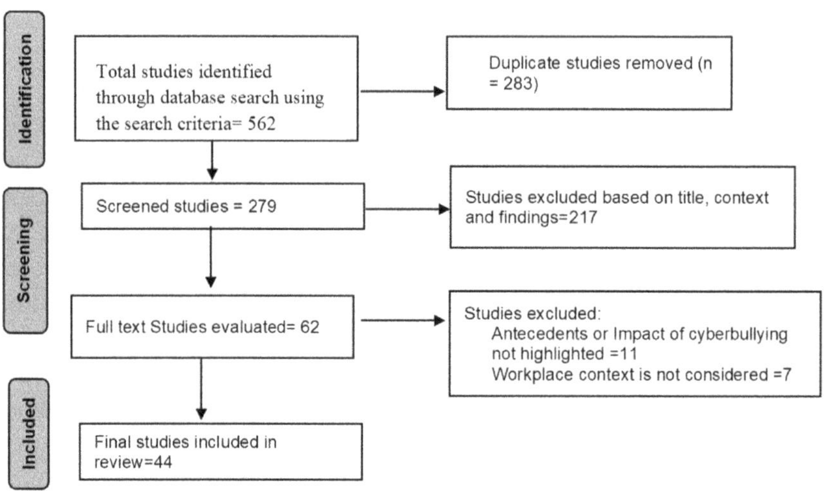

FIGURE 4.1 Flow diagram depicting study selection methodology.

Source: Authors' own work.

The subsequent sections highlight key findings related to the factors contributing to cyberbullying behavior in the workplace and the impact or outcomes of WCB on employees and organizations.

4.3 RESULTS AND DISCUSSIONS

Based on the reviewed articles and research papers, there is sufficient information and data available on the antecedents and impacts of WCB. This literature comes from various researchers across different geographical regions and academic backgrounds within the field of WCB. An overview of the 44 studies reviewed to identify the antecedents and impacts of WCB is presented in Table 4.1.

Based on the analysis of the findings from the 44 research studies, we have assembled the findings related to the antecedents of WCB into two categories: individual factors and organizational factors. The impact is divided into seven themes. The findings are presented and discussed to highlight the trends in the WCB literature.

4.3.1 ANTECEDENTS OF WCB

The antecedents of WCB have been divided into two aspects: the individual factors, which are the characteristics of the perpetrators that instigated him or her to bully the employee, and the organizational factors, which are those related to conditions within the organizations, processes to execute work, and operational aspects within the workplace that promote cyberbullying acts.

4.3.1.1 INDIVIDUAL FACTORS AS ANTECEDENTS

Zhang, Leidner et al. (2021) conducted an exhaustive study on the impact of low self-control on cyberbullying and the use of three organizational activities: mWork (working during family hours), boundary-spanning in enterprise social media (interaction with external members to accomplish goals), and regular email checking. The results revealed that low self-control and these three activities can be seen as compelling factors leading to WCB. The findings demonstrated that the effect of low self-control on workplace cyberbullying is intensified when employees engage in routine activities like mobile working, proactive email checking, and boundary

TABLE 4.1 Antecedents and Impact of Workplace Cyberbullying: An Overview of 44 Research Studies

SL. No.	Year and Author	Country	*Antecedents and Impact of Workplace Cyberbullying*
1.	Baruch (2005)	UK	The study focused on understanding the impact of bullying through email and other communication media. The findings highlighted the negative effects of bullying via information technology (IT), leading to increased anxiety, higher turnover intentions, lower job satisfaction, and reduced performance.
2.	Privitera and Campbell (2009)	Australia	This study contributes to bullying literature by analyzing the prevalence of both traditional bullying and cyberbullying. The findings suggest that the advent of information technology and increased applications of information and communication technology (ICT) are changing the nature of workplace bullying, taking a new form involving victimization through modern communication methods such as email and phones.
3.	D'Cruz and Noronha (2013)	India	The research findings highlight the coexistence of traditional bullying and cyberbullying in IT organizations. The study describes workplace cyberbullying (WCB) experiences as haunting, leading to physical and emotional strain, powerlessness, and a feeling of vulnerability.
4.	Zhang and Leidner (2014)	USA	The study used neutralization theory and rational choice theory to identify factors contributing to increased workplace cyberbullying. The findings suggest that formal company policies against cyberbullying, managerial intervention, employees' moral inhibitions, and a sense of fear or shame can reduce cyberbullying incidents. The research also highlights the negative effect of WCB on work motivation and its positive association with turnover intentions.
5.	Farley et al. (2015)	UK	The findings suggest that workplace cyberbullying negatively impacts job satisfaction and mental health. Victims of WCB experienced ill health following cyberbullying incidents.
6.	Snyman and Loh (2015)	Australia	The study highlights that workplace cyberbullying has a significant positive correlation with perceived stress and a negative effect on job satisfaction. WCB was also found to be negatively related to employee optimism.
7.	Farley (2015)	UK	This thesis explores the relationship between workplace cyberbullying and behavioral, attitudinal, and health outcomes. It finds that WCB results in increased anxiety, frustration, emotional exhaustion, and stress.
8.	Keskin et al. (2016)	Turkey	The study highlights that cyberbullying can lead to counterproductive workplace behaviors, including production deviance, sabotage, theft, and abuse.
9.	Vranjes et al. (2017)	UK	This study presents an understanding of environmental factors (e.g., work characteristics) and personal factors (e.g., emotional regulation tactics) that contribute to WCB incidents.

TABLE 4.1 *(Continued)*

SL. No.	Year and Author	Country	Antecedents and Impact of Workplace Cyberbullying
10.	Hollis (2016)	USA	This chapter highlights the public shaming aspect of cyberbullying, as content remains accessible in the public domain for years. The study also reveals that Black employees are more susceptible to cyberbullying compared to White employees.
11.	Gardner et al. (2016)	New Zealand	The study examines factors contributing to cyberbullying, finding that poor physical health, lack of organizational support, and ineffective strategies increase the likelihood of cyberbullying.
12.	Muhonen et al. (2017)	Sweden	This study asserts that the social organizational climate may mediate the relationship between workplace cyberbullying, employee well-being, work engagement, and job turnover. Unlike previous studies on traditional bullying, this research suggests that cyberbullying has stronger indirect effects on health, well-being, work engagement, and turnover.
13.	Coyne et al. (2017)	UK	The findings support the premise that the frequency and intensity of cyberbullying incidents significantly impact mental strain and job satisfaction.
14.	D'Souza et al. (2017)	New Zealand	This study presents insights from academicians and industry experts on workplace cyberbullying, highlighting its similarities and differences from traditional bullying. It also discusses measurement methods and management strategies for WCB.
15.	Kowalski et al. (2018)	USA	The study highlights that cyberbullying victims experience elevated levels of depression and social anxiety, along with reduced self-esteem. Victims report feelings of isolation, increased turnover, and engagement in counterproductive work behaviors. Job performance and satisfaction are also lower among victims of WCB.
16.	Van Geel et al. (2017)	Netherlands	The study examines the role of personality traits in predicting cyberbullying behavior at work. Findings indicate that agreeableness and sadism are linked to cyberbullying behaviors. Additionally, sadism is associated with antisocial behaviors, which contribute to workplace cyberbullying.
17.	Coyne and Farley (2018)	UK	This chapter provides a comprehensive view of workplace bullying, highlighting the increasing incidents of workplace cyberbullying (WCB). It explores the factors leading to cyberbullying and compares it with traditional workplace bullying.
18.	Madden and Loh (2018)	Australia	The study highlights that bystander intervention can play a crucial role during workplace cyberbullying incidents. Findings suggest that intervention is more likely when the bystander perceives the target as a friend rather than a colleague and when fewer bystanders are present.

TABLE 4.1 *(Continued)*

SL. No.	Year and Author	Country	Antecedents and Impact of Workplace Cyberbullying
19.	D'Souza et al. (2018)	New Zealand	The research suggests that cyberbullying has more severe outcomes than conventional bullying due to the permanence of digital content and the anonymity of perpetrators. The study emphasizes the role of job design and organizational culture in facilitating WCB. Competitive work environments and differential incentive schemes were also found to promote WCB. The findings suggest that WCB is deeply embedded in organizational systems and requires multi-level interventions.
20.	Iftikhar and Beh (2018)	Pakistan	The study highlights that excessive use of information and communication technology (ICT), social networking, and other digital communication tools has contributed to an increase in WCB incidents. Additionally, an organizational climate characterized by unclear job descriptions, time pressure, cultural norms, work arrangements, and managerial leadership styles can lead to workplace cyberbullying.
21.	Mijeong et al. (2019)	South Korea	The findings suggest that organizations need to effectively handle, manage, and prevent workplace cyberbullying, as it strongly impacts employees' psychological symptoms and turnover intentions.
22.	D'Souza et al. (2019)	New Zealand	This study presents individual accounts of cyberbullying experiences among nurses, highlighting its harmful effects, including feelings of sadness, exclusion, fear, and distrust.
23.	Anwar et al. (2020)	Malaysia	The study highlights a positive association between workplace cyberbullying and interpersonal deviance. Findings suggest that increased interpersonal deviance can lead to workplace disruptions and financial losses. Emotional exhaustion was found to mediate the relationship between cyberbullying and deviance. However, among employees who engage in "ineffectual silence," the relationship between cyberbullying and interpersonal deviance was found to be negative.
24.	Vranjes et al. (2020)	UK	The study explores the individual and organizational consequences of workplace cyberbullying. Individual outcomes include negative emotions, stress, mental strain, and depressive symptoms, while organizational outcomes include decreased job satisfaction, increased turnover intentions, absenteeism, lower organizational support, decreased engagement, counterproductive work behavior, and reduced performance.
25.	Loh and Snyman (2020)	Australia	Conducted among Australian employees, this study examines the relationship between workplace cyberbullying and job outcomes. Findings indicate that WCB increases perceived stress levels in employees, which in turn leads to job dissatisfaction. Female employees reported experiencing higher levels of stress and dissatisfaction compared to male employees.

TABLE 4.1 *(Continued)*

SL. No.	Year and Author	Country	Antecedents and Impact of Workplace Cyberbullying
26.	Alhujailli et al. (2020)	USA	This study investigates the effects of cyberbullying on employees' emotional state and stress levels, particularly in cases of social exclusion and verbal harassment. Findings reveal that social exclusion and verbal harassment significantly increase negative emotions and stress, with verbal harassment having a more severe impact.
27.	Kim et al. (2020)	Malaysia	This study is part of an ongoing project focused on developing and testing a mobile mental health intervention for healthcare professionals. Findings indicate that workplace cyberbullying negatively impacts communication and work behaviors, leading to increased role conflict and interpersonal conflict. The study suggests that organizations should adopt technological interventions to reduce conflict and enhance employee productivity.
28.	Kalyar et al. (2020)	Pakistan	This study explores the link between cyberbullying and employee creativity among nurses, focusing on the mediating role of psychological distress and psychological capital. Findings suggest that increased cyberbullying leads to psychological distress, which negatively impacts creativity. However, nurses with higher psychological capital—defined by resilience, hope, self-efficacy, and optimism—experience less distress, mitigating the negative effects of cyberbullying on creativity and performance. The study recommends training nurses to develop psychological capital to cope with cyberbullying.
29.	Oksanen et al. (2020)	Europe	This study examines the role of supervisor support and employee age in cyberbullying victimization. It also explores the impact of workplace cyberbullying on psychological distress, work exhaustion, and "technostress." Findings suggest that employees who strongly associate social media with their identity experience more severe effects of cyberbullying.
30.	Forssell (2020)	Sweden	The study emphasizes the role of organizational social climate in workplace cyberbullying. Findings indicate that employees with greater influence over work decisions experience lower cyberbullying incidents. Additionally, support from colleagues and managers negatively correlates with WCB. A supportive workplace climate was also found to reduce WCB behavior.
31.	Symons et al. (2020)	United States	This concept analysis identifies key characteristics of workplace cyberbullying, including its boundaryless nature, reliance on digital technology, persistence beyond the workplace, and involvement of anonymous perpetrators. The study highlights that cyberbullying leads to increased job dissatisfaction, reduced performance, lower physical and psychological well-being, heightened stress, and higher turnover. From an organizational perspective, WCB contributes to financial losses and reputational damage.

TABLE 4.1 *(Continued)*

SL. No.	Year and Author	Country	Antecedents and Impact of Workplace Cyberbullying
32.	Singthong (2020)	Thailand	Using a qualitative approach, this study examines the experiences and impact of cyberbullying incidents on victims. Interview results highlight severe psychological distress, depression, decreased productivity, increased intent to leave, and reputational damage to the victims' professional standing.
33.	Tiamboonprasert and Charoensukmongkol (2020)	Bangkok	The study emphasizes the role of ethical leadership in reducing cyberbullying in work units. Findings suggest that cyberbullying negatively affects employee commitment. Additionally, the use of computer-mediated platforms moderates the relationship between ethical leadership and exposure to cyberbullying, as well as the link between cyberbullying and employee commitment.
34.	Mushtaq et al. (2021)	Pakistan	The research study explores the linkage between cyberbullying and creativity, cyberbullying and burnout, and burnout and creativity. The findings suggest that cyberbullying decreases creativity and increases burnout. Increased burnout, in turn, decreases creativity. On the other hand, job burnout was not found to play a mediating role in the relationship between cyberbullying and creativity. The moderating factor of family social support, however, was found to weaken the association between cyberbullying and job burnout and vice versa.
35.	Farley et al. (2021)	USA	The study proposes that technological advancements can make bullying experiences more stressful as incidents of cyberbullying permeate through the office premises and can have long-ranging effects. The paper also highlights the role played by individual characteristics of employees, such as gender, age, and personality traits, in the WCB incidents.
36.	Czakert et al. (2021)	Germany and Spain	The paper had the objective of testing and validating the CBQ-S (Cyberbullying Behavior Questionnaire Short version) in Spanish and German languages to provide a reliable and valid questionnaire to measure workplace cyberbullying in Spanish and German organizations. The results substantiate the reliability and all forms of validity for CBQ-S in Spain and Germany. The results also suggested that cyberbullying has a direct link with workplace bullying as well as stressors at the workplace, such as role ambiguity and role conflict. Additionally, workplace cyberbullying has a positive relationship with stress and turnover intentions, and it decreases job satisfaction in both countries.
37.	Scott (2021)	New Zealand	The research findings emphasized that the personality of both perpetrators and victims may lead to cyberbullying behavior. A lower confidence level of victims and poor management competencies, along with the poor pressure coping abilities of perpetrators, can lead to WCB. Organizational factors like high performance pressures, lack of organizational support, and workplace culture can contribute to increased incidents of WCB.

TABLE 4.1 *(Continued)*

SL. No.	Year and Author	Country	Antecedents and Impact of Workplace Cyberbullying
38.	Zhang, Leidner et al. (2021)	USA	The study focused on understanding the role played by the traits of the perpetrator and the contextual situations in the increased incidents of workplace cyberbullying. The findings suggest that employees with low self-control have a higher tendency to engage in workplace cyberbullying. The results also highlighted that some routine activities, such as mobile working, the tendency for proactive email checking, and boundary spanning in enterprise social media, also contribute to the increased incidents of workplace cyberbullying by creating the right context for the perpetrators.
39.	Zhang, Wang et al. (2021)	China	The study results presented a new framework to understand the cognitive mechanism defining the relationship between workplace cyberbullying and interpersonal deviance in employees. The study suggests that workplace cyberbullying leads to personal ego depletion, which further results in interpersonal deviance. On the other hand, it also highlights the importance of supervisor support in buffering the negative effect of workplace cyberbullying on ego depletion and, hence, reduced interpersonal deviance.
40.	Zhang, Xiao et al. (2021)	China	The findings of the paper highlight that workplace cyberbullying leads to ego depletion, which further results in increased job strain in employees. The findings also highlight the importance of employees' self-efficacy in buffering the negative effect of ego depletion on job strain. It thus suggests that employees with low self-efficacy experience more job strain when experiencing workplace cyberbullying compared to those with high self-efficacy.
41.	Anwar et al. (2022)	Pakistan	The study presents unique findings that suggest the positive effect of workplace cyberbullying on work engagement in employees. The results also reveal that psychological well-being mediates the relationship between workplace cyberbullying and work engagement, and work meaningfulness also plays an important role in enhancing work engagement by moderating the linkage between psychological well-being and work engagement.
42.	Karthikeyan (2022)	India	The research provides a clear understanding of the various forms of cyberbullying behaviors used by employees in the organizational context. The study also provides a comprehensive view of the detrimental effects of WCB on employee motivation, leading to increased absenteeism and low productivity. The negative impact of WCB on the health and well-being of employees is highlighted, leading to increased pressure on employers to reduce workplace health bills and maintain a healthy and safe workplace for employees to meet statutory norms.
43.	Karthikeyan (2022)	India	The study highlights that the swelling psychological dependence and excessive usage of technological gadgets and social media vulnerability are the main causes of the ever-increasing incidents of WCB. The negative effect of WCB on the psychological health of employees, especially women, is also highlighted.
44.	Tiamboonprasert and Charoensukmongkol (2022)	Thailand	The research findings suggest the key role played by ethical leader behavior and organizational politics in reducing or increasing the WCB incidents. The findings also highlight the negative impact of WCB on organizational commitment and employee burnout.

spanning in enterprise social media. Similarly, Coyne and Farley (2018) found that individual characteristics that triggered cyberbullying incidents in organizations included low self-esteem, low empathy, and an inflated need for power.

In their study, Vranjes et al. (2016) highlighted work stressors as trigger points leading to emotions and thereby resulting in WCB. Stressors such as role conflict and interpersonal conflict lead to anger (emotion) in the perpetrator, thereby resulting in cyberbullying. The personality of both perpetrators and victims may lead to cyberbullying behavior. A low confidence level in victims and poor management competencies, along with the poor pressure coping abilities of perpetrators, can lead to WCB (Scott, 2021). Poor physical health is also a factor that promotes WCB, according to the findings of Gardner et al. (2016). Employees who possess these traits are more prone to resort to cyberbullying acts.

4.3.1.2 ORGANIZATIONAL FACTORS AS ANTECEDENTS

The research findings highlight that cyberbullying has more severe consequences compared to traditional bullying due to the permanency of cyber content and the anonymity of cyber communications, which are rapidly disseminated and invade personal boundaries. The results of the study conducted by D'Souza et al. (2018) emphasized the role of job design and organizational culture in facilitating workplace cyberbullying (WCB). Competitive work environments and differential incentive schemes were also found to promote WCB. The study further highlights that WCB is deeply embedded in organizational systems, necessitating multi-level interventions to address this concern. Employees' influence and control over work and decision-making can reduce WCB behavior. Additionally, support from colleagues and managers can negatively impact WCB incidents (Forssell, 2020). Thus, an encouraging and supportive social climate was also found to be negatively associated with WCB behavior.

Coyne and Farley (2018), in their research on "Cyberbullying within working contexts," revealed that some organizational factors acting as antecedents include organizational change, competition, poor management, and a lack of clear policies. Vranjes et al. (2016) also studied organizational change as a factor that promotes WCB. The study by Gardner et al. (2016) emphasized understanding the factors leading to cyberbullying, suggesting that a lack of support from the organization and ineffective organizational strategies lead to more incidents of cyberbullying. Similarly, the organizational climate characterized by unclear job descriptions, time pressure, cultural norms, working arrangements, and the leadership style of managers can lead to the occurrence of cyberbullying in the workplace (Iftikhar and Beh, 2018). Organizational factors such as high performance pressures, lack of organizational support, and workplace culture can contribute to increased incidents of WCB (Scott, 2021).

Some researchers, like Zhang and Leidner (2014), analyzed the factors that can curb cyberbullying and used neutralization theory and rational choice theory to identify the factors causing increased cyberbullying behavior in the workplace. The findings suggest that formal company policies against cyberbullying, managerial intervention against cyberbullying perpetrators, employees' moral inhibitions, and fear or shame among employees can negatively affect cyberbullying incidents in organizations. According to Tiamboonprasert and Charoensukmongkol (2020), supervisors' ethical leadership fosters a work climate that prevents WCB; thus, a lack of ethical leadership promotes cyberbullying. In their latest study, Tiamboonprasert and Charoensukmongkol (2022) highlighted the role of organizational politics in either reducing or increasing WCB incidents, along with the impact of ethical leadership.

4.3.2 IMPACT OF WCB

One of the key objectives of this study was to identify the impact or consequences of workplace cyberbullying. Based on a rigorous review of the literature published on workplace cyberbullying, we categorized the effects of WCB into seven themes as outlined below.

4.3.2.1 THEME 1: STRESS

The increasing stress levels among employees are a growing concern for individuals and organizations alike. Numerous studies have revealed a direct relationship between WCB and stress. According to Loh and Snyman (2020), cyberbullying resulted in perceived stress, which also leads to increased job dissatisfaction, and this is higher among female employees compared to their male counterparts. Czakert et al. (2021) and Kashif et al. (2017a) conducted comparative studies in Germany and Spain, finding a positive linkage between WCB and stress in both countries. Mushtaq et al. (2021) examined the relationship between cyberbullying, burnout, and creativity. The findings indicate that cyberbullying decreases creativity and increases burnout, with increased burnout also diminishing creativity. However, job burnout does not facilitate the relationship between cyberbullying and creativity. Earlier studies have also revealed similar results, such as Baruch (2005), who discussed increased anxiety levels, and Farley (2015), who asserted that WCB adversely impacts mental peace.

4.3.2.2 THEME 2: JOB SATISFACTION

The human resources department of every organization strives to enhance the job satisfaction of its employees. Organizations create employee-friendly policies to keep employees happy and satisfied. WCB can adversely affect employee satisfaction levels, as revealed by various studies. The volume and intensity of cyberbullying incidents significantly impact individual mental strain and job satisfaction, with WCB negatively affecting job satisfaction (Coyne et al., 2017). It is also highlighted that WCB has a significant and negative effect on employee job satisfaction (Snyman and Loh, 2015). Furthermore, WCB was found to be negatively related to optimism among employees.

4.3.2.3 THEME 3: PSYCHOLOGICAL WELL-BEING

In the current scenario of COVID-19, employee well-being is at the top of the priority list for organizations worldwide. Cyberbullying can have negative and long-lasting effects on employee well-being. Oksanen et al. (2020) revealed that victims of cyberbullying reported psychological distress, techno-stress, and work exhaustion, which was more prevalent among social media users. Previous studies on cyberbullying had similar outcomes (Fariya et al., 2024; Kowalski et al., 2018). The studies by Karthikeyan (2022) and Kashif et al. (2017b) also highlight the increasing psychological dependence and excessive use of technological gadgets and social media vulnerability as the main causes of the rising incidents of WCB. The negative effect of WCB on the psychological health of employees, especially women, is also emphasized.

Organizations must curb WCB, as it has a cascading effect on employee well-being, leading to increased absenteeism, turnover, and decreased productivity. Karthikeyan (2022) highlighted the negative impact of WCB on the health and well-being of employees, asserting that WCB increases pressure on employers to reduce workplace health costs and maintain a healthy and safe workplace to meet statutory norms.

Cyberbullying can occur even when the employee is not physically present in the organization. Contrary to earlier face-to-face bullying, Muhonen et al. (2017) proposed that cyberbullying behavior can have an indirect linkage with employee health and well-being, emphasizing the important role of the social organizational climate in mediating the relationship between cyberbullying behavior and employee well-being.

4.3.2.4 THEME 4: TURNOVER INTENTIONS

Employee turnover has always been a concern for organizations. The resignation of talented employees adversely affects organizational performance. Studies reveal that cyberbullying can increase the employee turnover rate within the organization. According to Czakert et al. (2021), WCB has a positive and direct relationship with turnover intentions. Similar findings were reported by Zhang and Leidner (2014), which showed a positive association between cyberbullying and turnover intentions.

WCB is a covert and ongoing issue; the victim undergoes systemic experiences, and if cyberbullying is repeated, it directly influences the turnover intention of the victimized employee. Park and Choi (2019) studied perceived organizational support and found that it plays a significant role in mediating the relationship between workplace cyberbullying and turnover intention. However, the research of Muhonen et al. (2017) indicated that WCB had an indirect rather than a direct relationship with employee intention to quit, with the social organizational climate mediating the relationship between cyberbullying behavior and intention to quit.

4.3.2.5 THEME 5: EMPLOYEE FEELINGS

Organizations strive to foster positive feelings among employees. Research in the area of workplace cyberbullying (WCB) indicates that cyberbullying can induce negative feelings among employees. The study by Kowalski et al. (2019) found that victims of cyberbullying experience higher levels of social anxiety and depression, exacerbated by lower self-esteem. Additionally, victims reported feelings of loneliness. The findings of D'Souza et al. (2019) revealed that individuals experiencing cyberbullying had feelings of sadness, exclusion, and an increased sense of fear and distrust. This aligns with the study by Alhujailli et al. (2020), which asserted that social exclusion and verbal harassment induce a negative emotional state among employees. Snyman and Loh (2015) examined the relationship between WCB and optimistic feelings among employees, finding a negative correlation. If organizations aim to keep their employees happy and promote positive feelings, they must control WCB within the workplace.

4.3.2.6 THEME 6: EMPLOYEE ENGAGEMENT

Employee engagement is another factor influenced by cyberbullying. However, the results differ significantly from both the expected outcomes and traditional face-to-face bullying. According to the study on the hotel industry by Anwar et al. (2020), workplace cyberbullying encourages work engagement. The study revealed a significant and positive association between workplace cyberbullying and work engagement. Similarly, the results of the study conducted by Muhonen et al. (2017) indicated that out of the four variables—namely well-being, work engagement, health, and intention to quit—only work engagement had a significant direct relationship with cyberbullying. The research concluded that this result could be attributed to cultural impacts. At times, superiors pressure or shout at subordinates to increase productivity. Victims may not even realize they are being bullied, as it is perceived as part of the culture and a method to extract work.

4.3.2.7 THEME 7: OTHER FACTORS

Researchers have also sought to study the impact of workplace cyberbullying (WCB) on employee loyalty, teamwork, trust (Symons et al., 2021), and creativity (Kalyar et al., 2021; Mushtaq et al., 2021). It was found that WCB negatively affected all these behavioral aspects within an organization. WCB has a positive correlation with interpersonal deviance, which in turn relates to financial costs and workplace disruptions (Anwar et al., 2020).

According to the findings of Czakert et al. (2021), there is a direct correlation between cyberbullying, role ambiguity, and role conflict. The research by Zhang and Leidner (2014) highlighted that employee motivation is negatively affected by WCB. Karthikeyan (2022), in his study, also provides a comprehensive view of the detrimental effects of WCB on employee motivation, leading to increased absenteeism and reduced productivity.

4.4 CONCLUSION

The current review was conducted to understand and explore the factors causing cyberbullying incidents in the workplace and to underline the key outcomes or impacts of WCB on employees and organizations. Considering modern workplace technologies characterized by online working, information sharing over the internet, the penetration of social media in workplaces, and the work-from-home scenario becoming the new normal, incidents of cyberbullying have increased. Numerous studies have been conducted to understand the prevalence of bullying and cyberbullying in adolescents and teenagers, but when it comes to organizations, policymakers have not emphasized understanding the relevance of cyberbullying and its impact on employees and the organizations themselves.

In line with traditional face-to-face bullying, it can be argued that cyberbullying will also have a detrimental impact on employees and organizations. However, to address the severity of WCB, organizations need to understand the possible antecedents to prevent cyberbullying incidents in the workplace. Based on this comprehensive review, it has been found that in most cases, incidents of cyberbullying can have severe negative effects on employees' physical and mental health, increasing stress levels. This impact is exacerbated by the anonymity element and the repetitive reproduction of abusive messages on social media, which can be daunting for employees' overall well-being. Some studies have also highlighted that organizations are negatively impacted in terms of reduced employee productivity, lower job satisfaction levels, higher turnover intentions, and increased negative feelings among employees.

To prevent and reduce incidents of cyberbullying, organizations must formulate and implement strict policies for employees engaged in WCB. Leaders must prioritize WCB and develop a culture and climate within the organization where perpetrators are deterred from bullying employees, and victims are empowered to voice their concerns against cyberbullying.

KEYWORDS

- **antecedents**
- **cyberbullying**
- **organizational climate**
- **traditional bullying**
- **victims**
- **work engagement**
- **workplace culture**
- **workplace cyberbullying**

REFERENCES

Alhujailli, A., Karwowski, W., Wan, T. T., & Hancock, P. (2020). Affective and stress consequences of cyberbullying. *Symmetry, 12*(9), 1536.

Anwar, A., Kee, D. M. H., & Ahmed, A. (2020). Workplace cyberbullying and interpersonal deviance: Understanding the mediating effect of silence and emotional exhaustion. *Cyberpsychology, Behavior, and Social Networking, 23*(5), 290–296. https://doi.org/10.1089/cyber.2019.0407.

Anwar, A., Kee, D. M. H., & Ijaz, M. F. (2022). Social media bullying in the workplace and its impact on work engagement: A case of psychological well-being. *Information, 13*(4), 165. https://doi.org/10.3390/info13040165.

Balducci, C., Fraccaroli, F., & Schaufeli, W. B. (2011). Workplace bullying and its relation with work characteristics, personality, and post-traumatic stress symptoms: An integrated model. *Anxiety, Stress & Coping, 24*(5), 499–513.

Baruch, Y. (2005). Bullying on the net: Adverse behavior on e-mail and its impact. *Information and Management, 42*(2), 361–371. https://doi.org/10.1016/j.im.2004.02.001.

Bhatnagar, M., Kumar, P., Taneja, S., Sood, K., & Grima, S. (2024). From digital overload to trading zen: The role of digital detox in enhancing intraday trading performance. In *Business Drivers in Promoting Digital Detoxification* (pp. 148–176). IGI Global.

Brotheridge, C. M. (2013). Explaining bullying: Using theory to answer practical questions. *Team Performance Management: An International Journal, 19*(3/4), 185–201.

Coyne, I., & Farley, S. (2018). Cyberbullying within working contexts. In *Cyberbullying at University in International Contexts* (pp. 80–96). Routledge.

Coyne, I., Farley, S., Axtell, C., Sprigg, C., Best, L., & Kwok, O. (2017). Understanding the relationship between experiencing workplace cyberbullying, employee mental strain and job satisfaction: A dysempowerment approach. *International Journal of Human Resource Management, 28*(7), 945–972. https://doi.org/10.1080/09585192.2015.1116454.

Cristian, B., & Wilmar, B. (2017). The job demands-resources model and counterproductive work behaviour: The role of job-related affect. *Work and Stress, 31*(3), 357–381.

Czakert, J. P., Reif, J., Glazer, S., & Berger, R. (2021). Adaptation and psychometric cross-cultural validation of a workplace cyberbullying questionnaire in Spain and Germany. *Cyberpsychology, Behavior, and Social Networking, 24*(12), 831–838. https://doi.org/10.1089/cyber.2020.0856.

D'Cruz, P., & Noronha, E. (2013). Navigating the extended reach: Target experiences of cyberbullying at work. *Information and Organization, 23*(4), 324–343.

D'Souza, N., Catley, B., Tappin, D., & Forsyth, D. (2019). "You live and breathe it…": Exploring experiences of workplace cyberbullying among New Zealand nurses. *Journal of Management and Organization*. https://doi.org/10.1017/jmo.2019.71.

D'Souza, N., Forsyth, D., Tappin, D., & Catley, B. (2017). Engaging industry specialists on the issue of workplace cyberbullying: A New Zealand study. *Journal of Health Safety and Environment, 33*(2), 105–124.

D'Souza, N., Forsyth, D., Tappin, D., & Catley, B. (2018). Conceptualizing workplace cyberbullying: Toward a definition for research and practice in nursing. *Journal of Nursing Management, 26*(7), 842–850. https://doi.org/10.1111/jonm.12614.

Fariya, Saini, A., & Kashif, M. (2024). Exploring the influence of factors driving financial accessibility, financial activities, and financial education on sustainable development. In *Artificial Intelligence and Machine Learning-Powered Smart Finance* (pp. 23–49). IGI Global.

Farley, S. (2015). The measurement and impact of workplace cyberbullying (Doctoral dissertation, University of Sheffield).

Farley, S., Coyne, I., & D'Cruz, P. (2021). Cyberbullying at work: Understanding the influence of technology. In *Concepts, Approaches and Methods* (pp. 233–263). IGI Global.

Farley, S., Coyne, I., Sprigg, C., Axtell, C., & Subramanian, G. (2015). Exploring the impact of workplace cyberbullying on trainee doctors. *Medical Education, 49*(4), 436–443. https://doi.org/10.1111/medu.12666.

Forssell, R. (2016). Exploring cyberbullying and face-to-face bullying in working life: Prevalence, targets, and expressions. *Computers in Human Behavior, 58*, 454–460.

Forssell, R. C. (2020). Gender and organizational position: Predicting victimization of cyberbullying behavior in working life. *International Journal of Human Resource Management, 31*(16), 2045–2064. https://doi.org/10.1080/09585192.2018.1424018.

Gardner, D., O'Driscoll, M., Cooper-Thomas, H. D., Roche, M., Bentley, T., Catley, B., Teo, S. T. T., & Trenberth, L. (2016). Predictors of workplace bullying and cyber-bullying in New Zealand. *International Journal of Environmental Research and Public Health, 13*(5). https://doi.org/10.3390/ijerph13050448.

Gradinger, P., Strohmeier, D., & Spiel, C. (2009). Traditional bullying and cyberbullying: Identification of risk groups for adjustment problems. *Zeitschrift für Psychologie/Journal of Psychology, 217*(4), 205.

Hershcovis, M. S. (2011). "Incivility, social undermining, bullying… oh my!": A call to reconcile constructs within workplace aggression research. *Journal of Organizational Behavior, 32*(3), 499–519.

Hollis, L. P. (2016). Cybershaming – Technology, cyberbullying, and the application to people of color (pp. 125–135). https://doi.org/10.1108/s1479-364420160000018014.

Iftikhar, M., & Beh, L.-S. (2018). Prevalence level and predictors of face-to-face and cyberbullying in selected service sectors of Pakistan. *International Journal of Engineering & Technology, 7*(2). www.sciencepubco.com/index.php/IJET (accessed on 17 January 2025).

Kalyar, M. N., Saeed, M., Usta, A., & Shafique, I. (2021). Workplace cyberbullying and creativity: Examining the roles of psychological distress and psychological capital. *Management Research Review, 44*(4), 607–624. https://doi.org/10.1108/MRR-03-2020-0130.

Karthikeyan, C. (2020). Workplace cyberbullying and its impact on productivity (pp. 197–214). https://doi.org/10.4018/978-1-7998-4912-4.ch010.

Karthikeyan, C. (2022). The escalating cyberbullying menace through social media platforms in developing countries including India (pp. 526–546). https://doi.org/10.4018/978-1-7998-9187-1.ch023.

Karthikeyan, C. (2022). The escalating cyberbullying menace through social media platforms in developing countries including India: The social media vulnerabilities due to excessive usage. In *Handbook of Research on Digital Violence and Discrimination Studies* (pp. 526–546). IGI Global.

Karthikeyan, C. (2022). Workplace cyberbullying and its impact on productivity. In *Research Anthology on Combating Cyber-Aggression and Online Negativity* (pp. 1498–1515). IGI Global.

Kashif, M., Kumar, P., Ghai, S., & Kumar, S. (2023b). Disruptive technologies in computational finance. In *Algorithmic Approaches to Financial Technology: Forecasting, Trading, and Optimization* (pp. 46–60). IGI Global.

Kashif, M., Shajar, S. N., Singhal, N., & Kumar, P. (2023a). Achieving sustainable investment practices through green finance: Challenges and opportunities. In *Sustainable Investments in Green Finance* (pp. 234–244). IGI Global.

Kashif, M., Sridharan, P., & Thiyagarajan, S. (2017a). Factors affecting international reserves with special reference to India. *Vision, 21*(4), 339–349.

Kashif, M., Thiyagarajan, S., & Sridharan, P. (2017b). Dynamics of Algeria's international reserves. *African Journal of Economic and Management Studies, 8*(4), 410–419.

Keskin, H., Akgün, A. E., Ayar, H., & Kayman, Ş. S. (2016). Cyberbullying victimization, counterproductive work behaviors, and emotional intelligence at the workplace. *Procedia – Social and Behavioral Sciences, 235*, 281–287. https://doi.org/10.1016/j.sbspro.2016.11.031.

Kim, Y. J., Qian, L., & Aslam, M. S. (2020). Development of a personalized mobile mental health intervention for workplace cyberbullying among health practitioners: Protocol for a mixed methods study. *JMIR Research Protocols, 9*(11). https://doi.org/10.2196/23112.

Kowalski, R. M., Toth, A., & Morgan, M. (2018). Bullying and cyberbullying in adulthood and the workplace. *Journal of Social Psychology, 158*(1), 64–81. https://doi.org/10.1080/00224545.2017.1302402.

Loh, J., & Snyman, R. (2020). The tangled web: Consequences of workplace cyberbullying in adult male and female employees. *Gender in Management, 35*(6), 567–584. https://doi.org/10.1108/GM-12-2019-0242.

Madden, C., & Loh, J. (2020). Workplace cyberbullying and bystander helping behavior. *International Journal of Human Resource Management, 31*(19), 2434–2458. https://doi.org/10.1080/09585192.2018.1449130.

Muhonen, T., Jönsson, S., & Bäckström, M. (2017). Consequences of cyberbullying behavior in working life: The mediating roles of social support and social organizational climate. *International Journal of Workplace Health Management, 10*(5), 376–390. https://doi.org/10.1108/IJWHM-10-2016-0075.

Mushtaq, W., Qammar, A., Shafique, I., & Anjum, Z. U. Z. (2021). Effect of cyberbullying on employee creativity: Examining the roles of family social support and job burnout. *Foresight*. https://doi.org/10.1108/FS-01-2021-0018.

Oksanen, A., Oksa, R., Savela, N., Kaakinen, M., & Ellonen, N. (2020). Cyberbullying victimization at work: Social media identity bubble approach. *Computers in Human Behavior, 109*. https://doi.org/10.1016/j.chb.2020.106363.

Park, M., & Choi, J. S. (2019). Effects of workplace cyberbullying on nurses' symptom experience and turnover intention. *Journal of Nursing Management, 27*(6), 1108–1115. https://doi.org/10.1111/jonm.12779.

Privitera, C., & Campbell, M. A. (2009). Cyberbullying: The new face of workplace bullying? *Cyberpsychology and Behavior, 12*(4), 395–400. https://doi.org/10.1089/cpb.2009.0025.

Raskauskas, J., & Stoltz, A. D. (2007). Involvement in traditional and electronic bullying among adolescents. *Developmental Psychology, 43*(3), 564–575. https://doi.org/10.1037/0012-1649.43.3.564.

Salin, D. (2008). The prevention of workplace bullying as a question of human resource management: Measures adopted and underlying organizational factors. *Scandinavian Journal of Management, 24*(3), 221–231.

Scott, K. (2021). Exploring experiences of cyberbullying in the New Zealand workplace: A victim's perspective. *Journal of Asia Entrepreneurship and Sustainability, 17*(5), 8–49.

Singthong, T. (2020). Impacts of cyberbullying in the workplace (Master's dissertation, Mahidol University).

Smith, P. K., Mahdavi, J., Carvalho, M., Fisher, S., Russell, S., & Tippett, N. (2008). Cyberbullying: Its nature and impact in secondary school pupils. *Journal of Child Psychology and Psychiatry, 49*(4), 376–385. https://doi.org/10.1111/j.1469-7610.2007.01846.x.

Snyman, R., & Loh, J. (2015). Cyberbullying at work: The mediating role of optimism between cyberbullying and job outcomes. *Computers in Human Behavior, 53*, 161–168. https://doi.org/10.1016/j.chb.2015.06.050.

Symons, M. M., di Carlo, H., & Caboral-Stevens, M. (2021). Workplace cyberbullying exposed: A concept analysis. *Nursing Forum, 56*(1), 141–150. https://doi.org/10.1111/nuf.12505.

Tiamboonprasert, W., & Charoensukmongkol, P. (2020). Effect of ethical leadership on workplace cyberbullying exposure and organizational commitment. *The Journal of Behavioral Science, 15*(3), 85–100.

Tiamboonprasert, W., & Charoensukmongkol, P. (2022). Effects of ethical leadership and organizational politics on workplace cyberbullying and job consequences of employees in a Thai educational institution: Moderating role of political skill of employees (Doctoral dissertation, National Institute of Development Administration).

Van Geel, M., Goemans, A., Toprak, F., & Vedder, P. (2017). Which personality traits are related to traditional bullying and cyberbullying? A study with the Big Five, Dark Triad, and sadism. *Personality and Individual Differences, 106*, 231–235.

Vranjes, I., Baillien, E., Vandebosch, H., & Erreygers, S. (2016). Design, development, and validation of a workplace cyberbullying measure. *Computers in Human Behavior, 44*, 207–211.

Vranjes, I., Baillien, E., Vandebosch, H., Erreygers, S., & de Witte, H. (2017). The dark side of working online: Towards a definition and an emotion reaction model of workplace cyberbullying. *Computers in Human Behavior, 69*, 324–334. https://doi.org/10.1016/j.chb.2016.12.055.

Vranjes, I., Farley, S., & Baillien, E. (2020). Harassment in the digital world. In *Bullying and Harassment in the Workplace* (pp. 409–433). CRC Press. https://doi.org/10.1201/9780429462528-15.

Zhang, S., & Leidner, D. (2014). Workplace cyberbullying: The antecedents and consequences. In *Social-Technical Issues and Social Inclusion Track (SIGSI)*, 20th Americas Conference on Information Systems.

Zhang, S., Leidner, D., Cao, X., & Liu, N. (2022). Workplace cyberbullying: A criminological and routine activity perspective. *Journal of Information Technology, 37*(1), 51–79. https://doi.org/10.1177/02683962211027888.

Zhang, Z., Wang, H., Zhang, L., & Zheng, J. (2021). Workplace cyberbullying and interpersonal deviance: Roles of depletion and perceived supervisor support. *Asia Pacific Journal of Human Resources*. https://doi.org/10.1111/1744-7941.12303.

Zhang, Z., Xiao, H., Zhang, L., & Zheng, J. (2021). Linking cyberbullying to job strain: Roles of ego depletion and self-efficacy. *Journal of Aggression, Maltreatment, and Trauma*. https://doi.org/10.1080/10926771.2021.1933288.

CHAPTER 5

Exploring the Future of FinTech: Innovations, Challenges, and Opportunities

SANJAY TANEJA,[1,*] KAPIL SHARMA,[2] JASPREET KAUR,[2] and LUAN VARDARI[3]

[1]*Department of Management, Graphic Era (Deemed to be University), Dehradun, Uttarakhand, India*

[2]*University School of Business, Chandigarh University, Mohali, Punjab, India*

[3]*University "Ukshin Hoti" Prizren, Kosovo*

**Corresponding author.*

ABSTRACT

This chapter presents a comprehensive exploration of the evolving landscape of financial technology (FinTech), highlighting the transformative role of innovations such as digitization, blockchain, artificial intelligence (AI), and data analytics. It traces the historical evolution of FinTech, from early electronic banking systems to the advent of decentralized finance and mobile payment solutions. The current FinTech ecosystem is examined through the lens of technological convergence, regulatory evolution, digital payment adoption, and the rise of ESG investing. Emerging trends, including open banking, robo-advisors, and RegTech, are discussed alongside the sector's pivotal challenges—ranging from data privacy to regulatory compliance and talent acquisition. The chapter also identifies key opportunities for collaboration and experimentation through ecosystem partnerships and regulatory sandboxes.

Transforming Business Finance in the Digital Era.
Sanjay Taneja, Mohammad Kashif, Ercan Özen, and Luan Vardari (Eds.)
© 2026 Apple Academic Press, Inc. Co-published with CRC Press (Taylor & Francis)

DOI: 10.1201/9781998511235-5

Looking ahead, it forecasts continued disruption, embedded finance growth, and the expanding impact of FinTech on financial inclusion and sustainability. This forward-looking analysis underscores the sector's potential to reshape global financial systems while emphasizing the need for adaptive strategies, robust governance, and inclusive innovation.

5.1 INTRODUCTION

The introduction provides an overview of the rapid growth and disruptive impact of financial technology (FinTech) on traditional financial services. It sets the stage for exploring the future of FinTech by highlighting key drivers such as digitization, data analytics, blockchain, and artificial intelligence (AI), along with regulatory reforms and changing consumer behaviors.

The convergence of digitization, data analytics, blockchain, and AI is transforming multiple industries and profoundly reshaping corporate processes in today's dynamic landscape. This section serves as a navigational tool, guiding readers through the complex interplay of emerging technologies, regulatory adaptations, and evolving consumer behaviors. The key aspects are as follows:

1. **Digitization – Unlocking New Horizons:** Digitization has become synonymous with the modern era, marking a shift from traditional analog processes to digital formats. It involves converting information, processes, and services into digital formats, enhancing efficiency, accessibility, and scalability. From automating routine tasks to digitizing customer interactions, organizations across sectors are embracing digitization to streamline operations, drive innovation, and maintain competitiveness in a digital-first world.
2. **Data Analytics – Harnessing the Power of Information:** At the heart of digital transformation is data analytics, the practice of deriving actionable insights from extensive datasets. With the expansion of data sources and the introduction of advanced analytical methods, businesses can leverage data to improve customer understanding, optimize operational processes, and uncover hidden patterns and trends. From descriptive analysis to predictive modeling and prescriptive analytics, data-driven decision-making has become essential for guiding strategic initiatives and achieving long-term success.

3. **Blockchain – Transforming Trust and Transparency:** Initially developed for cryptocurrencies, blockchain technology has evolved to impact various industries. At its core, blockchain functions as a decentralized, immutable ledger that records transactions across a distributed network of computers. By eliminating intermediaries and ensuring tamper-resistant data integrity, blockchain enhances trust, transparency, and security in digital transactions. Its applications extend across multiple domains, including supply chain management, digital identity verification, and smart contracts, with the potential to redefine trust-based interactions in the digital economy.
4. **Artificial Intelligence (AI) – Enhancing Automation and Innovation:** AI is a cutting-edge form of digital innovation that enables machines to mimic human cognitive abilities and perform tasks traditionally requiring human intelligence. AI technologies—including neural networks, natural language processing, computer vision, and robotics—are driving automation, personalization, and creativity across various industries. By augmenting human capabilities and unlocking new levels of productivity and innovation, AI has the potential to revolutionize industries, reshape business models, and redefine the future of work.
5. **Regulatory Reforms – Navigating the Regulatory Landscape:** As technology continues to disrupt traditional industries, policymakers must address the regulatory implications of this digital transformation. Regulatory adjustments seek to strike a delicate balance between fostering innovation and safeguarding consumer rights, privacy, and security. From data protection mandates such as the General Data Protection Regulation (GDPR) to financial regulations governing FinTech and digital assets, regulatory frameworks are evolving to mitigate emerging risks and capitalize on new opportunities in the digital age.
6. **Changing Consumer Behaviors – Adapting to Digital Experiences:** Alongside technological advancements and regulatory reforms, shifting consumer behaviors are reshaping market dynamics and fueling demand for digital experiences. From the expansion of e-commerce and mobile banking to the growing popularity of digital entertainment and telemedicine, consumers increasingly rely on digital channels for convenience, accessibility,

and personalized interactions. Businesses must understand and adapt to these evolving consumer preferences to remain competitive in the digital era.

5.2 EVOLUTION OF FINTECH

The evolution of financial technology (FinTech) has been marked by a series of transformative milestones that have reshaped the financial services landscape. This section explores the key stages in FinTech's evolution, from its inception to its current role as a driving force of digital innovation in the financial industry, as illustrated in Figure 5.1.

1. **Early Beginnings – Pioneering Innovations:** The origins of FinTech can be traced to the introduction of electronic trading systems, automated teller machines (ATMs), and early versions of online banking in the late 20th century. These groundbreaking advancements laid the foundation for digitizing financial services, streamlining operations, and expanding banking accessibility for both consumers and businesses.
2. **Internet Era – Dawn of Online Banking:** The rise of the internet in the 1990s marked a significant milestone in FinTech's

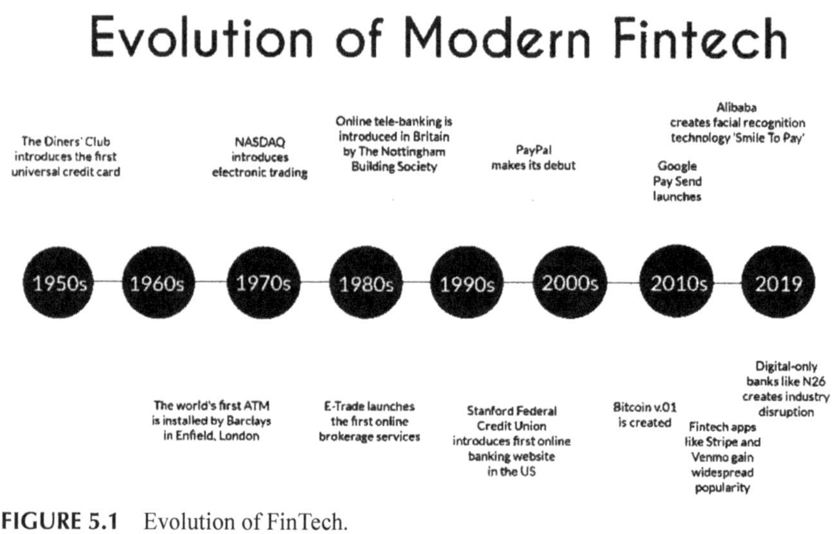

FIGURE 5.1 Evolution of FinTech.

Source: https://www.techtic.com/blog/best-fintech-apps/

evolution, enabling the expansion of online banking platforms, electronic payment systems, and e-commerce. The launch of PayPal in 1998 was a pivotal moment for online transactions, allowing individuals and businesses to transfer money electronically while bypassing traditional banking channels. This era also saw the emergence of online brokerage firms, peer-to-peer lending platforms, and digital wallets, offering consumers new ways to manage their finances and invest in the stock market.

3. **Mobile Revolution – Emergence of Digital Wallets and Mobile Banking:** The widespread adoption of smartphones and mobile devices in the early 21st century accelerated FinTech innovation, leading to the development of mobile banking apps, digital wallets, and contactless payment solutions. Mobile banking applications provided consumers with unprecedented convenience, enabling them to monitor their finances, transfer money, and make payments on the go. The introduction of Apple Pay in 2014 further popularized mobile payments, driving the shift toward a cashless society and fueling the growth of the digital economy.

4. **Blockchain and Cryptocurrencies – Disrupting Traditional Finance:** The introduction of blockchain technology and cryptocurrencies represented a paradigm shift in the financial industry, challenging traditional banking models and introducing new possibilities for decentralized finance (DeFi). The launch of Bitcoin in 2009 as the first decentralized cryptocurrency paved the way for the development of alternative digital assets and blockchain-based applications. Ethereum, launched in 2015, introduced smart contracts, enabling programmable, self-executing agreements that revolutionized crowdfunding, decentralized applications (DApps), and non-fungible tokens (NFTs). The emergence of blockchain and cryptocurrencies sparked a wave of innovation, attracting investment and driving experimentation with new financial instruments and business models.

5. **Regulatory Reforms – Adapting to a Changing Landscape:** The swift tempo of innovation within FinTech has spurred regulatory bodies globally to amend their frameworks to embrace new technologies and business models while upholding consumer protection and market integrity. Regulatory adaptations, including

open banking initiatives, PSD2 (Payment Services Directive 2), and GDPR, have aimed to foster competitiveness, bolster transparency, and safeguard consumer data privacy in the digital era. Furthermore, regulatory sandboxes have furnished a supervised arena for FinTech experimentation, empowering firms to trial novel products and services while upholding adherence to regulatory mandates.

5.3 CURRENT LANDSCAPE OF FINTECH

The current landscape of financial technology (FinTech) is a dynamic and rapidly evolving ecosystem characterized by innovation, disruption, and unprecedented growth. This section provides an in-depth analysis of the prevailing trends, challenges, and opportunities shaping the current state of FinTech. The details are as follows:

1. **Proliferation of FinTech Startups – Driving Innovation:** One of the defining features of the current FinTech landscape is the proliferation of startups leveraging technology to disrupt traditional financial services. These startups span a wide range of sectors, including payments, lending, wealth management, insurance, and regulatory technology (RegTech). With nimble operations, agile business models, and a focus on customer-centric solutions, FinTech startups are challenging incumbents, driving innovation, and reshaping the competitive landscape of the financial industry.
2. **Technological Convergence – Powering Digital Transformation:** The amalgamation of cutting-edge technologies such as AI, blockchain, data analytics, and cloud computing is propelling digital metamorphosis throughout the financial services domain. AI-driven chatbots and virtual assistants are elevating customer service and interaction, whereas blockchain technology is spearheading revolutions in payments, trade finance, and asset tokenization. Data analytics and machine learning algorithms are facilitating predictive analysis, risk evaluation, and personalized financial guidance, empowering financial institutions to furnish bespoke solutions and experiences to their clientele.

3. **Shift Towards Digital Payments – Embracing Cashless Transactions:** The transition to digital payments is rapidly gaining momentum, propelled by evolving consumer inclinations, technological progressions, and the surge of e-commerce and mobile commerce. Contactless payments, mobile wallets, peer-to-peer (P2P) transactions, and digital currencies are garnering increased acceptance, providing convenience, security, and efficiency in financial dealings. As digital payment platforms proliferate and open banking frameworks gain traction, consumers are presented with a myriad of payment alternatives, igniting innovation and fostering competition within the payments realm. Overall, the economic landscape of India has benefited from the implementation of FinTech (Figure 5.2), prompting the Indian government to launch a number of initiatives to promote its adoption in India.

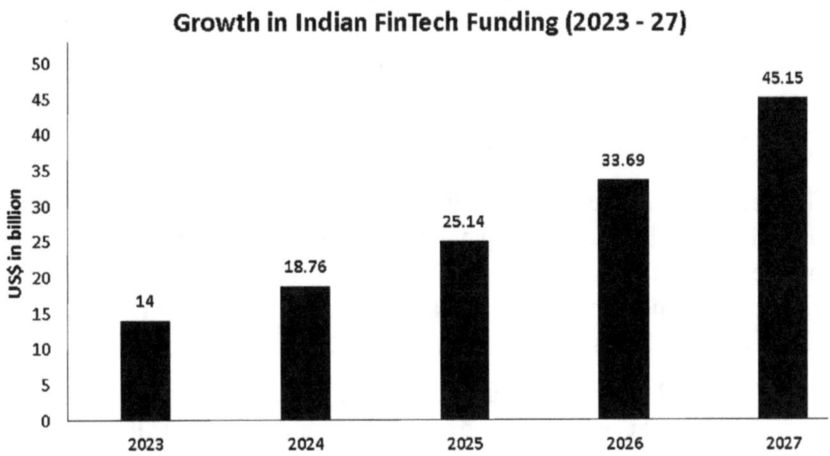

FIGURE 5.2 Funding boost for FinTech in India.

Source: Adapted from Momenitabar et al. (2022).

4. **Regulatory Evolution – Balancing Innovation and Compliance:** Regulatory frameworks governing FinTech are evolving to accommodate new technologies and business models while ensuring consumer protection, market integrity, and financial stability. Regulatory sandboxes, innovation hubs, and FinTech-friendly regulations

are providing a conducive environment for experimentation and innovation, enabling startups to test new products and services while adhering to regulatory requirements. However, regulatory compliance remains a significant challenge for FinTech firms, requiring robust risk management, compliance processes, and collaboration with regulators to navigate complex regulatory landscapes.

5. **Rise of Environmental, Social, and Governance (ESG) Investing – Embracing Sustainability:** ESG investing is gaining traction within the FinTech arena, spurred by heightened consciousness of environmental and social concerns, regulatory imperatives, and investor appetite for sustainable and ethical investment avenues. FinTech platforms are integrating ESG considerations into their investment methodologies, providing ESG-themed funds, impact investment opportunities, and financial products centered on sustainability. By harmonizing financial objectives with environmental and social aspirations, ESG investing is reshaping the investment panorama and catalyzing favorable transformations within the financial sector.

5.4 EMERGING TRENDS IN FINTECH

This section examines the latest trends and innovations shaping the future of FinTech, including digital payments and wallets, blockchain and cryptocurrencies, AI and ML, open banking and API integration, robo-advisors and wealth management, and innovations in InsurTech and RegTech. The details are as follows:

1. **Digital Payments and Wallets:** The emergence of mobile payments, contactless transactions, and digital wallets marks a transformative shift in financial transactions for both consumers and businesses. Digital payments and wallets represent a significant departure from traditional financial transaction methods for individuals and enterprises alike. Leveraging the widespread availability of smartphones and the proliferation of payment applications, consumers are increasingly adopting digital wallets due to their convenience, security, and speed. From peer-to-peer transfers to contactless payments and in-app purchases, digital wallets streamline transactions, reduce friction, and promote financial

inclusion by extending access to financial services to previously underserved populations, such as the unbanked and underbanked.

2. **Blockchain and Cryptocurrencies:** Blockchain and cryptocurrencies present new opportunities for DeFi, asset tokenization, and secure digital asset management. At the core of blockchain technology is a decentralized, immutable ledger that has the potential to revolutionize various industries, including finance. Cryptocurrencies such as Bitcoin and Ethereum, which are built on blockchain technology, offer decentralization, transparency, and security. Beyond cryptocurrencies, blockchain has applications in smart contracts, supply chain management, digital identity, and asset tokenization. By eliminating intermediaries and ensuring trust and transparency in transactions, blockchain has the potential to transform the future of finance and redefine trust-based interactions within the digital economy.

3. **AI and Machine Learning:** AI-driven solutions enable personalized financial advice, risk assessment, fraud detection, and algorithmic trading, enhancing efficiency and decision-making in financial services. AI and machine learning are driving a fundamental shift in how financial institutions analyze data, make decisions, and engage with customers. These technologies support a range of functions, including fraud detection, risk assessment, personalized recommendations, and algorithmic trading, empowering financial institutions to uncover valuable insights, enhance customer interactions, and improve operational efficiencies. By effectively utilizing large datasets and advanced algorithms, AI and machine learning equip financial institutions with the tools needed to remain competitive in an evolving digital and data-driven environment.

4. **Open Banking and API Integration:** The financial services landscape is being reshaped by open banking initiatives and the integration of APIs, fostering collaboration among traditional banks, FinTech startups, and third-party developers. Open banking and APIs enable the secure exchange of data and promote interoperability between financial institutions and external providers. This drives innovation, enhances customer experiences, and creates new opportunities for product development and service delivery. Open banking and APIs have the potential to support various

aspects of financial innovation, including account aggregation, payment initiation, lending, and wealth management, contributing to the ongoing evolution of financial systems.

5. **Robo-Advisors and Wealth Management – InsurTech and RegTech Innovations: Embracing Digital Transformation:** In addition to FinTech, innovations in InsurTech and RegTech are driving digital transformation across the insurance and regulatory compliance sectors. InsurTech startups harness technology to streamline insurance operations, bolster underwriting precision, and elevate customer satisfaction levels. Concurrently, RegTech solutions utilize AI, ML, and blockchain to automate regulatory compliance procedures, mitigate risks, and ensure alignment with evolving regulatory mandates. Through the adoption of InsurTech and RegTech advancements, insurance firms and regulatory entities can streamline operations, fortify risk management frameworks, and adeptly navigate the complexities of the digital era.

5.5 CHALLENGES AND REGULATORY CONSIDERATIONS

This section explores the challenges and regulatory considerations associated with the future of financial technology (FinTech), including data privacy and security, regulatory compliance, financial inclusion and accessibility, systemic risks and stability, and talent acquisition and the skills gap. The details are as follows:

1. **Data Privacy and Security:** In the digital era, safeguarding data privacy and security is of utmost importance, especially considering the vast repositories of sensitive financial information stored, processed, and transmitted online. Guaranteeing the confidentiality, integrity, and accessibility of financial data is indispensable for upholding consumer trust and fortifying defenses against cyber threats and data breaches. Robust cybersecurity measures, encryption protocols, and access controls are critical to mitigating risks and maintaining compliance with data protection regulations such as the GDPR and the California Consumer Privacy Act (CCPA).
2. **Regulatory Compliance:** Financial institutions must navigate a complex regulatory landscape characterized by stringent compliance requirements aimed at combating financial crime, protecting

consumer interests, and ensuring market integrity. Anti-money laundering (AML) regulations, know-your-customer (KYC) prerequisites, and consumer protection statutes represent merely a fraction of the regulatory obligations incumbent upon financial institutions. Establishing resilient AML/KYC protocols, conducting exhaustive due diligence on clientele, and scrutinizing transactions for indications of illicit conduct are imperative measures for fulfilling regulatory responsibilities and curtailing compliance vulnerabilities.

3. **Financial Inclusion and Accessibility:** Promoting financial inclusion and accessibility is essential to ensuring that underserved and marginalized populations have equitable access to financial services and opportunities. In many parts of the world, barriers such as limited access to banking infrastructure, lack of identification documents, and low financial literacy hinder financial inclusion efforts. Digital innovations such as mobile banking, digital wallets, and microfinance solutions have the potential to bridge the digital divide, empower individuals and businesses, and drive economic growth and development.

4. **Systemic Risks and Stability:** The interconnected nature of the financial system poses inherent risks to stability, as disruptions in one sector or market can have cascading effects across the entire ecosystem. Systemic risks, encompassing cyber threats, market instability, and liquidity emergencies, emphasize the significance of fortified risk management methodologies, stress testing, and regulatory supervision. Collaborative endeavors among financial institutions, regulators, and policymakers are indispensable for recognizing systemic risks, deploying efficient safeguards, and upholding the resilience and stability of the financial system (Fariya et al., 2024).

5. **Talent Acquisition and Skills Gap – Nurturing a Skilled Workforce:** As the financial sector progresses, there arises an increasing need for professionals proficient in emerging technologies, regulatory adherence, and data analytics. Nonetheless, a burgeoning skills deficit persists, as conventional educational frameworks frequently struggle to keep pace with rapid technological advancements. Financial establishments must allocate resources toward talent cultivation programs, retraining endeavors, and collaborations with educational entities to cultivate an adept workforce

capable of navigating the intricacies of the digital landscape. By fostering an environment conducive to perpetual learning and innovation, financial institutions can maintain a competitive edge and foster enduring growth in the digital epoch.

5.6 OPPORTUNITIES FOR COLLABORATION AND INNOVATION

This section highlights opportunities for collaboration and innovation in the future of financial technology (FinTech), including ecosystem partnerships, regulatory sandboxes and experimentation, and financial education and inclusion. The details are as follows:

1. **Ecosystem Partnerships:** Ecosystem partnerships play a pivotal role in fostering innovation and driving ecosystem growth by leveraging the complementary strengths and resources of diverse stakeholders. Collaboration between traditional financial institutions, FinTech startups, technology firms, regulatory bodies, and academia creates synergies that fuel innovation, enhance customer experiences, and accelerate digital transformation (Kashif et al., 2017). By forging strategic partnerships, sharing knowledge and expertise, and co-creating innovative solutions, ecosystem players can unlock new opportunities and address complex challenges in the rapidly evolving financial landscape.
2. **Regulatory Sandboxes and Experimentation:** Regulatory sandboxes offer a supervised setting for FinTech experimentation, allowing companies to trial novel products, services, and business models under regulatory oversight. By granting temporary regulatory relief and facilitating collaboration between regulators and innovators, sandboxes foster innovation while ensuring compliance with regulatory requirements. Through experimentation, firms can validate new ideas, identify potential risks, and refine their offerings before bringing them to market. Regulatory sandboxes promote a culture of innovation, regulatory compliance, and consumer protection, ultimately driving forward the evolution of the financial ecosystem.
3. **Financial Education and Inclusion:** Financial education and inclusion serve as pivotal elements of a resilient and equitable financial system, enabling individuals and communities to make informed financial choices, accumulate assets, and attain

financial stability. Providing access to high-quality financial education initiatives, resources, and tools furnishes individuals with the requisite knowledge and competencies to oversee their finances, strategize for the future, and comprehend intricate financial offerings. Furthermore, advancing financial inclusion by broadening access to banking amenities, credit facilities, and insurance coverage for marginalized communities promotes economic empowerment, diminishes disparities, and stimulates sustainable economic progress.

5.7 FUTURE OUTLOOK AND PREDICTIONS

The future of financial technology (FinTech) is poised for dynamic growth, fueled by technological advancements, shifting consumer behaviors, and evolving regulatory landscapes. This segment provides insights into the future prospects and forecasts for FinTech, delineating significant trends, opportunities, and challenges that will shape the sector in the coming years:

1. **Continued Innovation and Disruption:** The rate of innovation within FinTech remains unabated, propelled by emerging technologies such as AI, blockchain, and the Internet of things (IoT), catalyzing substantial transformations throughout the financial services sector. AI-driven chatbots and virtual assistants are poised to revolutionize customer service and interaction, whereas blockchain technology promises secure and transparent transactions, subsequently reducing costs and enhancing efficiency (Kashif et al., 2017). Furthermore, FinTech startups are expected to continue disrupting conventional banking paradigms, offering innovative solutions for payments, lending, wealth management, and insurance.
2. **Expansion of Digital Payments and Contactless Transactions:** The future of payments will be increasingly digital, with cashless transactions, mobile wallets, and contactless payments becoming the norm. The COVID-19 pandemic has accelerated the shift toward digital payments, as consumers seek safer and more convenient ways to transact. FinTech companies will capitalize on this trend by developing innovative payment solutions that offer seamless integration, enhanced security, and personalized experiences. Cross-border payments and remittances will also witness

significant innovation, as blockchain technology and digital currencies streamline processes and reduce transaction costs.

3. **Rise of Embedded Finance and Banking as a Service (BaaS):** Embedded finance, where financial services are seamlessly integrated into non-financial products and services, is set to become a dominant trend in the financial technology (FinTech) landscape. Companies across various industries, including e-commerce and ride-sharing, will increasingly offer financial products such as loans, insurance, and savings accounts as part of their core services.

   Banking as a Service (BaaS) platforms will drive this trend by providing the necessary infrastructure and application programming interfaces (APIs) for businesses to embed financial services into their platforms. The convergence of finance and technology will further democratize access to financial services, empowering both individuals and businesses to manage their finances more efficiently.

4. **Regulatory Evolution and Compliance Challenges:** As FinTech continues to disrupt traditional financial services, regulators will face new challenges related to consumer protection, data privacy, and systemic risk. Regulatory frameworks will evolve to accommodate new technologies and business models, with a focus on fostering innovation while ensuring market integrity and consumer trust (Kashif et al., 2023). However, navigating regulatory complexities will remain a significant challenge for FinTech firms, necessitating robust compliance programs, risk management processes, and collaboration with regulators to stay ahead of regulatory changes.

5. **Focus on Financial Inclusion and Environmental, Social, and Governance (ESG) Investing:** Financial inclusion and ESG investing will be key priorities for the future of FinTech. FinTech companies will leverage technology to expand access to financial services for underserved populations, including the unbanked and underbanked. Digital identity solutions, microfinance platforms, and mobile banking apps will drive financial inclusion by overcoming barriers such as limited access to banking infrastructure and lack of documentation. Additionally, ESG investing will gain momentum, with FinTech platforms offering sustainable and responsible investment options that align with investors' values and preferences.

5.8 CONCLUSION

The future of FinTech is poised for unprecedented growth, innovation, and transformation. With emerging technologies such as AI, blockchain, and the IoT driving profound changes across the financial landscape, the sector is experiencing a paradigm shift in how financial services are accessed, delivered, and experienced. AI-powered chatbots and virtual assistants are revolutionizing customer engagement, while blockchain technology is ensuring secure and transparent transactions, reducing costs, and enhancing efficiency.

Furthermore, FinTech startups continue to disrupt traditional banking models, offering innovative solutions for payments, lending, wealth management, and insurance. This convergence of finance and technology is democratizing access to financial services, empowering individuals and businesses to manage their finances more effectively.

As the FinTech ecosystem evolves, it is crucial for stakeholders to remain adaptable, resilient, and customer-centric. Collaboration between financial institutions, regulators, policymakers, and technology innovators will be essential in navigating regulatory complexities, addressing cyber-security threats, and ensuring responsible innovation.

Ultimately, the future of FinTech holds immense promise for driving financial inclusion, economic empowerment, and sustainable growth. By embracing innovation, fostering collaboration, and prioritizing consumer trust and protection, the FinTech industry can unlock new opportunities and reshape the financial landscape for the betterment of society as a whole.

KEYWORDS

- **artificial intelligence**
- **blockchain**
- **cryptocurrencies**
- **data analytics**
- **digitization**
- **FinTech**
- **machine learning**

REFERENCES

Agarwal, R., & Sweeney, D. J. (2021). *Financial Inclusion and The FinTech Ecosystem: Emerging Research and Opportunities*. IGI Global. https://doi.org/10.4018/978-1-7998-6827-5.

Arner, D. W., Barberis, J. N., & Buckley, R. P. (2015). The evolution of FinTech: A new post-crisis paradigm? *Georgetown Journal of International Law, 47*(4), 1271–1319.

Demirgüç-Kunt, A., Klapper, L., Singer, D., Ansar, S., & Hess, J. (2018). *The Global Findex Database 2017: Measuring Financial Inclusion and The FinTech Revolution*. The World Bank. https://doi.org/10.1596/978-1-4648-1259-0.

Fariya, Saini, A., & Kashif, M. (2024). Exploring the influence of factors driving financial accessibility, financial activities, and financial education on sustainable development. In *Artificial intelligence and machine learning-powered smart finance* (pp. 23–49). IGI Global.

Gai, K., Qiu, M., & Sun, X. (2020). *FinTech and Big Data: Understanding the new environment for financial services*. Springer. https://doi.org/10.1007/978-981-13-8168-4.

Haddad, C., Hornuf, L., & Vanini, P. (2020). FinTech: Financial innovation and its impact on the economy. *Annual Review of Financial Economics, 12*(1), 1–21. https://doi.org/10.1146/annurev-financial-111919-025753.

Iansiti, M., & Lakhani, K. R. (2017). The truth about blockchain. *Harvard Business Review, 95*(1), 118–127.

Kashif, M., Shajar, S. N., Singhal, N., & Kumar, P. (2023). Achieving sustainable investment practices through green finance: Challenges and opportunities. In *Sustainable Investments in Green Finance*. https://doi.org/10.4018/979-8-3693-1388-6.ch016.

Kashif, M., Sridharan, P., & Thiyagarajan, S. (2017). Factors affecting international reserves with special reference to India. *Vision-The Journal of Business Perspective, 21*(4), 339–349. https://doi.org/10.1177/0972262917733157.

Kashif, M., Thiyagarajan, S., & Sridharan, P. (2017). Dynamics of Algeria's international reserves. *African Journal of Economic and Management Studies, 8*(4). https://doi.org/10.1108/AJEMS-11-2016-0179.

Kaur, J. (2024). Green finance 2.0: Pioneering pathways for sustainable development and health through future trends and innovations. In *Sustainable investments in green finance* (pp. 294–319). IGI Global. https://doi.org/10.4018/978-1-7998-7701-0.

Kaur, J., & Ozen, E. (2024). Masters of the market: Unleashing algorithmic wizardry in finance. In *Algorithmic Approaches to Financial Technology: Forecasting, Trading, And Optimization* (pp. 93–120). IGI Global. https://doi.org/10.4018/978-1-7998-8927-1.

Lee, N. H. (2019). *The Handbook of Blockchain and Finance: Finance, Technology, and Applications*. Academic Press. https://doi.org/10.1016/C2016-0-02074-2.

Lenz, M. (2021). *Artificial Intelligence in Finance: From Buzzword to Value Creation*. Springer Nature. https://doi.org/10.1007/978-3-030-57600-5.

Momenitabar, M., Dehdari Ebrahimi, Z., Arani, M., Mattson, J., & Ghasemi, P. (2022). Designing a sustainable closed-loop supply chain network considering lateral resupply and backup suppliers using fuzzy inference system. *Environment, Development and Sustainability*, 1–34. https://doi.org/10.1007/s10668-022-02015-0.

Raskin, M., & Yermack, D. (2016). Digital currencies, decentralized ledgers, and the future of central banking. *NBER Working Paper No. 22238*. https://doi.org/10.3386/w22238.

Schueffel, P., & Händel, M. (2020). *Token Economy: How Blockchain and Smart Contracts Revolutionize the Economy*. Springer. https://doi.org/10.1007/978-3-030-47403-7.

CHAPTER 6

Reshaping Finance in the Digital Age: The Confluence of Social Commerce and Machine Learning

ABHAY GROVER and NILESH ARORA*

Chandigarh University, Mohali, Punjab, India

*Corresponding author.

ABSTRACT

This chapter explores the transformative intersection of social commerce and machine learning in reshaping financial analysis and decision-making in the digital era. Social commerce, which blends social media interaction with e-commerce, has revolutionized consumer engagement and business strategies by integrating real-time communication, peer influence, and in-app transactions. Concurrently, machine learning offers powerful tools for predictive analytics, personalization, and automated financial statement analysis. The convergence of these domains presents new opportunities for real-time insights, customer-centric financial services, and dynamic business intelligence. This study employs a systematic review methodology guided by PRISMA standards to synthesize current literature, identify trends, and highlight ethical and operational challenges, including data privacy and algorithmic transparency. It emphasizes the growing impact of machine learning on enhancing the accuracy, efficiency, and responsiveness of financial analysis within the evolving landscape of social commerce. The chapter concludes by outlining future research directions and strategic implications for businesses aiming to thrive in this hybrid, data-driven environment.

Transforming Business Finance in the Digital Era.
Sanjay Taneja, Mohammad Kashif, Ercan Özen, and Luan Vardari (Eds.)
© 2026 Apple Academic Press, Inc. Co-published with CRC Press (Taylor & Francis)

DOI: 10.1201/9781998511235-6

6.1 INTRODUCTION

Combining social commerce with machine learning can significantly alter how companies function, communicate with customers, and analyze financial data in today's dynamic digital environment. The fusion of online shopping with social networking, known as social commerce (s-commerce), has radically transformed the way businesses engage with their customer base (Arora et al., 2019; Grover et al., 2023a). This innovative concept has dissolved barriers between the traditionally separate spheres of marketing, sales, and customer relationships, resulting in a more cohesive and dynamic ecosystem. While the original purpose of social media was to facilitate communication and content sharing, it now seamlessly integrates commercial activity into everyday social interactions.

At the same time, machine learning (ML), a subset of artificial intelligence (AI), has become an invaluable resource for businesses interested in predictive analytics, personalization, and data-driven decision-making. ML has revolutionized financial statement analysis, enhancing efficiency and providing capabilities never seen before (Amel-Zadeh et al., 2020). When applied to large datasets, ML enables businesses to refine sales forecasts, improve customer service, and optimize pricing strategies in real time. This advancement grants organizations greater precision and adaptability in assessing their financial performance and making informed decisions.

The integration of social commerce and ML offers numerous benefits, including enhanced customer experiences and dynamic analytics (Amel-Zadeh et al., 2020; Arora et al., 2022). Customer engagement is increasingly defined by personalized recommendations, targeted advertising, and instantaneous responses. As consumers become more discerning, the synergy between social commerce and ML can help businesses differentiate themselves in an oversaturated online marketplace. While this convergence has the potential to drive profitability, it also raises complex ethical considerations. Issues such as data privacy, fairness, transparency, and the necessity of strong ethical guidelines remain critical concerns, despite the unprecedented opportunities this technological evolution presents (Rana and Arora, 2022; Tian and Liu, 2017).

6.1.1 SOCIAL COMMERCE: TRANSFORMING BUSINESS IN THE DIGITAL AGE

Business as we know it has undergone radical change with the advent of the digital age. One concept that has gained significance as technology has advanced and reshaped the corporate landscape is social commerce (s-commerce) (Grover et al., 2023b). This term signifies a fundamental shift in how corporations operate, engage with customers, and leverage technology to their advantage. Social commerce refers to the convergence of online shopping and social networking (Grover and Arora, 2023). It merges the best aspects of social networking sites and traditional e-commerce, allowing businesses to harness the large and active user base of social media to facilitate seamless buying, selling, and sharing of goods and services—all within the social network itself.

Social commerce encompasses a wide range of business practices, including but not limited to influencer marketing, live-stream shopping, customer reviews, and peer referrals. It transforms online shopping into an interactive and social experience where customers can not only research products and prices but also engage with one another, share recommendations, and promote brands within their networks. This transformation has had a profound impact on conventional business practices (Grover et al., 2023b). Traditionally, e-commerce platforms were standalone websites or online marketplaces where users browsed and purchased products. However, with social commerce, the boundaries between shopping and social interaction have become increasingly blurred.

One of the most significant changes brought about by social commerce is in advertising strategies. Brands now rely heavily on user-generated content, peer recommendations, and influencer endorsements to reach highly targeted and engaged audiences, rather than depending solely on traditional advertising or sponsored campaigns (Dinulescu and Prybutok, 2022). This shift not only enhances brand credibility but also reduces marketing expenditures.

The consumer experience has also been reimagined through the instant gratification and convenience offered by social commerce. Consumers can now shop and research products without leaving their favorite social media platforms. Businesses, in turn, can engage with customers and facilitate transactions within the same digital space where users socialize and consume content, thanks to integrated "buy" buttons and in-app purchasing features. The power of social influence plays a crucial role in this new landscape, with companies increasingly partnering with content creators and social media personalities who have built trust and rapport with their audiences. These influencers seamlessly integrate product recommendations into their content, making them feel more authentic and less like traditional advertisements. This type of marketing is particularly effective for e-commerce, as it leverages social media's vast networks and emphasis on transparency.

The shift brought about by social commerce is nothing short of revolutionary (Hansen et al., 2018). Consumers now have more control, access to greater information, and a wider array of choices than ever before. Unlike in traditional business models, where customers played a passive role in transactions, the new paradigm sees them as active participants who influence brand perception and purchasing decisions. However, businesses must adapt to this evolving landscape by prioritizing trust, value, and convenience in their products and services.

As social commerce continues to expand and evolve, its impact will be shaped by emerging technologies such as ML, which is expected to play a crucial role in its future development. Understanding the various dimensions and applications of social commerce—along with the role of ML in enhancing customer engagement, personalization, and business analytics—is essential for grasping the full scale and significance of this phenomenon.

6.1.2 *FINANCIAL STATEMENTS IN BUSINESS*

Fundamental to making informed decisions, gauging risk exposure, and assessing progress, the study of financial statements is an indispensable part of sound business practice. Analyzing and evaluating financial accounts is crucial for organizations that aim to survive, expand, and gain a competitive edge in today's volatile and uncertain business environment. An organization's financial health can be evaluated more thoroughly and accurately through financial statement analysis (Palepu et al., 2020). This analysis provides a comprehensive view of a company's financial stability, growth, and productivity. When business executives have access to this information, they are better equipped to make strategic decisions, such as allocating resources wisely and assessing the viability of potential investments.

Moreover, risk assessment heavily relies on financial statement analysis, helping companies determine their susceptibility to economic downturns and other financial risks. By analyzing key financial ratios, trends, and indicators, businesses can anticipate potential hazards and take proactive measures to ensure financial security. Additionally, financial statement analysis plays a crucial role in evaluating performance. Companies can assess their productivity, efficiency, and overall success through a transparent framework. Beyond self-evaluation, this analysis enables firms to compare their performance with industry peers, providing valuable insights into competitive positioning.

WeChat, with an astounding 980 million users, is poised to become a groundbreaking broker-dealer for high-net-worth Chinese investors. The platform leverages its parent company Tencent's recently acquired license to sell mutual funds, granting its users access to a broad range of financial opportunities (Macheel, 2018). This strategic move not only diversifies the services available within the messaging app but also reinforces Tencent's role as a key provider of financial solutions. WeChat's ability to facilitate seamless financial transactions reflects the growing dominance of messaging platforms in financial services, particularly in China. While Europe and North America continue to explore open platform-based financial service models, Asia has already embraced this strategy, marking a stark contrast to traditional financial methods. Unlike the conventional banking model where banks serve as the primary platform, WeChat's innovative approach highlights how social commerce platforms, combined with ML, can revolutionize financial statement analysis in today's increasingly digital economy.

6.1.3 THE MACHINE LEARNING REVOLUTION: TRANSFORMING FINANCIAL DATA ANALYSIS

Machine learning (ML), a branch of artificial intelligence (AI), has sparked a revolution across various fields, transforming how we address complex challenges and harness the power of data. The rapid advancement of ML is one of the most groundbreaking developments in technological history, leading to a fundamental shift in our ability to analyze and extract meaningful insights from vast and intricate datasets. One of the areas where ML's impact is most evident is financial data analysis, with the potential to revolutionize how businesses and financial institutions interpret and utilize their financial statements (Lokanan et al., 2019; Shiva et al., 2022).

The evolution of ML has been remarkable, characterized by rapid expansion and groundbreaking innovations. What was once a novel concept has quickly become an indispensable tool across industries. This rapid growth has been fueled by advancements in computing power, data storage, and algorithmic processing. ML is now widely applied beyond academic research to solve real-world problems across multiple disciplines (Jain et al., 2020; Rana and Arora, 2022). Its transformative effects are evident in fields such as healthcare, advertising, cybersecurity, and autonomous vehicles (Pugliese et al., 2021). In healthcare, ML is used for diagnostics, drug discovery, and personalized treatment plans. In marketing, it powers recommendation systems and customer segmentation. Additionally, ML is the key technology enabling self-driving cars. Its adaptability and versatility make ML a cornerstone of many recent technological advancements.

The transformative potential of ML is particularly evident in financial data processing (Pramanik et al., 2019). Traditional financial analysis relied primarily on manual techniques and rule-based models. However, the integration of ML has introduced predictive analytics, anomaly detection, and real-time insights, fundamentally reshaping financial data analysis. ML algorithms can efficiently and accurately process vast datasets, uncovering hidden patterns and correlations. One of the most prominent applications is predictive analytics, particularly in sales forecasting. By analyzing historical financial data and market trends, ML algorithms can generate accurate future sales forecasts (Rouf et al., 2021). This capability allows businesses to optimize inventory management, pricing strategies, and resource allocation, ultimately enhancing decision-making and operational efficiency.

ML also plays a crucial role in risk assessment by providing real-time insights into market volatility, credit risk, and fraud detection (Zennaro et al., 2021). Financial organizations leverage this information to assess borrowers' creditworthiness, detect fraudulent activities, and make informed lending decisions. By automating the risk assessment process, ML enhances efficiency and minimizes financial losses.

Another significant application of ML is personalization. Understanding consumer behavior and preferences is essential in today's era of social commerce. ML algorithms can analyze vast amounts of data to generate personalized recommendations and marketing strategies (Campbell et al., 2020). This level of customization enhances the customer experience, making interactions more engaging and increasing revenue for businesses.

Beyond algorithmic trading and portfolio management, ML also has a profound impact on regulatory compliance in financial data analysis. The financial sector, being highly regulated, faces challenges related to ethical concerns and the need for transparent, explainable models. ML addresses these challenges by enabling more efficient compliance monitoring and fraud detection. The emergence of ML in financial data analysis has been transformative (Kamalov and Gurrib, 2023). Its ability to revolutionize how businesses and financial institutions interpret and utilize financial statements stems from its diverse applications, including predictive analytics, risk assessment, and personalization. The continued advancements in ML have the potential to reshape financial analysis, unlocking new possibilities for data-driven insights and informed decision-making.

6.1.4 SOCIAL COMMERCE AND MACHINE LEARNING: CONVERGENCE

The fusion of social commerce with machine learning is a critical concept in the rapidly evolving digital age, with the potential to fundamentally alter how organizations operate (Ballestar et al., 2019). Social commerce, a hybrid of e-commerce and social media, integrates with the data-driven capabilities of machine learning, creating a powerful synthesis of these two transformative forces. As a result, businesses and customers benefit from this mutually advantageous relationship, particularly in financial statement analysis.

The way companies interact with customers has been fundamentally redefined by the growing field of social commerce. Social networking platforms with built-in e-commerce features create a thriving economic and social ecosystem. Businesses leverage social media's vast user base to build customer relationships, enhance brand recognition, and drive sales (Grover and Arora, 2023). Social commerce encompasses various strategies, including influencer marketing, live-stream shopping, customer reviews, and personalized product recommendations.

As a core component of artificial intelligence (AI), machine learning equips businesses with advanced capabilities such as predictive analytics, data-driven decision-making, and unprecedented customization. It has diverse applications across multiple industries, including healthcare, business, and marketing. Financial statement analysis is a complex domain, and machine learning serves as a catalyst for processing vast amounts of data, detecting hidden patterns, and providing real-time insights (Mishra and Tyagi, 2022). The convergence of social commerce and machine learning marks the onset of a new era in business. Machine learning algorithms undertake the intricate task of analyzing shoppers' online activities, leveraging data from social commerce platforms. This vast pool of information is used to generate personalized financial recommendations, enhancing the customer experience while driving sales and revenue (Majid et al., 2013).

Moreover, machine learning's dominance in real-time analytics enables businesses to swiftly adapt to evolving market dynamics and customer preferences. As these trends converge, the corporate landscape is poised for a radical transformation.

Integrating machine learning into financial statement analysis enables companies to process financial data more quickly and accurately (Ashta and Herrmann, 2021). Machine learning models can easily identify patterns and outliers in financial statements, aiding in fraud detection and financial performance evaluation. These models provide real-time insights that help organizations make data-driven decisions regarding pricing, stock levels, and sales projections. In the context of financial statements, the integration of social commerce and machine learning can have far-reaching effects on businesses. Previously, manual procedures and rule-based models were essential for analyzing financial statements. However, the implementation of machine learning has significantly improved the accuracy, efficiency, and timeliness of financial data analysis (Gerlein et al., 2016).

The implications of machine learning extend to various areas of financial statement analysis, such as predicting future sales by analyzing past financial data and consumer behavior. The ability to manage stock more effectively and set competitive prices directly impacts a company's bottom line. Additionally, machine learning provides valuable insights for real-time risk assessment in areas such as market volatility, credit risk, and fraud detection (Cheng et al., 2021). Enhanced risk management is possible due to improved loan decisions, creditworthiness assessments, and the detection of potentially fraudulent activity by financial institutions. In the era of social commerce, the ability to personalize offerings for each consumer is crucial (Grover et al., 2023b). Machine learning algorithms trained on large datasets can help businesses and individuals refine their marketing strategies and navigate the financial landscape with greater precision. As machine learning models take over tasks such as anomaly detection and data processing, automation and efficiency increase. This shift reduces the potential for human error in financial analysis and saves valuable time.

When applied to financial statements, the combination of social commerce and machine learning has the potential to transform the business environment completely. It can enhance company decision-making, improve the customer experience, and unlock new insights and data-driven decision-making opportunities. However, as businesses adapt to this evolving landscape, they must address ethical concerns arising from this convergence, particularly those related to data protection and transparency.

In this chapter, we explore the history and current state of social commerce and examine the significance of machine learning in financial statement analysis. To illuminate the intersection of technology and commerce in the modern era, this review chapter will analyze the complexities, benefits, and ethical considerations that shape this dynamic field. Specifically, it will investigate how machine learning enhances the capabilities of social commerce, particularly in financial statement analysis, creating new opportunities for businesses and consumers in the digital age.

This study is guided by the following research questions, which will be addressed throughout the chapter:

- What role does machine learning play in adapting financial statement analysis to account for shifting trends in social commerce that have altered traditional business structures and practices?
- In the context of social commerce, what are the key benefits and limitations associated with integrating machine learning into financial statement analysis, and how do these factors impact businesses and consumers?
- How are the emerging trends of social commerce and machine learning-driven financial statement analysis reshaping the digital business landscape, and what research gaps and unexplored areas remain?

6.2 METHODS AND RESULTS

The primary objective of this study is to conduct a thorough and insightful exploration, analysis, and synthesis to provide a comprehensive understanding of the evolving relationship between social commerce and machine learning, particularly in the context of financial statement analysis. As shown in Figure 6.1, the Preferred Reporting Items for Systematic Reviews and Meta-Analyses (PRISMA) guidelines have been strictly followed throughout this study.

While adherence to established rules is essential for ensuring replicability and maintaining scientific rigor, it has been observed that this is not always the case in systematic reviews. The PRISMA checklist serves as a crucial tool for facilitating a thorough and transparent review process, and the methodology employed in this study has been evaluated and validated by experts in the field. Throughout the research, strict compliance with PRISMA standards has been maintained to enhance the quality of the review and ensure its replicability.

6.2.1 ELIGIBILITY CRITERIA

Establishing clear eligibility criteria is crucial for ensuring the validity and significance of a review. The importance of cumulative and progressively stringent exclusion criteria cannot be overstated. For instance, if an article failed to meet the first exclusion criterion, it was automatically disqualified from further review and was not subjected to additional exclusion criteria checks. This careful planning ensures a thorough, multi-stage evaluation process, enhancing the trustworthiness and precision of the review.

A rigorous set of inclusion and exclusion criteria was applied during the article selection process to ensure that the chosen papers aligned with the research focus. These criteria were deliberately designed to allow for a comprehensive yet selective analysis.

1. **Acceptance Criteria (AC):**

    i. **AC-1 – Applicability:** A paper was considered eligible if it contained at least one of the required keywords—such as *Social Commerce*, *Machine Learning*, or *Finance*—in its title, abstract, or keywords. This criterion ensured that the selected publications were directly relevant to the study's focus.

    ii. **AC-2 – Document Type:** Only *Research Articles* and *Proceedings/Conference Articles* were included. These document types were chosen because they typically contain substantial scholarly content, reflecting the academic nature of this research.

    iii. **AC-3 – Language:** Language was the third important requirement; the paper had to be written in English to meet this criterion. For the sake of efficiency throughout the review process and uniformity of understanding within the study team, English was selected as the language of inclusion.

2. **Eligibility Restrictions (ER):**

    i. **ER-1 – Accessibility:** Articles that could not be accessed easily for the purpose of evaluation were disqualified. The content of the article can only be properly evaluated if it can be read by the intended audience.

    ii. **ER-2 – Language:** Papers not written in English were not considered for publication. To ensure linguistic uniformity and facilitate reliable assessment, articles written in languages other than English had to be excluded.

    iii. **ER-3 – Relevance:** Submissions that did not address either *Social Commerce* or *Machine Learning* were disqualified.

Using this criterion, we were able to guarantee that the papers we chose would make meaningful contributions to our study's primary goals.

We rigorously applied these inclusion and exclusion criteria to ensure that the selected publications align with the aims and scope of the research and uphold the highest standards of scholarly rigor.

6.2.2 SEARCH STRATEGY

The initial search term we utilized consisted of the phrases "Social Commerce," "Machine Learning," and "Finance," which are the three core components of our systematic literature review (SLR). This search term string, "Social Commerce" AND "Machine Learning" AND "Finance," formed the foundation of our approach. To ensure that no relevant studies were overlooked, we broadened our search string to include synonyms and related phrases, adopting a more comprehensive strategy.

The more specific search terms we employed included variations such as "Social Commerce" OR "S-commerce" OR "Social e-commerce" for the "Social Commerce" component, "Machine Learning" OR "ML" for the "Machine Learning" aspect, and "Finance" OR "Financial statements" to encompass the "Finance" dimension. Importantly, we did not impose any restrictions on publication years, aiming to include all pertinent research dating back to the inception of these domains. This strategy allowed us to gather all relevant material, effectively casting a wide net.

After retrieval, we efficiently managed and organized the selected documents. We imported the collected publications into Mendeley's reference management software using the BibTeX format. This process facilitated the removal of duplicate documents, thereby expediting the review process. Mendeley also provided a practical platform for modifying bibliographic information and citations, enhancing the quality of our dataset. The rigorously curated dataset was subsequently transferred to a spreadsheet for further analysis and comprehensive review.

6.2.3 STUDY SELECTION

We meticulously searched well-known databases during the first stage of our thorough literature analysis, which helped us find 242 documents. Following this, a careful procedure of removing duplicate articles was initiated to condense our dataset and ensure its integrity, resulting in the exclusion of 58 duplicate entries. Each of the 184 distinct papers that remained underwent a preliminary evaluation. After a thorough examination based on their titles, keywords, and abstracts, 95 records were excluded from the second phase as they did not meet our study goals. After this rigorous screening process, we were left with 89 papers that met the basic qualifying requirements.

The final stage of the review involved a comprehensive examination of the entire texts of the remaining 89 publications. During this stage, 61 papers that did not satisfy the stringent requirements for inclusion were eliminated. Following this strict procedure, only the most important and relevant documents were retained for further review. To enhance the thoroughness of our review, citations from the selected articles, found through a manual search across various search engines but not appearing in the original query results, were added. Notably, we also utilized Google Scholar as a resource to validate the inclusion of any pertinent papers within the scope of this systematic review, despite its recommendation against being a primary search system. This rigorous supplementary search resulted in the inclusion of two additional full-text publications, increasing the total number of papers for in-depth analysis to 29.

Figure 6.1 provides a comprehensive flow diagram that visually depicts the results obtained at each stage of the screening process. Additionally, Figure 6.2 illustrates a word cloud that graphically represents the terms associated with the included papers of the study.

6.3 DISCUSSION

6.3.1 FUTURE OF FINANCIAL STATEMENTS: SOCIAL COMMERCE AND MACHINE LEARNING

Due to the convergence of social commerce and the growing influence of machine learning, the business landscape is in a constant state of change (Singh et al., 2023). This amalgamation has far-reaching effects on the interpretation of financial statements because it fundamentally alters conventional company models and practices. In this investigation, we explore the role that machine learning has played in adapting financial statement analysis to these developments and how shifting trends in social commerce have sparked these revolutionary shifts. With the rise

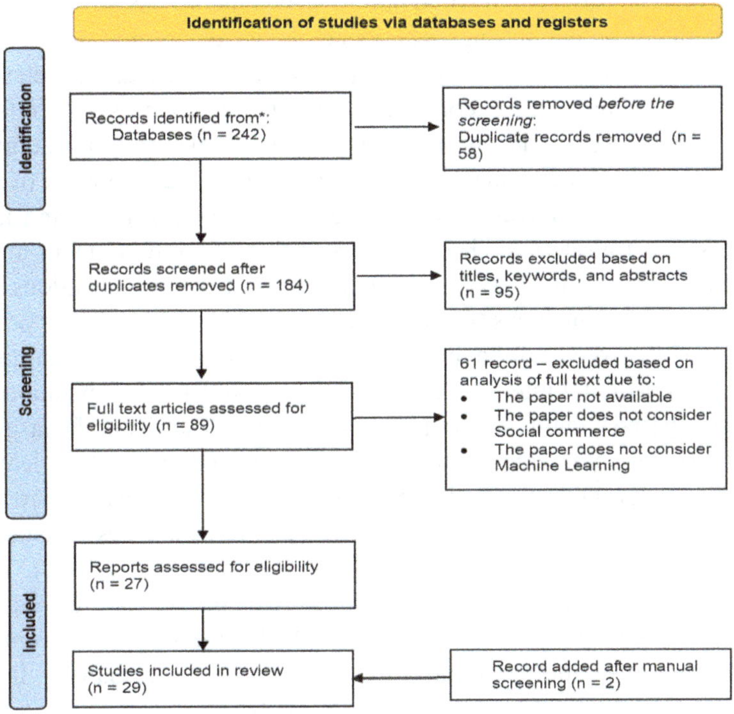

FIGURE 6.1 PRISMA flowchart.

Source: Author creation.

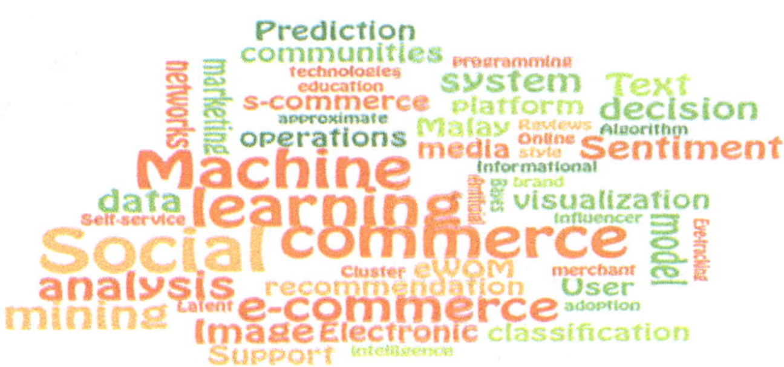

FIGURE 6.2 Word cloud.

Source: Author creation.

of social commerce, companies can now interact with their customers in entirely new ways (Grover et al., 2023b). This results from a union of online commerce and social networking sites, creating a fluid environment where buying, selling, and interacting with others coexist. To create a more immersive purchasing experience, social commerce goes beyond traditional online retail by incorporating community-driven elements and encouraging genuine consumer participation. In this environment, companies have shifted from static, one-dimensional outreach strategies to dynamic, multi-dimensional ones. They tap into the vast network of users on social media to spread their message, build brand loyalty, and facilitate business transactions. Key features of this new environment include influencer marketing, live-stream shopping, and recommendations from friends and acquaintances (Chen and Yang, 2023).

This shift would not have been possible without machine learning, a subfield of artificial intelligence. Predictive analytics, customization, and evidence-based judgment are all tools it provides to firms. Data generated by social commerce platforms can be analyzed by machine learning algorithms, revealing trends in consumer behavior and enabling remarkably precise recommendations to be made. This enhances satisfaction, increases client loyalty, and boosts revenue (Kashif et al., 2023). These shifting norms have caused significant changes in the way conventional financial statement analysis is conducted. Machine learning is instrumental in adapting to the new circumstances. In light of these changes, here is how financial statement analysis needs to evolve:

1. One application of machine learning is in forecasting revenues (Pundir et al., 2020), wherein past financial data and behavioral patterns of customers can be processed to produce remarkably accurate predictions of future revenue generation. By improving inventory management and pricing strategies, firms can positively affect their bottom lines.
2. Machine learning provides real-time insights into market volatility, credit risk, and fraud detection, making it a pivotal instrument for risk assessment in the era of social commerce (Federica Zennaro et al., 2021). The ability to make informed loan decisions, assess creditworthiness, and detect potentially fraudulent actions is particularly beneficial to the financial well-being of institutions.
3. In social commerce, one of the most critical aspects is understanding customers' preferences and behaviors through personalization. Algorithms that learn through machine learning can analyze massive datasets to generate individualized recommendations for financial forecasting and targeted campaign strategies (Eldridge et al., 2018).

This creates a more personalized and engaging experience for the customer and can lead to positive financial outcomes.

4. Machine learning streamlines and automates formerly labor-intensive tasks like anomaly detection and data processing. This not only accelerates the process but also reduces the likelihood of errors in the final financial reports.

Changes in social commerce are having far-reaching effects on conventional business models and procedures, calling for fresh methods of analyzing financial statements. Machine learning is crucial to this shift because of its predictive capabilities and data-driven insights. The impact of machine learning on financial statement analysis is expected to grow as social commerce expands. For companies to succeed in today's fast-paced market, they must be able to quickly and easily adapt to these shifting paradigms.

6.3.2 INCORPORATION OF MACHINE LEARNING IN THE ANALYSIS OF FINANCIAL STATEMENTS: SOCIAL COMMERCE CONTEXT

The application of machine learning to financial statement analysis in the context of social commerce raises numerous opportunities and threats for organizations and individuals. The consequences for all parties will be explored as we delve into the main benefits and drawbacks of such an integration.

Importance of machine learning in financial statement analysis for social commerce and its key benefits:

1. **Enhanced Efficiency:** The significant rise in productivity is one of the most important benefits brought about by this development. Machine learning algorithms can rapidly process enormous datasets, paving the way for real-time economic analysis (K et al., 2022). This kind of rapid analysis allows organizations to act quickly based on complex data.

2. **Accurate Predictive Analytics:** When it comes to predictive analytics, machine learning models perform exceptionally well (Gupta et al., 2023). They are remarkably accurate at predicting revenue, identifying trends, and analyzing customer behavior. This enables firms to optimize their pricing strategies and inventory management, ultimately resulting in improved financial performance.

3. **Risk Assessment:** In the context of examining financial statements, machine learning is an extremely important component of the risk assessment process. In addition to providing real-time insights into market sentiment, credit risks, and fraud detection, it can identify potential hazards related to financial transactions (Cheng et al., 2021). This, in turn, enhances risk management and allows firms to make well-informed financing decisions.

4. **Personalization:** Using machine learning, organizations can develop campaigns and financial advice that are highly tailored to each customer. By analyzing extensive data on customer habits, companies can better cater to individual preferences (Majid et al., 2013; Sharma and Arora, 2023). The improved client experience and subsequent financial gains are a direct result of this customization.

5. **Automation:** The manual analysis of financial statements has been replaced by automated systems. Tasks like anomaly detection, data processing, and report preparation are all within the capabilities of machine learning models. This not only accelerates the financial analysis process but also reduces the likelihood of human error.

The following are some of the primary challenges associated with integrating machine learning into the process of financial statement analysis in social commerce:

1. **Data Privacy and Security:** Machine learning integration requires access to massive amounts of data, including private and financial details (Pramanik et al., 2019). Protecting the confidentiality and security of this information is a major concern. Companies risk losing both money and credibility if their data is compromised.

2. **Complexity and Cost:** The incorporation of machine learning into financial analysis necessitates a significant investment in terms of both money and technology, as well as human capital (Corea, 2017). The complexity of these systems can be a hurdle for smaller organizations, reducing their capacity to benefit from modern technology.

3. **Ethical Concerns:** The application of machine learning in financial analysis raises several ethical questions (Rasheed et al., 2022).

Algorithmic decision-making has the potential to discriminate or be biased, affecting individuals' financial well-being. Maintaining transparency and equity in such systems is challenging.

4. **Data Quality and Preprocessing:** The quality of the input data plays a significant role in determining how effectively machine learning models perform their tasks. Using noisy or incomplete data may lead to erroneous conclusions. The data must be pre-processed and cleaned, which are both time-consuming operations that require careful management.

6.3.3 SOCIAL COMMERCE AND MACHINE LEARNING-DRIVEN FINANCIAL STATEMENT ANALYSIS: FUTURE TRENDS

The convergence of social commerce and machine learning is driving continuous change throughout the landscape of digital business. This evolution is being propelled by both of these trends. When we look into the future, it becomes clear that this dynamic field is about to be reshaped by several developing trends and new paths that are on the horizon. During the course of this examination, we will evaluate these patterns and their implications for the digital business landscape. In addition, we will highlight research gaps and unexplored areas that call for additional investigation.

6.3.3.1 FINANCIAL STATEMENT ANALYSIS: THE CONVERGENCE OF SOCIAL COMMERCE AND MACHINE LEARNING

1. **Impact of Social Commerce on Financial Statement Analysis:** Examine how the changing landscape of social commerce platforms affects the nuances of analyzing financial statements. Investigate how the influx of financial data from these platforms is altering the metrics and approaches typically utilized for such evaluations.

2. **Ethical Considerations in Social Commerce Financial Analysis:** Investigate the moral dilemmas that arise and the repercussions resulting from utilizing machine learning for the financial statement analysis of social commerce. Analyze data

privacy, transparency, and fairness concerns, and provide ethical frameworks for organizations to follow.

3. **Consumer Behavior Analysis in Social Commerce:** Explore how machine learning can offer more in-depth insights into customer behavior using social commerce platforms. Consider the effects on revenue projections, individual segmentation, and personalized investment advice, as these factors all contribute to your examination of financial statements.
4. **The Role of Chatbots and AI in Social Commerce:** Examine the effect of chatbots and AI-powered customer support on social commerce platforms with respect to the bottom line. Investigate their role in boosting sales, resolving customer concerns, and enhancing customer engagement, as well as how this impacts the company's financial reporting.
5. **Machine Learning for Risk Assessment in Social Commerce:** Investigate how machine learning algorithms are being employed to evaluate and mitigate the financial risks of social commerce in areas such as fraud detection, payment processing, and cybersecurity.

Opportunities for in-depth inquiry and significant contributions to the field exist across a wide range of issues related to the dynamic changes in social commerce and the application of machine learning in financial statement analysis. It is anticipated that the rising trends and future directions in social commerce and machine learning-driven financial statement analysis will completely alter the current status of the online business world. Companies that leverage these trends to their advantage will secure a foothold in the market by providing customers with unique and personalized services (Kashif et al., 2023). However, to gain and maintain customer trust, they must overcome ethical, legal, and privacy concerns.

There are significant managerial takeaways for companies operating in the digital sphere from the research on shifting tendencies in social commerce and the incorporation of machine learning in financial statement analysis. These ramifications encompass a wide variety of strategic factors that can influence managerial and leadership decisions in this fluid environment. Managers should strategically invest in machine learning due to its substantial impact on the future analysis of financial statements. This technology is not optional but rather crucial to the company's success.

To harness machine learning's potential in predictive analytics and automation, the study emphasizes the importance of investing in the appropriate tools, talent, and infrastructure. The necessity of keeping personal information confidential is underscored throughout the research. Managers must develop rigorous data protection methods to preserve sensitive financial and consumer data. Consumer trust can be cultivated by adhering to data privacy standards and implementing measures such as encryption and access limits. Managers should establish ethical AI frameworks within their organizations, as machine learning significantly influences financial decisions. Defining ethical guidelines, ensuring algorithmic transparency, and routinely assessing AI-driven processes are essential to mitigate discrimination and bias. The nature of the digital landscape is one that is constantly evolving, necessitating ongoing adaptation. The ability to adjust quickly and effectively is crucial to navigating the changing landscape of social commerce, and this fact must be acknowledged. To maintain competitiveness in the face of such rapid change, companies should foster a culture of lifelong learning and transformation.

6.4 CONCLUSION

This research delves into the evolving relationship between social commerce and machine learning-driven financial statement analysis to illuminate the current landscape and possible future developments in this space. It is clear that the convergence of e-commerce and social media is altering the social commerce environment and, by extension, the way businesses operate. Machine learning is crucial here, enabling organizations to make more informed, data-driven decisions and engage in predictive analytics and customer customization. Financial statement analysis is significantly enhanced by machine learning due to the immediate insights it provides into sales forecasting, risk assessment, and consumer behavior. Machine learning's ability to facilitate hyper-personalization and automation is radically transforming how businesses operate. Key factors in the ever-changing landscape of social commerce and machine learning in financial statement analysis include ethical considerations, data protection, and the implications of sustainability. The research has also highlighted the importance of collaboration among professionals from various fields, including data scientists, financial analysts, ethicists, and legal experts, to address the numerous challenges in this area.

The inevitable intersection of social commerce and machine learning is rapidly transforming the digital business landscape. Embracing this change will provide businesses with a competitive advantage by enabling them to make better decisions, increase their profits, and offer more personalized service to their clients. However, they must also confront issues related to data protection, ethical considerations, and constantly evolving regulations. The limitations of this study must be acknowledged. The interdisciplinary nature of the field makes it challenging to explore each component of the research comprehensively, leading to a broad scope. Furthermore, due to the ever-changing nature of the digital ecosystem, certain new discoveries and trends may have been overlooked.

Promising opportunities await researchers in this area. Scholars can construct multidisciplinary frameworks to explore the ethical issues that arise from employing AI in financial decision-making and the legal and regulatory ramifications of this evolving landscape. Future studies can greatly benefit from examining emerging phenomena such as augmented reality shopping and voice commerce. New developments in social commerce and machine learning-driven financial statement analysis are reshaping the competitive landscape. This research lays the groundwork for future studies on the subject and its implications for businesses and consumers.

KEYWORDS

- **customer customization**
- **decision-making**
- **digital age**
- **digital ecosystem**
- **digital environment**
- **e-commerce**
- **financial data**
- **machine learning**
- **social commerce**

REFERENCES

Amel-zadeh, A., Calliess, J., Roberts, S., & Kaiser, D. (2020). Machine learning-based financial statement analysis. *3rd Conference on Intelligent Information Retrieval in Accounting and Finance.*

Arora, N., Prashar, S., Parsad, C., & Tata, S. V. (2019). Influence of celebrity factors, consumer attitude, and involvement on shoppers' purchase intention using hierarchical regression. *Decision, 46*(3), 179–195.

Arora, N., Prashar, S., Vijay, T. S., & Parsad, C. (2022). A consumer typology based on celebrity endorsement factors. *FIIB Business Review*. https://doi.org/10.1177/23197145221112749.

Ashta, A., & Herrmann, H. (2021). Artificial intelligence and FinTech: An overview of opportunities and risks for banking, investments, and microfinance. *Strategic Change*. https://doi.org/10.1002/jsc.2404.

Ballestar, M. T., Grau-Carles, P., & Sainz, J. (2019). Predicting customer quality in e-commerce social networks: A machine learning approach. *Review of Managerial Science, 13*(3), 589–603. https://doi.org/10.1007/s11846-018-0316-x.

Campbell, C., Sands, S., Ferraro, C., Tsao, H.-Y. (Jody), & Mavrommatis, A. (2020). From data to action: How marketers can leverage AI. *Business Horizons, 63*(2), 227–243. https://doi.org/10.1016/j.bushor.2019.12.002.

Chen, N., & Yang, Y. (2023). The role of influencers in live streaming e-commerce: Influencer trust, attachment, and consumer purchase intention. *Journal of Theoretical and Applied Electronic Commerce Research, 18*(3), 1601–1618. https://doi.org/10.3390/jtaer18030081.

Cheng, X., Liu, S., Sun, X., Wang, Z., Zhou, H., Shao, Y., & Shen, H. (2021). Combating emerging financial risks in the big data era: A perspective review. *Fundamental Research, 1*(5), 595–606. https://doi.org/10.1016/j.fmre.2021.08.017.

Corea, F. (2017). *Artificial Intelligence and Exponential Technologies: Business Models Evolution and New Investment Opportunities*. Springer Cham. https://doi.org/10.1007/978-3-319-51550-2.

Dinulescu, C. C., & Prybutok, V. R. (2022). In authority, or peers we trust? Reviews and recommendations in social commerce. *Behaviour & Information Technology, 41*(13), 2887–2904. https://doi.org/10.1080/0144929X.2021.1957016.

Eldridge, C., Hobbs, C., & Moran, M. (2018). Fusing algorithms and analysts: Open-source intelligence in the age of 'Big Data.' *Intelligence and National Security, 33*(3), 391–406. https://doi.org/10.1080/02684527.2017.1406677.

Gerlein, E. A., McGinnity, M., Belatreche, A., & Coleman, S. (2016). Evaluating machine learning classification for financial trading: An empirical approach. *Expert Systems with Applications, 54*, 193–207. https://doi.org/10.1016/j.eswa.2016.01.018.

Grover, A., & Arora, N. (2023). Green marketing magic: Fostering lasting brand loyalty on social commerce platforms. *International Journal of Membrane Science and Technology, 10*(3). https://doi.org/10.15379/ijmst.v10i3.2570.

Grover, A., Arora, N., & Sharma, P. (2023a). Examining the influence of HEXACO personality traits on impulse buying tendency, perceived enjoyment, and impulse buying behavior in the context of Instagram commerce. *International Journal of Electronic Marketing and Retailing*. https://doi.org/10.1504/IJEMR.2023.10054386.

Grover, A., Arora, N., & Sharma, P. (2023b). Social commerce and metaverse in a new virtual world: Exploring women's adoption intentions. In *Cultural Marketing and Metaverse for Consumer Engagement* (p. 25).

Gupta, A., Tadanki, N., Berry, N., Bardae, R., Harikrishnan, R., & Wagle, S. A. (2023). A comparative study on different machine learning algorithms for predictive analysis of stock prices. *Proceedings of Fourth International Conference on Computing, Communications, and Cyber-Security*. https://doi.org/10.1007/978-981-99-1479-1_44.

Hansen, J. M., Saridakis, G., & Benson, V. (2018). Risk, trust, and the interaction of perceived ease of use and behavioral control in predicting consumers' use of social media for transactions. *Computers in Human Behavior, 80*, 197–206. https://doi.org/10.1016/j.chb.2017.11.010.

Hemachandran, K., Khanra, S., Rodriguez, R. V., & Jaramillo, J. (2022). *Machine Learning for Business Analytics: Real-Time Data Analysis for Decision-Making*. Productivity Press. https://doi.org/10.4324/9781003206316.

Jain, A., Patel, H., Nagalapatti, L., Gupta, N., Mehta, S., Guttula, S., Mujumdar, S., Afzal, S., Mittal, R. S., & Munigala, V. (2020). Overview and importance of data quality for machine learning tasks. *Proceedings of the 26th ACM SIGKDD International Conference on Knowledge Discovery & Data Mining*. https://doi.org/10.1145/3394486.3406477.

Kamalov, F., & Gurrib, I. (2023). A new era of artificial intelligence in education: A multifaceted revolution. *Computers and Society*. https://doi.org/10.48550/arXiv.2305.18303.

Kashif, M., Kumar, P., Ghai, S., & Kumar, S. (2023). Disruptive technologies in computational finance. In *Algorithmic Approaches to Financial Technology: Forecasting, Trading, and Optimization* (pp. 46–60). IGI Global.

Kashif, M., Shajar, S. N., Singhal, N., & Kumar, P. (2023). Achieving sustainable investment practices through green finance: Challenges and opportunities. *Sustainable Investments in Green Finance*, 234–244. IGI Global.

Lokanan, M., Tran, V., & Vuong, N. H. (2019). Detecting anomalies in financial statements using machine learning algorithm: The case of Vietnamese listed firms. *Asian Journal of Accounting Research, 4*(2), 181–201. https://doi.org/10.1108/AJAR-09-2018-0032.

Macheel, T. (2018). WeChat shows messaging is the future of financial services 'platforms.' *Tear Sheet*. https://tearsheet.co/future-of-investing/wechat-shows-messaging-is-the-future-of-financial-services-platforms/ (accessed on 17 January 2025).

Majid, A., Chen, L., Chen, G., Mirza, H. T., Hussain, I., & Woodward, J. (2013). A context-aware personalized travel recommendation system based on geotagged social media data mining. *International Journal of Geographical Information Science, 4*, 662–684. https://doi.org/10.1080/13658816.2012.696649.

Mishra, S., & Tyagi, A. K. (2022). The role of machine learning techniques in Internet of Things-based cloud applications. In *Artificial Intelligence-Based Internet of Things Systems* (pp. 45–66). https://doi.org/10.1007/978-3-030-87059-1_4.

Palepu, K. G., Healy, P. M., Wright, S., Bradbury, M., & Coulton, J. (2020). *Business Analysis and Valuation: Using Financial Statements*. Cengage Learning Australia.

Pramanik, H. S., Kirtania, M., & Pani, A. K. (2019). Essence of digital transformation—Manifestations at large financial institutions from North America. *Future Generation Computer Systems, 95*, 323–343. https://doi.org/10.1016/j.future.2018.12.003.

Pugliese, R., Regondi, S., & Marini, R. (2021). Machine learning-based approach: Global trends, research directions, and regulatory standpoints. *Data Science and Management, 4*(December), 19–29. https://doi.org/10.1016/j.dsm.2021.12.002.

Pundir, A. K., Ganapathy, L., Maheshwari, P., & Kumar, M. N. (2020). Machine learning for revenue forecasting: A case study in retail business. *11th Annual IEEE Information Technology, Electronics and Mobile Communication Conference, IEMCON 2020*, 201–207. https://doi.org/10.1109/IEMCON51383.2020.9284819.

Rana, M., & Arora, N. (2022). How does social media advertising persuade? An investigation of the moderation effects of corporate reputation, privacy concerns, and intrusiveness. *Journal of Global Marketing, 35*(3), 248–267.

Rana, M., & Arora, N. (2022). Predicting user response behaviour towards social media advertising and e-WoM antecedents. *Review of Marketing Science, 20*(1), 83–112.

Rasheed, K., Qayyum, A., Ghaly, M., Al-Fuqaha, A., Razi, A., & Qadir, J. (2022). Explainable, trustworthy, and ethical machine learning for healthcare: A survey. *Computers in Biology and Medicine, 149*(September), 106043. https://doi.org/10.1016/j.compbiomed.2022.106043.

Rouf, N., Malik, M. B., Arif, T., Sharma, S., Singh, S., Aich, S., & Kim, H. C. (2021). Stock market prediction using machine learning techniques: A decade survey on methodologies, recent developments, and future directions. *Electronics (Switzerland), 10*(21). https://doi.org/10.3390/electronics10212717.

Sharma, N., & Arora, N. (2023). Past, present, and future of cultural marketing: A bibliometric analysis. In *Cultural Marketing and Metaverse for Consumer Engagement* (pp. 234–248). IGI Global.

Shiva, A., Arora, N., & Rishi, B. (2022). Do celebrity endorsements influence stock investment intentions? *Marketing Intelligence & Planning, 40*(6), 804–819.

Singh, A., Taneja, S., & Kumar, P. (2023). Algorithmic approaches to financial technology: Forecasting, trading, and optimization. In *Algorithmic Approaches to Financial Technology: Forecasting, Trading, and Optimization*. https://doi.org/10.4018/9798369317464.

Tian, X., & Liu, L. (2017). Does big data mean big knowledge? Integration of big data analysis and conceptual model for social commerce research. *Electronic Commerce Research, 17*(1), 169–183. https://doi.org/10.1007/s10660-016-9242-7.

Zennaro, F., Furlan, E., Simeoni, C., Torresan, S., Aslan, S., Critto, A., & Marcomini, A. (2021). Exploring machine learning potential for climate change risk assessment. *Earth-Science Reviews*. https://doi.org/10.1016/j.earscirev.2021.103752.

CHAPTER 7

Mapping the Landscape: A Bibliometric Journey Through Machine Learning Research

DIXIT KALRA,[1,*] MEDHA GUPTA,[1] SWATI GUPTA,[2] and HARPREET SINGH[3]

[1]*University School of Business, Chandigarh University, Mohali, Punjab, India*

[2]*Chitkara Business School, Chitkara University, Punjab, India*

[3]*School of Management Studies, Punjabi University, Patiala, Punjab, India*

**Corresponding author.*

ABSTRACT

This chapter presents a comprehensive bibliometric analysis of the evolving landscape of machine learning (ML) research, with a specific focus on its applications in financial statement analysis and accounting-based anomalies. By leveraging bibliometric methods and Scopus data, the study systematically examines 502 key publications from 1995 to 2023, identifying prominent authors, influential journals, significant research clusters, and international collaborations. The analysis reveals critical research trends, thematic clusters—including forecasting, data mining, and algorithm development—and key contributors shaping the field. Findings highlight the growing integration of ML techniques like neural networks, clustering, and random forests in complex financial domains, offering predictive insights and enhancing decision-making. The chapter underscores the importance of interdisciplinary collaboration and outlines

Transforming Business Finance in the Digital Era.
Sanjay Taneja, Mohammad Kashif, Ercan Özen, and Luan Vardari (Eds.)
© 2026 Apple Academic Press, Inc. Co-published with CRC Press (Taylor & Francis)

DOI: 10.1201/9781998511235-7

future research directions while addressing limitations in data sources and scope. This study serves as a valuable resource for researchers, practitioners, and policymakers seeking to navigate and contribute to the rapidly advancing domain of machine learning in finance.

7.1 INTRODUCTION

Machine learning is the application of statistical techniques, procedures, and proficient or untutored data to accomplish tasks (Mitchell, 1997). As a cornerstone of artificial intelligence, machine learning has witnessed exceptional expansion in a short time, driven by improvements in computational supremacy, information accessibility, and algorithmic novelty. The sheer volume of research output can be overwhelming, making it imperative to employ systematic methods to comprehend the intricacies of this ever-expanding domain. Bibliometrics, a quantitative analysis of publications, offers a powerful lens through which we can distill valuable insights, discern pivotal research themes, and identify critical contributors in the machine learning landscape. Educationalists and societal experts are delving into this knowledge to enhance their ability to serve and respond to various segments of the population (Gray and Perkins, 2019).

"In machine learning, comprehension is achieved by assimilating knowledge and revolves around six fundamental pillars: large-scale data, volume, value, diversity, speed, and accuracy (Bowen et al., 2022). Computational linguistics has made noteworthy contributions to theory and real-world applications in tackling practical issues. Enhancements in computing power have hastened this progression, leading to the development of advanced architectures and machine learning models, as well as the emergence of Web 4.0 as a valuable repository of information. Natural Language Processing (NLP) is extensively employed in these contexts, from elementary solutions that utilize part-of-speech (POS) data to more intricate designs that leverage syntactic and semantic relationships (Fariya et al., 2024; Silvia et al., 2022). Recently, innovations in computing power have led to the development of machine learning (ML) techniques capable of scrutinizing non-linear connections among intricate environmental factors and policies amidst uncertainty. Studies in macroeconomics and finance have employed ML-based predictions, showcasing superior performance compared to predictions based on linear relationships (Feng and Zhang, 2014; Moscato et al., 2021; Siami-Namini et al., 2018).

The commonly used machine learning algorithms encompass a variety of techniques (IBM, 2020), including:

1. **Neural Networks:** These algorithms replicate the functioning of the human mind, employing numerous interconnected processing nodes. They demonstrate proficiency in identifying patterns and are applicable in natural language translation, image recognition, speech recognition, and image generation.
2. **Linear Regression:** This method forecasts numeric outcomes by establishing a linear correlation among various variables. For instance, it can forecast house prices using historical data about the area.
3. **Logistic Regression:** As a supervised learning technique, logistic regression generates predictions for categorical outcome variables, such as responding with "yes" or "no" to specific inquiries. It proves beneficial in spam classification and quality control in production lines.
4. **Clustering:** By utilizing unsupervised learning, clustering algorithms uncover patterns within data and group them accordingly. This aids data scientists in identifying discrepancies between data points that human observation may have missed.
5. **Decision Trees:** Decision trees predict mathematical values (regression) and categorize data. They visually categorize interconnected decisions as a tree diagram. One advantage of decision trees is their transparency and ease of validation, unlike the opaque nature of neural networks.
6. **Random Forests:** In this approach, a machine learning algorithm combines outcomes from multiple decision trees to predict values or categories.

In the swiftly advancing domain of machine learning, where new methodologies, algorithms, and applications surface at an unprecedented rate, it becomes imperative to grasp the field's current state. This research paper initiates a bibliometric exploration to systematically investigate and chart the extensive landscape of machine learning research alongside financial statement analysis (Kashif et al., 2024). The challenge of comprehending the true meaning of a text at a discourse level, including its temporal aspects, remains unsolved in research in artificial intelligence. Present efforts in extracting knowledge from text using AI techniques only address certain aspects, leaving much to be explored (Collobert et al., 2011). This paper navigates through the vast sea of machine learning literature, leveraging bibliometric techniques to analyze publication patterns, identify seminal works, and trace the evolution of fundamental concepts of financial statement analysis and accounting-based anomalies over time. The study specifically aims to address the following research concerns:

- What is the current state of machine learning research?
- Which critical researchers, institutions, and nations are spearheading developments in machine learning related to financial statement analysis?
- Which research journals and publishers are the focal points for cutting-edge machine learning studies?
- Which significant publications have shaped the path of machine learning research?

This bibliometric exploration aims to showcase the richness of machine learning research and contribute to the ongoing discourse on its trajectory, impact, and potential growth areas within financial statement analysis and accounting-based anomalies. By systematically mapping the landscape, the aim is to provide researchers, practitioners, and enthusiasts alike with a valuable resource for understanding the past, present, and potential future of machine learning.

7.2 RESEARCH METHODOLOGY

The study intends to investigate advancements in research within financial statement analysis and accounting-based anomalies, particularly in machine learning. Consequently, a bibliometric analysis was undertaken to accomplish this goal. It is a commonly employed approach for plotting the conceptual understanding of a research subject (Gupta et al., 2023; Kashif et al., 2023). At the outset, a comprehensive literature review was conducted in this study to acquire pertinent literature. The process involves pinpointing keywords, conducting keyword searches, and selecting the most appropriate works based on specified norms (Jain et al., 2021). Additionally, the research employed bibliometric methods to investigate the works, providing valuable insights into progressive trends of papers, prominent authors, leading journals, and impactful education (Eduardsen and Marinova, 2020; Ren et al., 2019).

7.3 EXPLORATION PARAMETERS AND CONTENT CHOICE

The Scopus database, being a vast collection of articles, was employed in this study. The findings of the conducted and published research contribute to a pool of current information. The references reflect the vital variables that were revealed and analyzed, as well as the numerous connections that were identified (Singh et al., 2023). The literature exploration centers on machine learning. Figure 7.1 illustrates the methodical approach we employed to reach the ultimate compilation of 502 publications. Originally, there were 1,610 articles in the Scopus record related to machine learning, financial statement analysis, and accounting-based anomalies prediction. The final selection of 502 papers was determined after screening based on different criteria, as discussed in Figure 7.1.

7.4 RESULTS

This section of the results aims to address the aforementioned research queries outlined in the paper. It explores publication patterns, prominent authors with the highest citation counts, country-specific citation peaks, leading journals in machine learning and financial statement analysis, and more.

7.4.1 SEQUENTIAL PUBLISHING PATTERN

The depiction of financial statement analysis and fundamental value, utilizing machine learning, is presented in Figure 7.2. Figure 7.2 distinctly shows that the initial publication occurred in 1995. Nevertheless, there was a heightened research emphasis on this topic in 2022, with 117 articles published to date. This was followed by 84 in 2023, 83 in 2021, 56 in 2019, and so forth.

7.4.2 EXAMINATION OF LEADING AUTHORS WITH THE HIGHEST CITATION COUNTS

The leading authors with the highest number of citations were derived from the Scopus record. Table 7.1 presents the peak citations along with

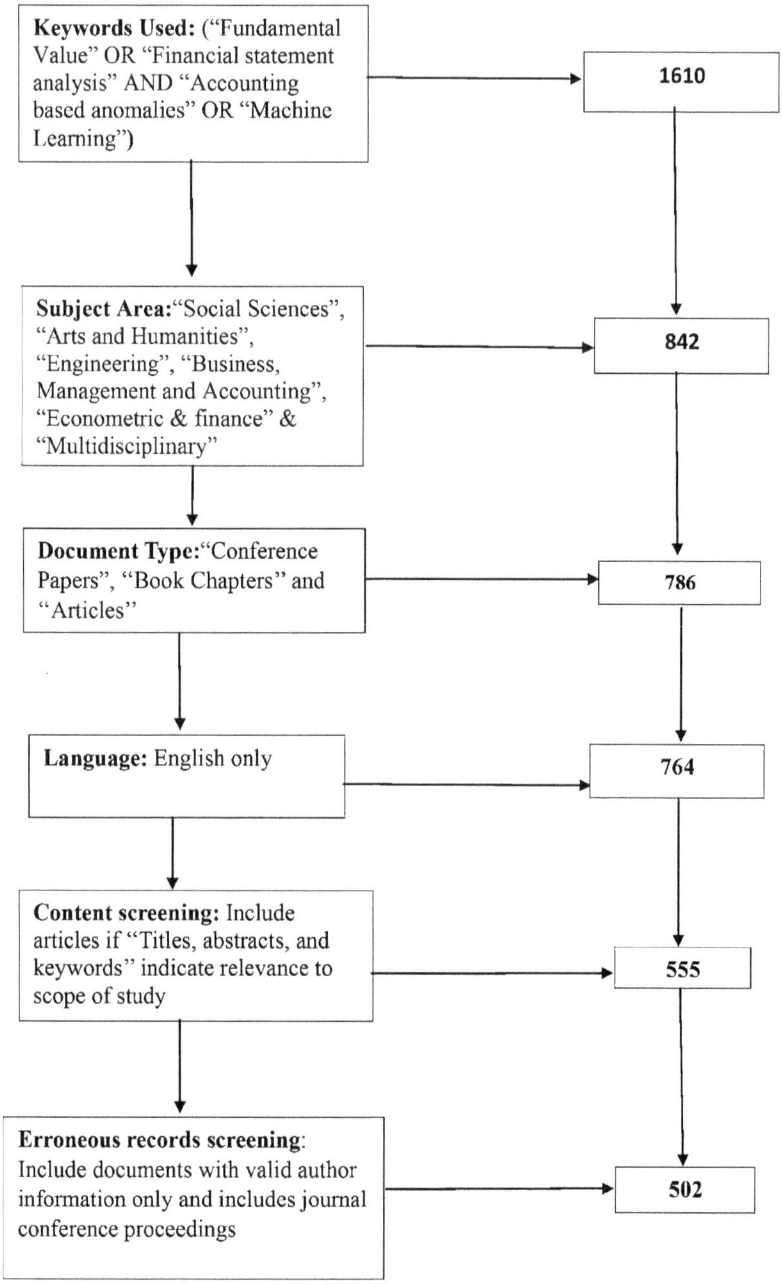

FIGURE 7.1 Exploration parameters and content choice.

Source: Author's own work.

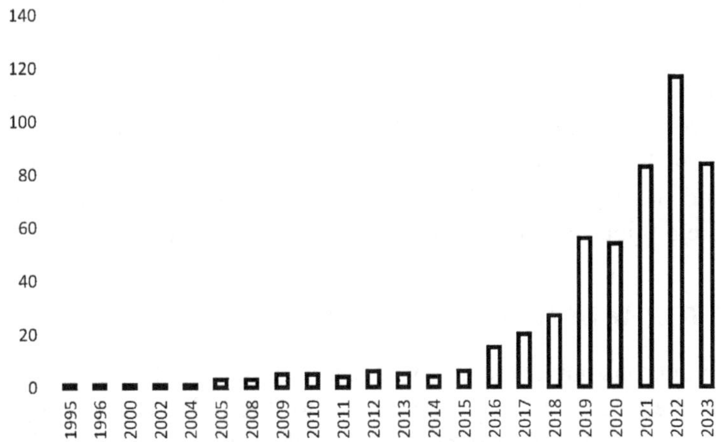

FIGURE 7.2 Sequential publishing pattern.

Source: Author's own work.

the roster of top authors. Table 7.1 provides information on the top 10 authors with the highest citation counts. Based on the citations, the highest is Faloutsos C., Fu X., Huang K., De Lathauwer L., Papalexakis E.E., and Sidiropoulos N.D. with 927 citations, followed by Rasheed A., San O., and Kvamsdal T. with 631 citations, and Liu J., Cao X., Wong D.W.K., Fu H., Xu Y., and Cheng J. with 582 citations.

TABLE 7.1 Leading Authors with Highest Citation Counts

Author	No. of Citations
Faloutsos C.; Fu X.; Huang K.; De Lathauwer L.; Papalexakis E.E.; Sidiropoulos N.D.	927
Rasheed A.; San O.; Kvamsdal T.	631
Liu J.; Cao X.; Wong D.W.K.; Fu H.; Xu Y.; Cheng J.	582
Bergmeir C.; Benítez J.M.	511
Tomiyama T.; Umeda Y.; Ishii M.; Yoshioka M.; Shimomura Y.	496
Štrumbelj E.; Kononenko I.	357
Doyle A.G.; Shields B.J.; Stevens J.; Li J.; Parasram M.; Damani F.; Alvarado J.I.M.; Janey J.M.; Adams R.P.	280
Narayanaswamy B.E. et al.	274
Ratcliff R.; Philiastides M.G.; Sajda P.	212
Chen C.-T.; Gu G.X.	153

Source: Author's own work.

7.4.3 LEADING JOURNALS FOR MACHINE LEARNING

The premier periodicals in the field of machine learning are *IEEE Transactions on Signal Processing* and *IEEE Access*, with 974 and 763 citations, respectively. With the help of Table 7.2, we can deduce that most articles on machine learning are published in *IEEE* conferences, followed by *PLoS ONE* and the *Information Sciences* journal. Table 7.2 provides insights about the top journal with the maximum number of citations.

7.4.4 TOP ARTICLES ON MACHINE LEARNING

While numerous publications have addressed machine learning, Table 7.3 presents the foremost articles pertaining to this field. The primary work by Faloutsos, C., Fu, X., Huang, K., De Lathauwer, L., Papalexakis, E.E., and Sidiropoulos, N.D. boasts 927 citations. Additionally, the second

TABLE 7.2 Top Journals for Machine Learning

Top Journals for Machine Learning	TC
IEEE Transactions on Signal Processing	974
IEEE Access	763
IEEE Transactions on Medical Imaging	582
PLoS ONE	580
Information Sciences	511
Artificial Intelligence for Engineering Design, Analysis, and Manufacturing (AIEDAM)	496
Journal of Machine Learning Research	377
Nature	280
Expert Systems with Applications	228
Proceedings of the National Academy of Sciences of the United States of America	213
Advanced Science	153
Journal of Civil Structural Health Monitoring	149
Procedia CIRP	119
IEEE Systems Journal	116
Journal of Neuroscience	111
Journal of Computer Assisted Learning	109
IEEE Journal on Selected Topics in Signal Processing	103

Source: Author's own work.

renowned article authored by Rasheed, A., San, O., and Kvamsdal, T. has accumulated 631 citations to date.

7.4.5 THEMATIC STRUCTURE ON MACHINE LEARNING

The depiction of various clusters in Figure 7.3 illustrates the simultaneous existence of all keywords employed by the writers in the discussed subject, including:

1. **Cluster 1: Machine Learning:** Cluster 1 is highlighted in red, showcasing the words associated with machine learning, such as algorithm, signal processing, prediction, and support vector machine.

TABLE 7.3 Top Articles on Machine Learning

Author(s)	Title	TC
Sidiropoulos N.D. et al.	Tensor Decomposition for Signal Processing and Machine Learning	927
Rasheed A. et al.	Digital Twin: Values, Challenges, and Enablers from a Modeling Perspective	631
Fu H. et al.	Joint Optic Disc and Cup Segmentation Based on Multi-Label Deep Network and Polar Transformation	582
Bergmeir C. et al.	On the Use of Cross-Validation for Time Series Predictor Evaluation	511
Umeda Y. et al.	Supporting Conceptual Design Based on the Function-Behavior-State Modeler	496
Štrumbelj E. et al.	An Efficient Explanation of Individual Classifications Using Game Theory	357
Shields B.J. et al.	Bayesian Reaction Optimization as a Tool for Chemical Synthesis	280
Wei C.-L. et al.	Global Patterns and Predictions of Seafloor Biomass Using Random Forests	274
Ratcliff R. et al.	Quality of Evidence for Perceptual Decision-Making Is Indexed by Trial-to-Trial Variability of the EEG	212
Chen C.-T.; Gu G.X.	Generative Deep Neural Networks for Inverse Materials Design Using Backpropagation and Active Learning	153

Source: Author's own work.

2. **Cluster 2: Forecasting:** Cluster 2 is highlighted in green, showcasing the words associated with forecasting, such as uncertainty analysis, time series, mean square error, nearest neighbor search, and so forth.
3. **Cluster 3: Learning Algorithm:** Cluster 3 is highlighted in blue, showcasing the words associated with learning algorithms, such as natural language processing, financial markets, decision making, investments, and so forth.
4. **Cluster 4: Data Mining:** Cluster 4 is highlighted in yellow, showcasing the words associated with data mining, such as data handling, learning systems, artificial intelligence, internet of things, and so forth.

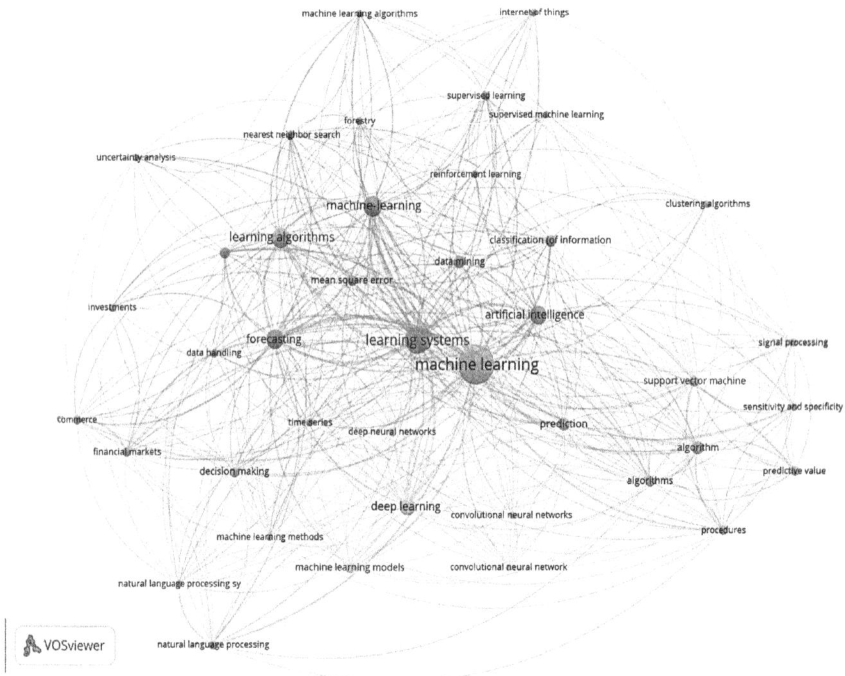

FIGURE 7.3 Thematic clusters based on keywords.

Source: Author's own work.

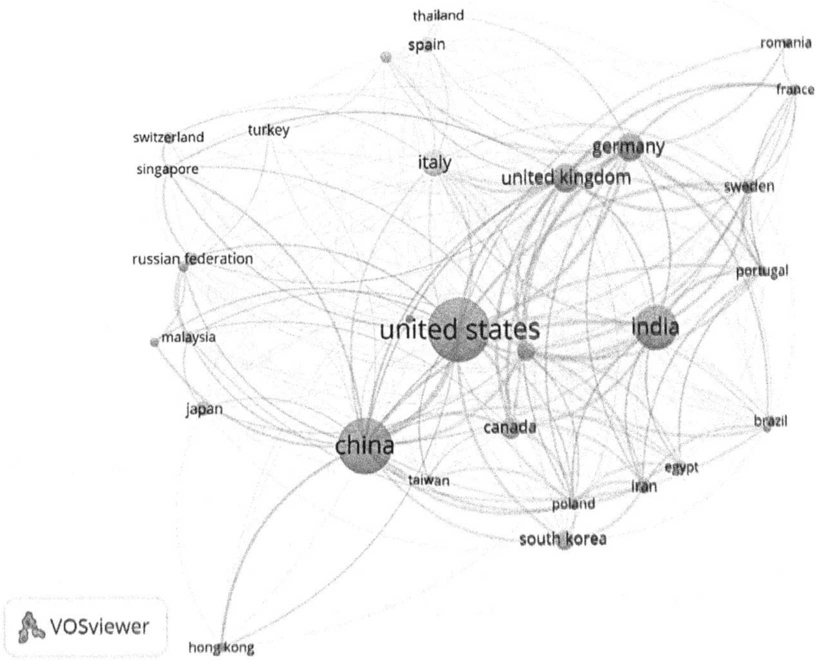

FIGURE 7.4 Cross country bibliographic linkage.

Source: Author's own work.

7.4.6 CROSS COUNTRY BIBLIOGRAPHIC LINKAGE

Figure 7.4 illustrates the nations that have authored the highest number of papers in collaboration with authors from other countries. The United States has produced the most papers in collaboration with the United Kingdom, India, China, Germany, Thailand, and Canada. Following the United States, China has authored the second-highest number of papers, with India in third place.

7.5 DISCUSSIONS AND FUTURE RESEARCH

The current investigation begins by reviewing the existing literature related to "Financial Statement Analysis" or "Fundamental Value" and "Machine Learning" or "Accounting-Based Anomalies." The study gathered a total of 1,610 documents from 1995 to 2023 using the Scopus database. However, after a thorough examination and thoughtful consideration,

502 papers were chosen for detailed analysis. The VOS Viewer method was utilized for comprehensive qualitative and quantitative assessments. This section covers key articles, authors, journals, affiliated institutions, countries, keywords, and references. The VOS Viewer provided profound insights and quantitative evaluations on specific topics. This inquiry serves as a benchmark for efficiently and rapidly exploring new areas. The geographic distribution of the investigation reveals that India, China, and the United States have highly impactful publications.

Despite being an exhaustive examination, it has some limitations. The study utilized data extracted from the Scopus record. Subsequent research could involve selecting papers from an alternative database. This investigation exclusively encompassed review papers and articles, excluding all other conference and book proceedings. Taking these into account will yield more profound insights for future research. The Scopus and VOS Viewer databases provide a succinct summary of the thesis or paper, which may result in overlooking vital information during the course of the thesis or paper. Utilizing a uniform research methodology can aid in investigating interconnected topics to achieve enduring progress.

KEYWORDS

- **artificial intelligence**
- **bibliometrics**
- **financial statement analysis**
- **machine learning**
- **qualitative assessment**
- **quantitative assessment**
- **Scopus database**

REFERENCES

Bowen, F., Gentle-Genitty, C., Siegler, J., & Jackson, M. (2022). Revealing underlying factors of absenteeism: A machine learning approach. *Frontiers in Psychology, 13*, 958748. https://doi.org/10.3389/fpsyg.2022.958748.

Collobert, R., Weston, J., Bottou, L., Karlen, M., Kavukcuoglu, K., & Kuksa, P. (2011). Natural language processing (almost) from scratch. *Journal of Machine Learning Research, 12*, 2493–2537.

Fariya, Saini, A., & Kashif, M. (2024). Exploring the influence of factors driving financial accessibility, financial activities, and financial education on sustainable development. In *Artificial Intelligence and Machine Learning-Powered Smart Finance* (pp. 23–49). IGI Global.

Feng, L., & Zhang, J. (2014). Application of artificial neural networks in tendency forecasting of economic growth. *Economic Modelling, 40*, 76–80. https://doi.org/10.1016/j.econmod.2014.02.015.

García-Méndez, S., de Arriba-Pérez, F., Barros-Vila, A., & González-Castaño, F. J. (2022). Detection of temporality at discourse level on financial news by combining natural language processing and machine learning. *Expert Systems with Applications, 197*, 116648. https://doi.org/10.1016/j.eswa.2022.116648.

Gray, C. C., & Perkins, D. (2019). Utilizing early engagement and machine learning to predict student outcomes. *Computers & Education, 131*, 22–32. https://doi.org/10.1016/j.compedu.2018.12.007.

Gupta, M., Arora, R., & Taneja, S. (2023). Bibliometric analysis on employee engagement and human resource management. In *Enhancing Customer Engagement Through Location-Based Marketing* (pp. 185–205). IGI Global.

IBM. (2020). What is machine learning? https://www.ibm.com/topics/machine-learning (accessed on 17 January 2025).

Jain, J., Walia, N., Singh, S., & Jain, E. (2021). Mapping the field of behavioural biases: A literature review using bibliometric analysis. *Management Review Quarterly*, 1–33. https://doi.org/10.1007/s11301-021-00178-1.

Kashif, M., David, A., Gupta, V. P., & Alam, S. (2024). Integration of artificial intelligence in the financial sector. In *Artificial Intelligence and Machine Learning-Powered Smart Finance* (pp. 96–108). IGI Global.

Kashif, M., Kumar, P., Ghai, S., & Kumar, S. (2023). Disruptive technologies in computational finance. In *Algorithmic Approaches to Financial Technology: Forecasting, Trading, and Optimization* (pp. 46–60). IGI Global.

Kashif, M., Shajar, S. N., Singhal, N., & Kumar, P. (2023). Achieving sustainable investment practices through green finance: Challenges and opportunities. *Sustainable Investments in Green Finance*, 234–244. IGI Global.

Kashif, M., Thiyagarajan, S., & Sridharan, P. (2017). Dynamics of Algeria's international reserves. *African Journal of Economic and Management Studies, 8*(4), 410–419. https://doi.org/10.1108/AJEMS-01-2017-0024.

Kumar, S., Sureka, R., & Colombage, S. (2020). Capital structure of SMEs: A systematic literature review and bibliometric analysis. *Management Review Quarterly, 70*, 535–565. https://doi.org/10.1007/s11301-020-00175-9.

Mitchell, T. M. (1997). Does machine learning really work? *AI Magazine, 18*(3), 11–11.

Moscato, V., Picariello, A., & Sperlí, G. (2021). A benchmark of machine learning approaches for credit score prediction. *Expert Systems with Applications, 165*, 113986. https://doi.org/10.1016/j.eswa.2020.113986.

Ren, R., Hu, W., Dong, J., Sun, B., Chen, Y., & Chen, Z. (2020). A systematic literature review of green and sustainable logistics: Bibliometric analysis, research trend, and knowledge taxonomy. *International Journal of Environmental Research and Public Health, 17*(1), 261. https://doi.org/10.3390/ijerph17010261.

Singh, A., Taneja, S., & Kumar, P. (2023). Algorithmic approaches to financial technology: Forecasting, trading, and optimization. In *Algorithmic Approaches to Financial Technology: Forecasting, Trading, and Optimization.* https://doi.org/10.4018/9798369317464.

Singh, S., & Walia, N. (2022). Momentum investing: A systematic literature review and bibliometric analysis. *Management Review Quarterly, 72*(1), 87–113. https://doi.org/10.1007/s11301-022-00225-6.

CHAPTER 8

Financial Services Employing Artificial Intelligence and Machine Learning

NEEMA GUPTA,[1,*] SHIKHA SALONI,[1] K. K. MISHRA,[1] and MOHAMMAD KASHIF[2]

[1]*University School of Business, Chandigarh University, Mohali, Punjab, India*

[2]*Graphic Era (Deemed to be University), Dehradun, Uttarakhand, India*

**Corresponding author.*

ABSTRACT

This chapter explores the transformative role of Artificial Intelligence (AI) and Machine Learning (ML) in revolutionizing financial services, particularly in the context of post-pandemic risk assessment and investment strategies. It delves into how AI-driven tools, such as robo-advisors and intelligent financial applications, have redefined decision-making processes, risk management, fraud detection, and customer interaction in the financial sector. The study highlights the application of supervised ML algorithms in analyzing financial behavior, predicting cryptocurrency trends, and managing the complexities of unbalanced data in financial modeling. Emphasis is placed on AI's capacity for real-time data processing, personalized financial guidance, and improved forecasting capabilities. Furthermore, the chapter introduces the concept of Explainable AI (XAI) as a pivotal advancement toward financial transparency and accountability. Drawing on empirical data and machine learning methodologies, the chapter provides theoretical and practical insights into AI/ML's expanding influence on household investment behavior, regulatory frameworks, and

Transforming Business Finance in the Digital Era.
Sanjay Taneja, Mohammad Kashif, Ercan Özen, and Luan Vardari (Eds.)
© 2026 Apple Academic Press, Inc. Co-published with CRC Press (Taylor & Francis)

DOI: 10.1201/9781998511235-8

digital financial literacy. The findings underscore the need for ethical AI integration and intelligent regulatory strategies to enhance financial stability and investor trust in an increasingly data-driven economic landscape.

8.1 INTRODUCTION

Even though artificial intelligence (AI) has been around for a while, there has been a significant explosion in both interest and advancements in the field over the last 10 years. The falling costs of computing have resulted in the production of ever-more-powerful computers. These computers are equipped with the necessary hardware and processing power to draw accurate conclusions from the data they collect. AI development will change how individuals live and how they perform even the most basic tasks. Concurrently, the Internet of Things (IoT) is spreading rapidly and will inevitably rely more on AI. A computer can readily comprehend and analyze the vast amount of data being aggregated due to the interconnection of all the computational devices in our immediate environment. From there, the computer can determine the best use of the data, as it is far too extensive for human manipulation (Bhuvana et al., 2016). In addition to affecting our lives, these two developments are likely to impact numerous future business sectors, shaping and altering the future. Financial services providers are one sector that is particularly poised for significant growth.

Higher education is among the many industries where AI is becoming increasingly common. Applications of AI have become essential for colleges and universities. Software programs driven by AI that simulate human-to-human dialogue are known as chatbots (Sharma et al., 2021). These software programs function by conducting evaluations in the lexicon of formulating and conversing responses that they deem suitable. Given that they are well-trained and capable of using a wide array of languages, they can effectively handle various queries in different languages without limitation (Hong et al., 2021). According to Pranavi et al. (2022), chatbots like ChatGPT and Google Bard can be particularly advantageous for different establishments such as schools and institutions. One of their greatest assets is their ability to offer individualized instruction.

Globally, the coronavirus (COVID-19) pandemic has ravaged almost every aspect of life, including politics, the economy, the workplace, and daily activities. The International Monetary Fund (IMF) reported that 2020 saw the largest global economic decline since the 1930s Great Depression, at 4.4% (Jones et al., 2021). The long-term effects of COVID-19 are still felt in the post-epidemic era, with volatility and fluctuation affecting the labor and stock markets (Topçu and Gülal, 2020). The pandemic's economic aftermath significantly altered households' attitudes and practices regarding investments. Digital financial investments have become more popular than traditional financial investments (Guesmi et al., 2019), as they allow for portfolio diversification and hedging (Akhtaruzzaman et al., 2020). Recent years have seen increased interest in cryptocurrency investments from both academia and industry due to advancements made possible by blockchain technology. Aini and Lutfi (2019) indicate that risk assessment illustrates how hazards are perceived from different perspectives and circumstances. When investing in unpredictable environments, risk assessment is particularly crucial (Forlani and Mullins, 2000). Consequently, households perceive and respond to risks differently in unpredictable circumstances, necessitating further study to deepen our understanding of the investment landscape in the aftermath of the pandemic.

Forecasting has become more challenging due to significant global political and economic events that have affected stock price volatility, such as the conflict between the US and China, the Russia-Ukraine war, and the global financial crisis of 2008, along with the COVID-19 pandemic in recent years. Investors' decisions to purchase stocks are frequently influenced by news about such events or business operations. Numerous relevant research studies indicate that new information influences investors' decisions, which, in turn, affects changes in the stock price index; additionally, quantitative variables of finance-related indicators also play a role (Wei et al., 2017; Huang, 2016). In addition to traditional media sources, investors are referencing social media opinions and sharing their perspectives on various online platforms (Sezer et al., 2020). Thus, when estimating stock prices, investor sentiment is a significant variable alongside finance-related indicators. Automated financial advisors employ AI to assist users in managing and making decisions related to their financial concerns. These robo-advisors monitor both the stock market and the user's financial goals to recommend which stocks or bonds to buy or sell. Artificial intelligence-powered applications that users download, install, and use on their devices evaluate vast amounts of data to generate accurate financial forecasts and recommendations (Chakraborty and Joseph, 2017). Through the application of AI, intelligent wallets analyze users' habits and needs before offering feedback on their expenditures to help them develop self-control. The application of Big Data is causing a rapid transformation in the financial services sector. Businesses are utilizing advanced analytics to enhance decision-making, optimize operations, and gain new insights into customer behavior. Big Data in finance can be applied to various areas, including risk management, pricing optimization, product development, and fraud detection.

8.2 LITERATURE REVIEW

8.2.1 MACHINE LEARNING

"A field of study that gives computers the ability to learn without being explicitly programmed" (Munoz et al., 2014) defines machine learning (ML). ML is practically associated with ML algorithms, which employ statistical methods to identify patterns in massive amounts of data with little to no human involvement, thereby facilitating pattern recognition and decision-making (Hao et al., 2018; SAS, 2022). The three types of ML algorithms are supervised, semi-supervised, and unsupervised. The distinction between these types is based on whether datasets have labels and how the labeled dataset is used to train the models to attain a certain level of performance (Brownlee, 2016). In simple terms, the semi-supervised mode of learning uses a limited combination of input–output pairs and only input sets for model optimization. The supervised method offers a set of input–output pairs so that inputs can be accurately mapped to outputs via an intermediary system, whereas unsupervised learning involves only inputs without matching labels or classifications (Cheng, 2021).

To predict cryptocurrency prices, Le et al. (2018) employed a conglomerate of machine learning techniques, such as stochastic gradient descent, multi-layer perceptron, support vector machines, and K-nearest neighbors. Predicting cryptocurrency prices has been a primary application of machine learning algorithms. To investigate cryptocurrency investment habits, Le et al. (2019) utilized logistic regression (LR). Additionally, the co-movement and prices of cryptocurrencies, including Bitcoin, Ethereum, Litecoin, and Monero, were forecasted using neural networks and random forests (Aggarwal et al., 2019). Awotunde et al. (2021) discovered that the association between perceived benefits and cryptocurrency investment decisions was reinforced by machine learning forecasting. Samaddar et al. (2021) incorporated four machine learning algorithms and procured results for investment with the resampled series in cryptocurrency cash injection; the four algorithms were support vector classifier (SVC), logistic regression (LR), random forest (RF), and gradient tree boosting (GTB). Veerasingam and Teoh (2022) developed a hierarchical risk parity strategy to manage cryptocurrency portfolio risk. Borges and Neves (2020) categorized individuals based on their cryptocurrency investment interests using K-means clustering analysis. However, from a household perspective, the machine learning approach has rarely been used to assess risk, particularly in cryptocurrency investments, highlighting the significance of this work.

8.2.2 MACHINE LEARNING IN TODAY'S TIME

Numerous financial issues can be formulated as classification tasks from a machine learning perspective, where the arena to be classified is frequently much more compact than the specimen in the other arena (Burggraf, 2021; Sittivangkul et al., 2022). For example, in the financial market, if one aims to classify the companies with the highest likelihood of failing, there are far fewer bankrupt companies compared to other companies. This discrepancy makes it challenging to determine an appropriate decision boundary to differentiate between bankrupt and healthy companies based on limited observations. Consequently, the performance of any classifier trained on this data is usually insufficient (Wei et al., 2017). However, from a household perspective, the machine learning approach has rarely been utilized for assessing risk, particularly in cryptocurrency investments, which emphasizes the significance of this work.

Nevertheless, a higher recall of insolvency events but a very low precision of events involving healthy companies is the outcome of the design choice to sample an extensive class of healthy companies. According to Lombardo et al. (2022), in both cases, performance is subpar, especially in temporal and dynamic contexts where the data distribution is not unchanging over time. Unbalanced data in the financial domain must be addressed, which is why numerous research studies have been published in the literature. Prior to training a classifier to handle a range of financial issues, these studies recalibrate data to equalize minority and majority classes (Santoso et al., 2019). In particular, augmentation techniques produce a balanced dataset by adding new synthetic samples to the minority class. These techniques are typically used when handling highly unbalanced data (Wen et al., 2022).

In this situation, various approaches can be used to control varying over-sampling or data augmentation. The Synthetic Minority Oversampling Technique (SMOTE) by Chawla (2009) is perhaps the most popular and successful of these. Using the shared characteristics determined by k-Nearest Neighbors (kNN) for every minority sample, it generates artificial information for the minority class. SMOTE was employed by Veganzones and Séverin (2018) to forecast bankruptcy based on the financial ratios of a sizable group of French businesses. Pozzolo et al. (2015) employed SMOTE in conjunction with a combination of incrementally learning classifiers to identify unauthorized transactions with credit cards.

Variations of this approach have also surfaced in the literature to address this problem. Previous papers examined a range of SMOTE-based resampling strategies to enhance the efficacy of fundamental classifiers on bankruptcy data from Korean businesses between 2016 and 2017. In a similar vein, in 2022, the authors evaluated a hybrid approach for forecasting bankruptcy using an actual dataset from Spain that combined SMOTE with a group of classification algorithms. SMOTE and a Random Forest were combined to identify fraudulent transactions, achieving an impressive overall classification accuracy of 90%. A promising classification result for bankruptcy prediction was obtained by Garcia (2022) using a combination of cluster-based undersampling and SMOTE. According to Santoso et al. (2019), the authors developed a quick and precise machine learning model called XGBS. The technique is validated on imbalanced datasets for Korean, US, and Japanese companies. It tackles the insolvency forecasting problem using the squared logistics loss (SqLL) and an extreme gradient boosting model. The k-means clustering algorithm is used by CBoost to calculate the initial weight vector for the training set. A set of poor classifiers is found after multiple CBoost iterations, and XGBS integrates them to create the final classifier.

8.2.3 MACHINE LEARNING AND FINANCE

Conditional heteroscedasticity is a frequent problem in financial time series. In these situations, it is impossible to forecast the degree of volatility over time; moreover, weighted regressions are a common method for generating estimates (Loshchilov and Hutter, 2016). Heteroscedasticity violates the least squares presumption of constant variance in the residuals. Weighted regression produces residuals with constant variance by lowering the combined value of the weighted squared residuals when the appropriate weight is applied (Opitz, 2019).

The literature has also included proposals for other pertinent augmentation methods for financial imbalanced issues. A conditional variational autoencoder serves as the foundation for the authors' innovative boosting regression data resampling method, which can be used for a range of regression tasks, including those involving unbalanced datasets. Opitz (2019) reported that other researchers developed deep learning techniques to forecast the hourly movements of various banking stocks by utilizing technical characteristics and stock prices. Recursive feature elimination selection was employed to reduce these characteristics. A new metric for class sample separation that yields decision tree solutions with improved performance was developed by Alfaiz and Fati (2022) through a comparison of various decision tree splitting criteria for credit card fraud detection. Chugh and Malik (2022) examined the use of over-sampling in multiple machine learning techniques, such as logistic regression, random forests, support vector machines, decision trees, and artificial neural networks, to identify fraudulent credit card transactions (Table 8.1). Their findings indicated that the inclusion of data augmentation resulted in superior performance compared to the models used alone (Table 8.1). Finally, to identify fraudulent transactions across multiple nations, Chugh and Malik (2022) used data augmentation in conjunction with the AdaBoost algorithm and random forest. A further significant issue that should be considered when working with economic and financial data is data imputation, in addition to the problem of imbalanced data. Missing values are frequently discovered in financial time series, such as stock market data. The causes could be numerous and include factors such as market closures during holidays, the inability to obtain financial data promptly, noise, recording errors, and more (Machado et al., 2022). The challenge of forecasting future financial series analysis points with the most recent market data is heightened by missing data. Therefore, it is imperative to address the issue of missing data as soon as it arises (Mai et al., 2019). The literature has presented a wide range of data imputation techniques.

TABLE 8.1 Fraud Detection Techniques in Existing Literature

Fraud Detection Method	References
Random forests	Chugh and Malik (2022)
Support vector machines	Chugh and Malik (2022)
Logistic regression	Chugh and Malik (2022)
Decision trees	Chugh and Malik (2022)
Artificial neural networks	Chugh and Malik (2022)
Data augmentation	Chugh and Malik (2022)
Data imputation	Machado et al. (2022)

Source: Author's own.

8.2.4 ROLE OF MACHINE LEARNING IN FINANCE

The financial crisis has many different, twisted, and unexpected causes. According to Santoso et al. (2019), several of them can be attributed to the fraudulent execution of financial procedures, including excessive leverage, liquidity mismatches, erroneous tax and subsidy assessments, and an increase in bank and investor borrowing. Additionally, unexpected global occurrences like the COVID-19 pandemic can trigger financial crises (Kashif et al., 2024). As a result, no agreed-upon definition for the financial crisis is available; nonetheless, it can be characterized as an abrupt and severe disruption of certain economic equilibriums, followed by the failure of multiple financial establishments and its consequences for other entities. The global economic outlook for 2022 was released by the IMF last year, predicting it to be worse than anticipated. Simultaneously, it mentioned the notable decline in purchasing managers' surveys in the past few months, suggesting the fragility of the majority of G-20 economies. Furthermore, the IMF stated that the most recent data "confirms that the outlook is bleaker," particularly in Europe, in a blog post ahead of the G20 leaders' meeting in Indonesia. Recent managers' indices of purchases, which track manufacturing and services activity, indicate weakness in the majority of G-20 economies, continuing with a contraction in economic activity predicted in the face of high inflation. Moreover, it is anticipated that the escalation of the European energy crisis will seriously harm economic expansion and drive up inflation, which could prompt further tightening of international financial conditions and interest rate policy hikes if it continues to rise. Additionally, the IMF clarified that weak economies are consequently at greater risk of a sovereign debt crisis.

According to Mai et al. (2019), the frequency of hazardous weather events will be detrimental to global growth. Computational intelligence (CI) and AI are increasingly being applied in the financial domain to tasks like credit risk assessment, algorithmic trading, asset pricing and derivatives, and stock market forecasting.

8.3 THEORETICAL IMPLICATIONS

This research represents a pioneering effort in the literature on cryptocurrency investments for households, as it compares the classification performance of multiple supervised machine learning algorithms, thereby integrating potential risk factors. Subsequently, these are the study's theoretical ramifications. The chief role of the present study is to evaluate the post-pandemic risk associated with household cryptocurrency investments. We discovered that the impact of the worldwide outbreak on risk assessment has primarily focused on financial investments generally, with little research conducted on it during the early phases of the pandemic (Angrisani et al., 2020; Shachat et al., 2020). Household risk assessments of cryptocurrency investments have been significantly impacted by the COVID-19 pandemic, and this influence persists into the post-pandemic period as well. On the other hand, this study explored the post-pandemic risk assessment. Additionally, this research broadens the scope of the exhaustive examination of the variables influencing risk evaluation in household cryptocurrency investments (Yue et al., 2020). This is in addition to the partial factor analysis that examines financial literacy, education, occupation, gender, and investment experience, as well as financial connectivity (Charfeddine et al., 2022; Zhao and Zhang, 2021).

Furthermore, by extending the ML approach for domestic investments in cryptocurrency, this study makes a valuable contribution. It is found that the majority of existing studies concentrate on applying ML to forecast cryptocurrency co-movements and prices. The approach can be applied with a single or a collection of different algorithms. Thus, this work broadens the application of ML beyond predicting prices and movements and elucidates the literature on risk assessment concerning the prediction of risk and the automatic construction of analytical models, especially regarding investments in cryptocurrencies by households. Additionally, this study aims to solve the "black box" problem of the ML approach and makes a general contribution to interpretability for the same.

This study utilized various machine learning algorithms to train a supervised classification model, compared performance metrics to validate the ML algorithms, and used the best-performing model, RF, to examine the significance of 13 potential determinants. It should be noted, however, that algorithm effectiveness will depend on the size of datasets, training, validation configurations, and other factors, so RF may not always be the best algorithm for assessment and prediction of risk. Rather, the cutting-edge methodological approach used in this study to assess the investing risk associated with household cryptocurrency investments will inform future research methodologies.

8.4 PRACTICAL IMPLICATIONS

This research has applications for four groups of people: government regulators, financial educators, investment managers, and household cryptocurrency investors. By applying the ML approach, this study also helps average cryptocurrency investors make better investment choices. Because machine learning effectively turns data into interpretable insights for risk assessment, it enables average cryptocurrency investors to make more informed decisions. Thus, when estimating stock prices, investor sentiment is a significant variable in addition to finance-related indicators. Automated financial advisors employ AI to assist users in managing and making decisions related to their various financial concerns. When it comes to recommending which stocks or bonds a user should buy or sell, these robo-advisors monitor both the stock market and the user's financial goals. Through data processing and analysis, the AI approach can assist in making more transparent, reliable, and trustworthy investment decisions for prospective household investors. Moreover, this research helps to motivate investment managers and financial regulators to lessen the distortion of the cryptocurrency market and to efficiently manage risk in times of extreme circumstances, like pandemics (Kashif et al., 2023a). According to the research findings, investment duration is deemed less significant for risk assessment than investment amount, even though the interaction between investment amount and duration matters. This suggests that many households may be reluctant to consider investing in cryptocurrencies as a long-term or short-term strategy and that the market's notorious volatility makes it more difficult for investors to accurately assess the risks. Consequently, risk controls and market stabilization could be implemented by investment managers and financial regulators. For instance, more platforms could be created to offer hosting, staking, and monitoring services to safeguard individual cryptocurrency investors and prevent fraud. Third, our results have significant ramifications for how government regulators should establish rules governing financial institutions' exposure to and participation in cryptocurrency and investment activities. According to the results, one of the top five factors in determining risk assessment was one's perception of traditional investments.

In the discussion section, we further argued that this may relate to how traditional financial assets and cryptocurrencies are connected in the post-pandemic era. Since crypto-assets are no longer viewed as being on the periphery of the financial system (Adrian, 2022), government regulators may issue guidelines regarding cryptocurrency regulations and reduce the risks associated with cryptocurrency investments related to financial stability. To limit the amount of cryptocurrency investment advertisements, for instance, there could be some restrictions put in place on online platforms like Twitter. These restrictions could apply to ads for cryptocurrency exchanges, cryptocurrency wallet services, and cryptocurrency debit or credit cards. Finally, this study adds to the body of evidence suggesting that financial advisors and educators can educate investors about cryptocurrencies via various channels, including Twitter communities. The information may be used to help investors become more cryptocurrency literate as well as for short- and long-term cryptocurrency planning. Because of this, it was discovered that the prime factors influencing risk assessment were cryptocurrency literacy (Kashif et al., 2017). Due to the high volatility of cryptocurrencies and the possibility that many investors will only have limited exposure through word of mouth, cryptocurrency literacy is imperative. Therefore, when it comes to household cryptocurrency investments, specific knowledge about cryptocurrencies may be more significant than general financial knowledge (Fujiki, 2020), particularly when determining whether or not to accept the associated risks.

8.5 DISCUSSION

To develop a more intelligent model for identifying, forecasting, and categorizing the causes of financial crises than traditional techniques that depend on intricate computations, such as those employed in statistical and operations research methodologies, machine learning and deep learning technologies have attracted the interest of numerous researchers. AI-based techniques offer two main advantages over classical methods in identifying the causes of financial crises. First, the AI-based approach can process and learn from unbalanced and random data. This means that AI-based techniques can identify the causes of financial crises without relying on the statistical distribution of financial data. Second, AI-based techniques fall under the category of nonlinear approaches, which allows them to analyze complex financial data patterns more accurately.

Moreover, a new concept has emerged: Explainable AI (XAI). This innovative idea may provide a miraculous solution to the issue of financial transparency in the financial services industry. The latest AI models can enhance the accuracy, speed, and efficacy of various financial services, including credit score assignment, investment portfolio optimization, and liquidity balance prediction (Figure 8.1). To prevent financial bias, all stakeholders—banks, investors, staff, clients, and others—must understand the rationale and logic behind the use of these AI models. Consequently, XAI is capable of addressing this challenge.

While the market for this technology is still developing and XAI standards are being established, current trends suggest that XAI will be crucial for future economic AI applications. By 2025, the Gartner website predicts that contracts for AI application purchases by the government and 30% of large companies will require explainable and ethical AI (Singh et al., 2023).

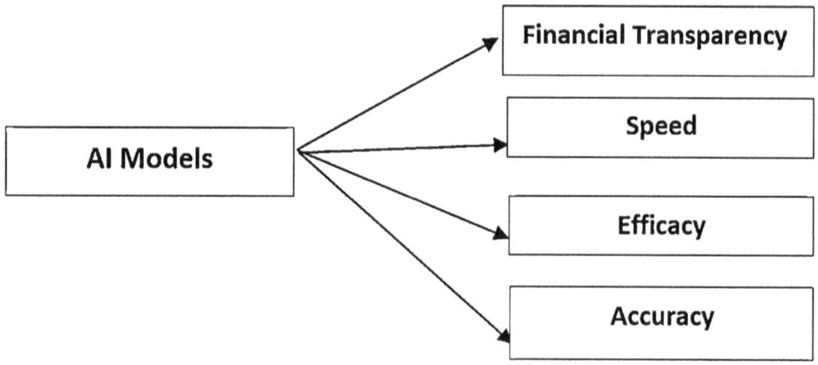

FIGURE 8.1 Benefits of AI models.

Source: Author's own.

AI is becoming increasingly prevalent across various sectors, including higher education. AI applications are becoming essential for higher education institutions, whether for staff support, personalized learning, smart educational systems, or automated assessment. They provide support that enhances learning outcomes while reducing costs. Chatbots are AI-powered software applications that simulate human-to-human communication. They generate what they perceive to be appropriate responses after evaluating the context of the conversation (Kashif et al., 2023b). Trained on extensive linguistic datasets, they can address a wide range of inquiries. Educational institutions, including professional development programs, universities, and elementary and secondary schools, can benefit from chatbots like Google Bard and ChatGPT, which have the significant advantage of offering customized instruction.

The global coronavirus pandemic, known as COVID-19, has affected nearly every aspect of life, including politics, the economy, the workplace, and daily activities. The IMF estimates that the world economy contracted by 4.4% in 2020, marking the most significant decline since the Great Depression of the 1930s. The COVID-19 pandemic has left a lasting impact on the post-pandemic era, as evidenced by the fluctuations and turbulence experienced in the labor and stock markets. The economic aftermath of the pandemic has significantly altered households' attitudes and practices regarding investments. Consequently, digital financial investments have garnered comparatively more attention than traditional financial investments for portfolio diversification and hedging (Table 8.2). In recent years, there has been a growing interest in cryptocurrency investments from both academia and industry, facilitated by advancements in blockchain technology. Risk assessment illustrates how various perspectives and realities are used to interpret risks. This is particularly important when investing in unpredictable environments. As a result, households' access to and responses to risks in uncertain circumstances vary, necessitating further study to gain a deeper understanding of the post-pandemic investment response.

TABLE 8.2 Post-Pandemic Trends

Trend	Example
Portfolio diversification	Blockchain technology
Digital financial investments	Crypto currency investments
Supervised classification model	–

Source: Author's own.

8.6 CONCLUSION

Artificial Intelligence (AI), renowned for its flexibility, excels at making decisions based on information. These devices can exhibit emotional and contextual responses. AI is effective in encryption and detecting suspicious activity. Customers can choose loan amounts at competitive interest rates. It demonstrates a superior understanding of customers and their behaviors based on previous interactions. The daily advancements in AI render banking security increasingly reliable. Complete encryption can be achieved with skill and appropriate application. With AI's implementation, processes could accelerate significantly. AI possesses self-control and emotional intelligence. By reducing costs, banks can save millions of dollars. As Bitcoin and other cryptocurrencies are digital currencies, it is crucial to mitigate investment risks, make accurate forecasts, and safeguard them against fraud. Enhanced forecasting and outcomes for cryptocurrencies are under investigation, with both AI and Machine Learning (ML) being applied. Methods utilizing AI and ML were discussed. Overall, the best-performing models included the Support Vector Machine, Long Short-Term Memory Model, and Artificial Neural Network. Neural network models require long-term data, while long short-term data is optimal for LSTM models. Bitcoin and cryptocurrencies are more influenced by market dynamics. Consequently, they may be integrated into AI-based price prediction models and emotional analysis. To predict Bitcoin's future, a novel cointegration method utilizes data from other cryptocurrencies.

KEYWORDS

- **artificial intelligence**
- **blockchain technology**
- **chatbots**
- **cryptocurrencies**
- **financial services**
- **machine learning**

REFERENCES

Adrian, T., Iyer, T., & Qureshi, M. S. (2022). Crypto prices move more in sync with stocks, posing new risks. *IMF Blog*. Available online: https://www.imf.org/en/Blogs/Articles/2022/01/11/crypto-prices-move-more-in-sync-with-stocksposing-new-risks/ (accessed on 17 January 2025).

Aggarwal, A., Gupta, I., Garg, N., & Goel, A. (2019). Deep learning approach to determine the impact of socio-economic factors on Bitcoin price prediction. In *Twelfth International Conference on Contemporary Computing* (https://doi.org/10.1109/ic3.2019.8844928).

Aini, N. S. N., & Lutfi, L. (2019). The influence of risk perception, risk tolerance, overconfidence, and loss aversion towards investment decision making. *Journal of Economics, Business, and Accountancy | Ventura, 21*(3), 401. https://doi.org/10.14414/jebav.v21i3.1663.

Akhtaruzzaman, M., Şensoy, A., & Corbet, S. (2020). The influence of Bitcoin on portfolio diversification and design. *Finance Research Letters, 37*, 101344. https://doi.org/10.1016/j.frl.2019.101344.

Alarfaj, F. K., Malik, I., Khan, H. U., Almusallam, N., Ramzan, M., & Khan, H. M. (2022). Credit card fraud detection using state-of-the-art machine learning and deep learning algorithms. *IEEE Access, 10*, 39700–39715. https://doi.org/10.1109/access.2022.3166891.

Alfaiz, N. S., & Fati, S. M. (2022). Enhanced credit card fraud detection model using machine learning. *Electronics, 11*(4), 662. https://doi.org/10.3390/electronics11040662.

Angrisani, M., Cipriani, M., Guarino, A., Kendall, R., & De Zarate, J. O. (2020). Risk preferences at the time of COVID-19: An experiment with professional traders and students. *Social Science Research Network*. https://doi.org/10.2139/ssrn.3609586.

Awotunde, J. B., Ogundokun, R. O., Jimoh, R. G., Misra, S., & Aro, T. O. (2021). Machine learning algorithm for cryptocurrencies price prediction. In *Studies in Computational Intelligence* (pp. 421–447). https://doi.org/10.1007/978-3-030-72236-4_17.

Bhuvana, M., Thirumagal, P. G., & Vasantha, S. (2016). Big data analytics – A leveraging technology for Indian commercial banks. *Indian Journal of Science and Technology, 9*(32). https://doi.org/10.17485/ijst/2016/v9i32/98643.

Borges, T. A., & Neves, R. (2020). Ensemble of machine learning algorithms for cryptocurrency investment with different data resampling methods. *Applied Soft Computing, 90*, 106187. https://doi.org/10.1016/j.asoc.2020.106187.

Brownlee, J. (2016). Supervised and unsupervised machine learning algorithms. *Machine Learning Mastery, 16*(03).

Burggraf, T. (2021). Beyond risk parity – A machine learning-based hierarchical risk parity approach on cryptocurrencies. *Finance Research Letters, 38*, 101523. https://doi.org/10.1016/j.frl.2020.101523.

Chakraborty, C., & Joseph, A. (2017). Machine learning at central banks. *Social Science Research Network*. https://doi.org/10.2139/ssrn.3031796.

Charfeddine, L., Benlagha, N., & Khediri, K. B. (2022). An intra-cryptocurrency analysis of volatility connectedness and its determinants: Evidence from mining coins, non-mining coins, and tokens. *Research in International Business and Finance, 62*, 101699. https://doi.org/10.1016/j.ribaf.2022.101699.

Chawla, N. V. (2009). Data mining for imbalanced datasets: An overview. In *Springer eBooks* (pp. 875–886). https://doi.org/10.1007/978-0-387-09823-4_45.

Cheng, T. (2021). Supervised, semi-supervised, unsupervised, and self-supervised learning. *Towards Data Science*. https://towardsdatascience.com/supervised-semi-supervised-unsupervised-and-self-supervised-learning-7fa79aa9247c (accessed on 17 January 2025).

Chugh, B., & Malik, N. (2022). Machine learning classifiers for detecting credit card fraudulent transactions. In *Lecture Notes in Networks and Systems* (pp. 223–231). https://doi.org/10.1007/978-981-19-0095-2_23.

Forlani, D., & Mullins, J. (2000). Perceived risks and choices in entrepreneurs' new venture decisions. *Journal of Business Venturing, 15*(4), 305–322. https://doi.org/10.1016/s0883-9026(98)00017-2.

Fujiki, H. (2020). Who adopts crypto assets in Japan? Evidence from the 2019 financial literacy survey. *Journal of the Japanese and International Economies, 58*, 101107. https://doi.org/10.1016/j.jjie.2020.101107.

García, J. (2022). Bankruptcy prediction using synthetic sampling. *Machine Learning with Applications, 9*, 100343. https://doi.org/10.1016/j.mlwa.2022.100343.

Guesmi, K., Saadi, S., Abid, I., & Ftiti, Z. (2019). Portfolio diversification with virtual currency: Evidence from bitcoin. *International Review of Financial Analysis, 63*, 431–437. https://doi.org/10.1016/j.irfa.2018.03.004.

Hao, K. (2018). What is machine learning. *Posts & Telecom Press: Beijing, China.*

Hong, H., Bian, Z., & Lee, C. (2021). COVID-19 and instability of stock market performance: Evidence from the U.S. *Financial Innovation, 7*(1). https://doi.org/10.1186/s40854-021-00229-1.

Huang, J. (2016). Patent network analysis of cloud computing by text mining. *技術學刊, 31*(2), 127–146. https://www.airitilibrary.com/Publication/Index?FirstID=10123407-201606-201607120012-201607120012-127-146 (accessed on 17 January 2025).

Jones, L., Palumbo, D., & Brown, D. (2021). Coronavirus: How the pandemic has changed the world economy. *BBC News, 24.*

Kashif, M., David, A., Gupta, V. P., & Alam, S. (2024). Integration of artificial intelligence in the financial sector. In *Artificial Intelligence and Machine Learning-Powered Smart Finance* (pp. 96–108). IGI Global.

Kashif, M., Kumar, P., Ghai, S., & Kumar, S. (2023). Disruptive technologies in computational finance. In *Algorithmic Approaches to Financial Technology: Forecasting, Trading, and Optimization* (pp. 46–60). IGI Global.

Kashif, M., Shajar, S. N., Singhal, N., & Kumar, P. (2023). Achieving sustainable investment practices through green finance: Challenges and opportunities. In *Sustainable Investments in Green Finance* (pp. 234–244). IGI Global.

Kashif, M., Thiyagarajan, S., & Sridharan, P. (2017). Dynamics of Algeria's international reserves. *African Journal of Economic and Management Studies, 8*(4), 410–419.

Le, T., Lee, M. Y., Park, J. R., & Baik, S. W. (2018). Oversampling techniques for bankruptcy prediction: Novel features from a transaction dataset. *Symmetry, 10*(4), 79. https://doi.org/10.3390/sym10040079.

Le, T., Vo, B., Fujita, H., Nguyen, N. T., & Baik, S. W. (2019). A fast and accurate approach for bankruptcy forecasting using squared logistics loss with GPU-based extreme gradient boosting. *Information Sciences, 494*, 294–310. https://doi.org/10.1016/j.ins.2019.04.060.

Lombardo, G., Pellegrino, M., Adosoglou, G., Cagnoni, S., Pardalos, P. M., & Poggi, A. (2022). Machine learning for bankruptcy prediction in the American stock market: Dataset and benchmarks. *Future Internet, 14*(8), 244. https://doi.org/10.3390/fi14080244.

Loshchilov, I., & Hutter, F. (2016). SGDR: Stochastic gradient descent with warm restarts. *arXiv*. https://arxiv.org/pdf/1608.03983.pdf.

Machado, P., Fernandes, B., & Nováis, P. (2022). Benchmarking data augmentation techniques for tabular data. In *Lecture Notes in Computer Science* (pp. 104–112). https://doi.org/10.1007/978-3-031-21753-1_11.

Mai, F., Tian, S., Lee, C., & Ma, L. (2019). Deep learning models for bankruptcy prediction using textual disclosures. *European Journal of Operational Research, 274*(2), 743–758. https://doi.org/10.1016/j.ejor.2018.10.024.

Maiti, M., Vyklyuk, Y., & Vuković, D. (2020). Cryptocurrencies chaotic co-movement forecasting with neural networks. *Internet Technology Letters, 3*(3). https://doi.org/10.1002/itl2.157.

Munoz, A. (2014). Machine learning and optimization. *Courant Institute of Mathematical Sciences, 1, 2*.

Opitz, J., & Burst, S. (2019). Macro F1 and macro F1. *arXiv preprint arXiv:1911.03347*.

Pozzolo, A. D., Caelen, O., & Bontempi, G. (2015). When is undersampling effective in unbalanced classification tasks? In *Lecture Notes in Computer Science* (pp. 200–215). https://doi.org/10.1007/978-3-319-23528-8_13.

Pranavi, N. S. S., Sruthi, T. K. S. S., Sirisha, B. J. N., Nayak, M. S. D. P., & Thadikemalla, V. S. G. (2022). Credit card fraud detection using minority oversampling and random forest technique. In *2022 3rd International Conference for Emerging Technology (INCET)*. https://doi.org/10.1109/incet54531.2022.9824146.

Samaddar, M., Roy, R. S., De, S., & Karmakar, R. (2021). A comparative study of different machine learning algorithms on bitcoin value prediction. In *2021 International Conference on Advances in Electrical, Computing, Communication and Sustainable Technologies (ICAECT)*. https://doi.org/10.1109/icaect49130.2021.9392629.

Santoso, N., Wibowo, W., & Hikmawati, H. (2019). Integration of synthetic minority oversampling technique for imbalanced class. *Indonesian Journal of Electrical Engineering and Computer Science, 13*(1), 102–108. https://doi.org/10.11591/ijeecs.v13.i1.pp102-108.

SAS. (2022). Machine learning, what it is and why it matters. *SAS Insights*. https://www.sas.com/enca/insights/analytics/machine-learning.html (accessed on 17 January 2025).

Sezer, Ö. B., Gudelek, M. U., & Özbayoğlu, A. M. (2020). Financial time series forecasting with deep learning: A systematic literature review: 2005–2019. *Applied Soft Computing, 90*, 106181. https://doi.org/10.1016/j.asoc.2020.106181.

Shachat, J., Walker, M. J., & Wei, L. (2020). The impact of the COVID-19 pandemic on economic behaviours and preferences: Experimental evidence from Wuhan. *RePEc: Research Papers in Economics*. https://digitalcommons.chapman.edu/cgi/viewcontent.cgi?article=1328&context=esi_working_papers (accessed on 17 January 2025).

Sharma, D. K., Hota, H. S., Brown, K., & Handa, R. (2021). Integration of genetic algorithm with artificial neural network for stock market forecasting. *International*

Journal of Systems Assurance Engineering and Management, 13(S2), 828–841. https://doi.org/10.1007/s13198-021-01209-5.

Singh, A., Taneja, S., & Kumar, P. (2023). Algorithmic approaches to financial technology: Forecasting, trading, and optimization. In *Algorithmic Approaches to Financial Technology: Forecasting, Trading, and Optimization*. https://doi.org/10.4018/9798369317464.

Sittivangkul, K., Arreeras, T., & Tiwong, S. (2022). Perception and clustering analysis towards cryptocurrency investment decision using machine learning. In *2022 International Conference on Decision Aid Sciences and Applications (DASA)*. https://doi.org/10.1109/dasa54658.2022.9764969.

Topçu, M., & Gülal, Ö. S. (2020). The impact of COVID-19 on emerging stock markets. *Finance Research Letters, 36*, 101691. https://doi.org/10.1016/j.frl.2020.101691.

Veerasingam, N., & Teoh, A. P. (2022). Modeling cryptocurrency investment decision: Evidence from Islamic emerging market. *Journal of Islamic Marketing, 14*(7), 1817–1835. https://doi.org/10.1108/jima-07-2021-0234.

Veganzones, D., & Séverin, É. (2018). An investigation of bankruptcy prediction in imbalanced datasets. *Decision Support Systems, 112*, 111–124. https://doi.org/10.1016/j.dss.2018.06.011.

Wei, B., Yue, J., & Rao, Y. (2017). A deep learning framework for financial time series using stacked autoencoders and long-short term memory. *PLOS ONE, 12*(7), e0180944. https://doi.org/10.1371/journal.pone.0180944.

Wei, Y., Lu, Y., Chen, J., & Hsu, Y. (2017). Informativeness of the market news sentiment in the Taiwan stock market. *The North American Journal of Economics and Finance, 39*, 158–181. https://doi.org/10.1016/j.najef.2016.10.004.

Wen, Q., Tian, Z., Zhang, C., Chen, W., Ma, Z., Yan, J., & Sun, L. (2022). Transformers in time series: A survey. *arXiv*. https://doi.org/10.48550/arxiv.2202.07125.

Yue, P., Korkmaz, A. G., & Zhou, H. (2020). Household financial decision making amidst the COVID-19 pandemic. *Emerging Markets Finance and Trade, 56*(10), 2363–2377. https://doi.org/10.1080/1540496x.2020.1784717.

Zhao, H., & Zhang, L. (2021). Financial literacy or investment experience: Which is more influential in cryptocurrency investment? *International Journal of Bank Marketing, 39*(7), 1208–1226. https://doi.org/10.1108/ijbm-11-2020-0552.

CHAPTER 9

Artificial Intelligence (AI) and Machine Learning (ML) in Indian Finance: Present Landscape and Future Trajectory

RIZWAN KHAN,[1,*] MOHD. TAQI,[2] MANJU BABU,[2] and MOHD. ATIF AFZAL[3]

[1]*University School of Business, Chandigarh University, Mohali, Punjab, India*

[2]*School of Business, Bahrain Polytechnic, Isa Town, Bahrain*

[3]*Center for Distance and Online Education, Aligarh Muslim University, Aligarh, Uttar Pradesh, India*

**Corresponding author.*

ABSTRACT

This chapter provides a comprehensive analysis of the evolving role of Artificial Intelligence (AI) and Machine Learning (ML) in the Indian financial sector, examining both current applications and future directions. Through a detailed literature review, qualitative research, and empirical insights, the study explores how AI and ML are transforming asset management, algorithmic trading, credit underwriting, risk management, and regulatory compliance. Emphasizing India's unique financial landscape, the chapter investigates how digital transformation and data-driven innovations have enabled more informed, efficient, and personalized financial services. Key applications such as robo-advisory, sentiment analysis, fraud detection, and financial chatbots are discussed, alongside

Transforming Business Finance in the Digital Era.
Sanjay Taneja, Mohammad Kashif, Ercan Özen, and Luan Vardari (Eds.)
© 2026 Apple Academic Press, Inc. Co-published with CRC Press (Taylor & Francis)

DOI: 10.1201/9781998511235-9

challenges like data privacy, algorithmic bias, and regulatory fragmentation. The study also addresses the impact of COVID-19 on accelerating AI adoption and highlights strategies for optimizing AI/ML deployment in finance. Ultimately, the chapter underscores AI and ML's potential to reshape financial services by enhancing operational efficiency, financial inclusion, and decision-making while calling for responsible innovation and skill development in the Indian financial ecosystem.

9.1 INTRODUCTION

Machine learning (ML) is utilized in asset management, algorithmic trading, credit underwriting, and blockchain-based finance. The availability of data and affordable computational resources has facilitated this development. Machine learning models leverage big data to self-teach and enhance performance and predictability without human intervention. Prominent figures such as Elon Musk, Chairman of Tesla Inc. and SpaceX Inc., Jeff Bezos, Executive Chairman of Amazon Inc., and Mark Zuckerberg, CEO of Meta Inc., have emphasized the importance of machine learning techniques and AI technologies for ensuring their companies' financial sustainability. The fourth phase of the Fourth Industrial Revolution, driven by digital transformation, has resulted in numerous opportunities and breakthroughs in finance, healthcare, and education through AI. AI has emerged as a dominant technology in the 2020s, and machine learning has rapidly advanced due to improvements in computer technology; however, the evolution of AI necessitates the creativity of top data scientists and engineers. Consequently, this study employs a scoping review and an embedding review to assess the conceptual development of AI and ML in finance research in India. The aim is to elucidate the complexities of AI and ML research in finance, particularly in the Indian context. This study synthesizes and expands upon portfolio management and robo-advisory, risk management and financial distress, sentiment analysis and investor behavior, algorithmic stock market prediction and high-frequency trading, data protection and cybersecurity, big data analytics, blockchain, and FinTech.

Financial and investment decisions significantly impact individuals and businesses today. Each financial scenario demands precise decision-making. Modern AI and ML are evolving and committed to facilitating optimal financial choices. In computer science, AI fosters machine intelligence to make sound decisions. Machines are developing human-like expert systems that think, learn, and act. AI and ML are crucial for enabling machines to perform intelligent tasks. Enhanced financial and investment decisions are vital across various aspects of life. AI is emerging as a trend in finance, employing scientific methods to achieve flawless financial and investment decisions through financial modeling, e-financing, e-trading, and more.

AI and machine learning play a pivotal role in computer science, finance, economics, transportation, marketing, engineering, and beyond. This chapter examines the role and conceptual epistemology of AI and ML in the evolving banking trends in India. The study reveals that artificial intelligence and machine learning provide significant advantages to financial learners, youth, and students aspiring to work in finance. The research aims to familiarize readers with AI in finance, illustrate its classical and modern forms, and review the literature and best practices. The conceptual review of artificial intelligence and machine learning as financial trends is conducted for these reasons. This study showcases AI's classical and modern financial manifestations. Furthermore, it investigates machine- or AI-based financial transactions that are free from fraud, errors, or mistakes. The research utilizes books, journal articles, research papers, periodicals, websites, newspapers, and personal observations for its analysis. Tables and historical data are also examined.

9.2 SIGNIFICANCE OF THE STUDY

While the literature extensively covers the topics of machine learning, artificial intelligence, and their implementations in the financial sector, scholarly investigations into the advantages of AI in financial services remain scarce. This qualitative investigation constructs theories related to finance, AI, and ML. According to the study, AI and ML have rendered financial operations more systematic and practical. Additionally, the study demonstrates the advantages that AI and ML provide to organizations, finance experts, and personnel. The analysis illustrates why every Indian firm should implement AI and ML in finance.

9.3 REVIEW OF LITERATURE

Artificial intelligence mimics human intelligence using algorithms and computers. AI extrapolates patterns from massive data sets using advanced mathematics to solve issues through optimization mechanisms. Rather than equipment aptitude, this study utilized computer program information

(Chan et al., 2019). Advances in artificial intelligence provide applications for economic experts. These applications might destabilize the economy. Fethi and Pasiouras (2009) anticipate that AI will outperform humans and replace them.

The phenomenon found in AI involves pattern recognition that detects abnormalities. Security, money laundering, unusual financial arrangements, and illicit behavior can be detected by AI. Comprehensive investing applies it (Chan et al., 2019). By portfolio management recommendations, automated consulting is achieved. Individual shareholders typically engage in this. Financial algorithm trading employs bespoke algorithms to analyze market and price data for rapid, planned trades. Quick trades are referred to as "high-frequency trading" (Kraus and Palmer, 2018).

AI offers numerous financial advantages. Automated processes enhance creativity and efficiency. It also reduces emotional or mental errors. Understanding long-term trends and improvements that current methods cannot detect can increase data management precision and clarity. These criteria are especially crucial when principles like the Financial Instrument Directive II for MiFID II or EU markets increase senior management's analysis-related obligations and business-related data (Ho et al., 2012). AI utilizes semantic grammar, news, and text. Articles, novels, and social media posts can be understood and assessed by AI. Economics depend on AI systems' ability to quickly process all relevant news and information, while humans would require hours to handle all the nuances that could affect inventory performance. Data mining simplifies market price forecasting and research. Findings and predictions may influence legislative and institutional improvements (Kraus and Palmer, 2018).

Big data from social media and the internet can be utilized to examine market behavior. Social media sentiment analysis enhances election prediction. AI may be integrated into credit risk analysis, bond rates, scoring, and rating rates. In various studies, artificial neural networks improve credit judgment and default prediction (Kashif et al., 2017; Zavadskaya, 2017). Douglas Merrill, former Google CIO, founded Zest Finance, a lender-borrower software site. After 50 years, banking operations still utilize less than 50 data points and make biased decisions. Zest Finance's ZAML ended the indemnity chase by finding millions of new consumers using vast data points. They assert that loan analysis has not improved after years of study. ZAML can identify better borrowers using thousands of data points, which reduces bias. According to the founder, late loan repayment does not always signify poor borrowing. The additional risk factors for human default surprised him. This applies to credit-free youth, who are often excluded by traditional industries. However, employing ZAML to reveal the machine learning black box that creates tests and delivers law-related facts to candidates when unfavorable impacts arise is advised.

The research has partially succeeded based on AI and finance studies. Financial applications affect uncertain financial decision-making, according to Bahrammirzaee (2010). It begins with the historical financial patterns of technology reform. This study explored how hybrid models, neural networks, and expert systems have transformed financial application patterns. Investment portfolio management, credit evaluation, financial planning, and forecasting utilize intelligent systems. AI in banking is more accurate than traditional financial applications, according to research. The financial impact and performance of AI should be studied. AI-based banking performance assessment and operations research for employment analysis and data operation were explained by Meryem Duygun Fethi (2009). Bank underperformance was studied utilizing neural networks, multi-criteria assessments, and support vector machines (SVMs). The bank achieved profit efficiency and capacity efficiency but predicted bank and employee credit ratings using non-bootstrapping methods, which biased the results. Future AI research should suggest predicting individual models into integrated meta-classifiers. Computing intelligence was related to financial AI in 2005. The study examined Herbert Simon's history and economic finance. Herbert Simon proposed AI in finance and economics measurement. This study proved the necessity of constructing economic models. Economic and financial stock prices should inform future strong computation structure judgments. Yu (2005) identified a genetic programming capital flow model. Global short-term capital market techniques and trading rules are identified by the model (Kashif et al., 2024). Capital market techniques might be influenced by simulation modeling. This simulation model works for short-term capital markets. Lin (2019) noted that artificial intelligence is making financial transactions easier, more profitable, cheaper, more accessible, and more efficient for smooth operations. AI assesses structural risk and financial restrictions. AI in finance feeds data coding, bias, and risk. The data code performs systematic finance risk using AI. AI research should explore many financial issues from an internal perspective. Lin (2016) found AI changing banking technologies. It offers tech-based compliance, trading, banking, analysis, financial forecasting, optimization, and financial change evaluation. The study created new financial technologies and modernized financial technical settings. Therefore, developing finance technology must be investigated to generate new modern finance technology to revolutionize finance. Innovation in finance using AI and ML is discussed by Kristin Johnson (2019). Financial judgments from robots should be fraud-free. FinTech is used on smartphones and tablets. This FinTech company has made credit and money safety decisions for banks and non-banks. Accounting, transparency, and financial technology are their goals in finance operations. Bharti Kumari (January 2021) explained artificial intelligence in finance and offered the best financial technology design and technique for better financial services. The study promotes innovative financial models to enhance AI awareness in finance. In this design, a feedforward loop, dynamic approaches, and an AI in finance conceptual framework model are utilized. Further research on financial AI implementation is needed.

Artificial intelligence mimics human intelligence using algorithms and computers. AI extrapolates patterns from massive data sets using advanced mathematics to solve issues. The mechanism of optimization is employed. Rather than equipment aptitude, this study utilized computer program information (Chan et al., 2019; Kashif et al., 2023a, b). Recent AI advances allow economic specialists to use applications. These applications might destabilize the economy. Fethi and Pasiouras (2009) expect AI to outperform humans and replace them.

The AI-found phenomenon involves pattern recognition that detects abnormalities. Security, money laundering, unusual financial arrangements, and illicit behavior can be detected by AI. Comprehensive investing applies it (Chan et al., 2019). By portfolio management recommendations, automated consulting is achieved. Individual shareholders typically engage in this. Financial algorithm trading employs bespoke algorithms to analyze market and price data for rapid, planned trades. Quick trades are referred to as "high-frequency trading" (Kraus and Palmer, 2018).

AI provides numerous financial advantages. Automated processes enhance creativity and efficiency while reducing emotional or mental errors. Understanding long-term trends and improvements that current methods cannot detect can increase data management precision and conciseness. These criteria are particularly crucial when principles such as the Financial Instrument Directive II for MiFID II or EU markets increase senior management's analysis-related obligations and business-related data (Ho et al., 2012). AI utilizes semantic grammar, news, and text. Articles, novels, and social media posts can be understood and assessed by AI. Economics rely on AI systems' ability to swiftly process all relevant news and information, whereas humans would require hours to manage all the nuances that could impact inventory performance. Data mining simplifies market price forecasting and research. Findings and predictions may influence legislative and institutional improvements (Kraus and Palmer, 2018).

Big data from social media and the internet can be leveraged to examine market behavior. Social media sentiment analysis enhances election predictions. AI may be integrated into credit risk analysis, bond rates, scoring, and rating rates. Various studies indicate that artificial neural networks improve credit judgment and default prediction (Kashif et al., 2017; Zavadskaya, 2017). Douglas Merrill, former Google CIO, founded Zest Finance, a lending and borrowing software platform.

9.4 OBJECTIVES OF THE STUDY

AI and ML revolutionize financial management in India, offering advanced analytics, risk assessment, and personalized recommendations while confronting challenges such as data privacy concerns and algorithmic biases.

9.5 RESEARCH QUESTIONS

How prevalent are AI and ML applications across various finance functions within Indian corporations, and what specific benefits, challenges, and opportunities do they present for professionals, employees, and businesses, particularly within the banking sector?

9.6 RESEARCH METHODOLOGY

This study utilizes only secondary data. Researchers obtained data from online and offline papers, publications, and other materials. Well-analyzed secondary data is employed. As no core AI or financial research exists, the study relies on secondary data. Research was conducted to identify and select papers from JSTOR, Google Scholar, and ProQuest. Additional data was sourced from AI websites, newspapers, and magazines. Financial professionals in major banks and finance companies were surveyed and interviewed for this study. This study examined the adoption of AI and ML in accounting and finance using primary data from 117 financial specialists.

We employ desk and conceptual research. New financial learners and management students acquire financial knowledge through this research. The research design focused on personal reading, observation, and the role of AI in financial performance, including:

1. **Collecting Data:** Secondary sources included books, research papers, journal articles, web reports, and newspaper articles.
2. **Data Coverage:** The data encompasses B2B, B2G, and B2C companies. The figures are based on market funding from various industries.
3. **Modeling Approach/Market Size:** Market sizes are determined top-down and validated bottom-up using market-specific rationale. We analyze markets using annual financial reports, funding data, and third-party data. Gross domestic product (GDP), internet users, secure internet servers, and internet penetration are also considered. We estimate country markets using this data.
4. **Forecasts:** Researchers employ several predictive approaches. Market behavior determines forecasting methods. The S-curve function and exponential trend smoothing are appropriate for projecting digital products and services since technological adoption is non-linear. Digitalization, secure internet servers, and public cloud revenue drive this trend. Models utilize current currency rates. Country-specific COVID-19 and Russian-Ukraine war effects are examined. Markets are updated biannually. Ad hoc market updates may occur when new, pertinent data or significant market developments alter predicted growth. Statista Consumer Insights Global representatively weights survey data.

9.7 ARTIFICIAL INTELLIGENCE IN FINANCE: AN OVERVIEW

Financial institutions face pressure to incorporate public expectations into their business plans. All these companies desire stakeholders and employees to explore new possibilities to gain a competitive advantage, which has extended corporate sustainability. Sustainable financial development requires effective financial management. AI is employed in chief monetary administration to monitor, appraise, and issue development on time. AI has enhanced financial scrutiny to improve credit decisions. This strategy has assisted financial managers in managing all administrative and transactional responsibilities in businesses. Figure 9.1 illustrates the benefits of AI in finance.

Business and finance have transformed due to AI. AI has enabled financial institutions to reduce costs and increase value more rapidly. Global financial institutions utilize AI to enhance customer service. Functional assistance includes fraud detection chatbots, recheck testing, robotic instruction, simulated customer subordinates, market investigation, supervisory, and trial assessment testing.

Previous technology could not manage complex projects. AI addresses multi-solution complicated problems. AI can recommend financial products, calculate insurance premiums, predict stock prices, and forecast gains and losses. The list continues. The above demonstrates how Financial Business Management has evolved. It manages new operations more effectively. Financial management heavily collects customer data, illustrating its use of data mining. Thus, it must define finance's primary AI and ML applications. Many companies and governments safeguard consumers through AI and ML. AI and ML combat fraud in banking,

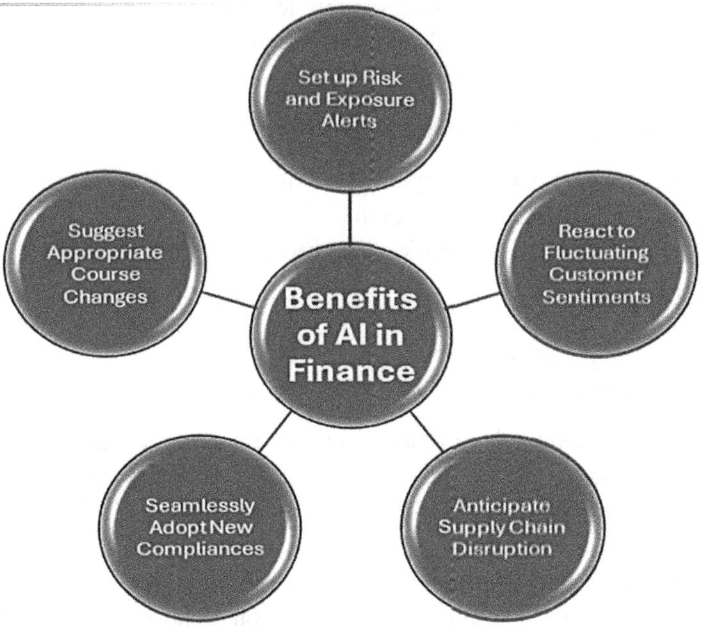

FIGURE 9.1 Benefits of artificial intelligence in finance.

Source: Authors' Compilation.

insurance, and businesses (mortgage, credit card, money laundering, healthcare, auto insurance, financial statement modifications, share market fraud). Numerous innovative fraud detection technologies exist. These technologies assist customers, institutions, and transaction partners.

9.8 IMPORTANT ISSUES AND RISKS COMING FROM FINANCE AI DEPLOYMENT

- **Governance and Accountability:**
  - Model governance arrangements;
  - Accountability and responsibility lines;
  - Outsourced infrastructure models.
- **Non-Financial Risks:**
  - Biases, unfair deals, and discrimination;
  - Data protection and confidentiality.
- **Policy Frameworks:**
  - AI complexity hinders technology-neutral approach;
  - Potential compatibility with regulatory frameworks;
  - Policy fragmentation risk.
- **Durable and Resilient:**
  - Unintended consequences at firm/market level;
  - Overfitting and model drift;
  - Interpreted correlations as causality.
- **Clarity:**
  - Model results generation;
  - Strategy inflexibility during stress.

Reasoning, knowledge representation, planning, learning, natural language processing, vision, and movement and manipulation are AI research goals. Long-term AI goals include general intelligence. The approaches utilize statistical methodologies, machine intelligence, and symbolic AI. AI tools encompass search optimization, artificial neural networks, statistical, probable, and economical methods. Information technology, mathematics, languages, psychology, philosophy, and other fields underpin AI. Figure 9.2 depicts the best use of artificial intelligence in finance.

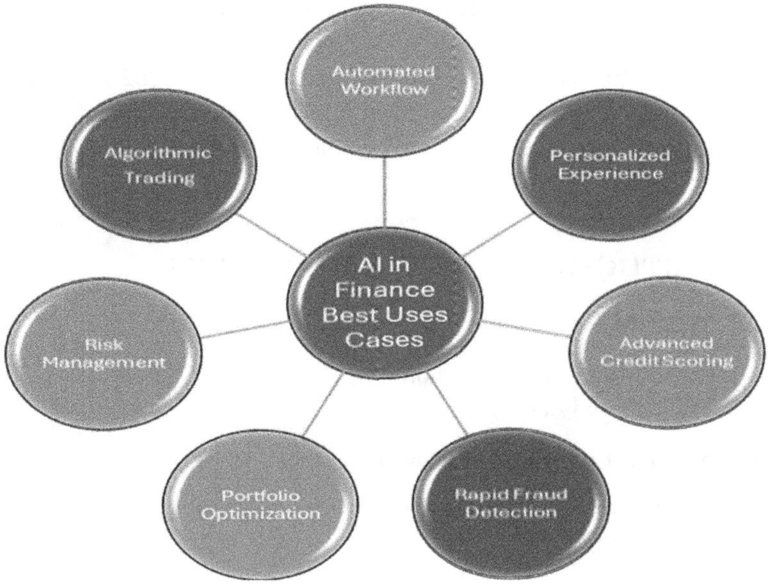

FIGURE 9.2 Best use case of artificial intelligence in finance.
Source: Authors' compilation.

Statistics and computing researchers have developed new strategies for large, heterogeneous data analysis, categorizing organized or unstructured data. These strategies teach machines natural language processing (NLP) and image recognition through practice. AI performs human-like tasks utilizing cognitive tools. Stability Board (2017). AI evolves across industries, with limitless applications. This technique could be applied across sectors. AI is being researched for surgery and drug administration. AI can assist a bank's fraud department in identifying unusual debit card usage and significant account deposits. Trading is streamlined using AI, which estimates output, demand, and stock prices (Investopedia, 2019).

9.9 ARTIFICIAL INTELLIGENCE (AI) IN FINANCE

Machines with variable autonomy can foresee, recommend, or decide based on human-defined goals. AI employs extensive "big data" and diverse sources. Machine learning (ML) models enhance predictability and performance without human programming by leveraging experience and data.

COVID-19 has accelerated and deepened pre-pandemic digitization, including AI. Global AI spending is projected to triple from USD 50 billion in 2020 to over USD 110 billion in 2024 (IDC, 2020). AI can be utilized in asset management, algorithmic trading, credit underwriting, and blockchain-based financial services due to abundant data and reduced processing costs.

9.10 AI APPLICATIONS IN FINANCIAL SERVICES

- **Machine Learning:**
  - Customer recommendation;
  - Robo-advice.
- **Natural Language Processing:**
  - Anti-money laundering (AML) and fraud detection;
  - Chatbot.
- **Cognitive Computing:**
  - Algorithmic trading.

AI in finance is expected to provide financial firms with two main competitive advantages: (i) cost reduction and productivity enhancement, driving higher profitability (e.g., enhanced decision-making processes, automated execution, risk management, regulatory compliance gains, and optimization of back-office and other processes); and (ii) quality improvement. Competitive advantage can lead to lower prices, improved quality, variety, and personalization, or support for financial customers.

9.11 OPPORTUNITIES AND CHALLENGES OF ARTIFICIAL INTELLIGENCE

AI is utilized in finance and healthcare, with demands varying based on tasks. AI can identify aviation engine or line assembly issues by analyzing vast amounts of data from images to audio, enhancing predictive maintenance and company efficiency. Optimization of logistics traffic reduces fuel utilization and delivery times. Customer service benefits from voice recognition. Many merchants tailor suggestions using social media, demographics, and transactions (Manyika and Bughin, 2018).

Building new competitive policies across their value chains with AI can significantly benefit financial institutions in the coming years. By assessing and deciding (credit adjudication), AI accelerates loan distribution. AI reduces errors, integrates new data, and automates risk modeling in underwriting (Manyika and Bughin, 2018).

AI will most improve employment by substituting and contributing to output. It will enhance labor market skills and create jobs by freeing up workers to engage in more complex tasks. AI can replace dangerous jobs in oil and mining, potentially saving more lives in these sectors (Manyika and Bughin, 2018).

9.12 IMPACT OF AI ON BUSINESS MODELS AND ACTIVITY IN THE FINANCIAL SECTOR

- **Asset Management:**
  - Identify and capture big data signals and relationships;
  - Optimize workflows and risk management;
  - Possibly alpha-generating.
- **Credit Intermediation:**
  - Lower underwriting costs and improve efficiency;
  - Extension of credit to low-scoring clients;
  - Addressing financial inclusion and SME financing gaps.
- **Blockchain-based Finance:**
  - Improve smart contract autonomy;
  - Manage risk;
  - Support decentralized finance (DeFi) applications and autonomous chains.
- **Algo Trading:**
  - Improve risk and liquidity management;
  - Optimize order flow and execute huge orders.

People process data more slowly than computers. This is how IBM's Watson outperformed Jeopardy contestants with pinpoint accuracy and speed. Although human minds are versatile, machines analyze data quickly and accurately. Our minds cannot process data like the latest computer chips.

Companies seek these advancements in their systems. Given the volume of quality and quantitative data organizations manage daily, AI and its processing capabilities are essential (Jaslove, 2017).

Innovative, effective, fast, and scalable are the benefits of AI. Economics, workers, consumers, and communities will significantly benefit from these advantages (MMC Ventures, 2019). AI has revolutionized business. Some sectors cannot function without human assistance, notwithstanding machines' remarkable changes. Misuse of AI can damage a company's brand (Manyika and Bughin, 2018). Creating or obtaining sufficient clinical trial data to predict healthcare treatment for training is similarly challenging. Deep learning techniques must demonstrate how specific decisions or predictions were made. Generalized learning approaches present another difficulty due to AI's struggle to generalize its experience (Frue, 2019; Manyika and Bughin, 2018).

9.13 MACHINE LEARNING IN FINANCE

Machine learning is a powerful tool for evaluating various concerns and financial operations, including stock trading, a key component of finance. Stock markets are significant and desirable in the financial sector as they allow traders to critically analyze and evaluate daily rate fluctuations, which are not random. While predicting stock market changes is challenging, it is not impossible; predictive automatic trading decisions based on detailed features are more effective than traditional methods based solely on numerical data. Every stock market trader must identify lucrative stocks and trade them without error or personal bias.

9.14 MACHINE LEARNING USE CASES IN FINANCE

- Financial monitoring;
- Making investment predictions;
- Process automation;
- Secure transactions;
- Risk management;
- Algorithmic trading;
- Financial advisory;
- Customer data management;
- Decision making;

- Customer service level improvement;
- Marketing.

Chandrika Kadirvel Mani and Carol Ane (2016) proposed a solution using machine learning and other applications to predict stocks using technical and fundamental variables. The results were positive, as they identified high-return healthcare stocks. Additionally, these stocks were traded using an auto trading tool to eliminate human error and sentiment intervention, yielding a 16.64% revenue increase in three months.

Many studies have tested statistical and machine learning algorithms, such as logistic regression and artificial neural networks, to enhance financial fraud detection. Three important features that remained unchanged in the ERC investigation were training prior fraud probabilities, relative error costs, and threshold classifications to improve fraud detection. To clarify whether statistical and machine learning algorithms could enhance classification performance, the article noted that several other studies in the same context have shown that classification algorithms like SYM and bagging can improve fraud detection (Perols, 2011).

9.15 EMERGING APPLICATION OF MACHINE LEARNING IN FINANCE

The financial industry is poised to leverage machine learning for a competitive edge as complex models run on high-power computing processors with vast data storage become more affordable. Some use cases are currently in operation, while others must overcome business and operational challenges before being adopted. A few applications are listed here.

9.15.1 RISK MODELING

AI/ML models and algorithms are widely used in risk modeling and management. Machine learning is vital for risk modeling in credit and market sectors, as well as for operational risk management, compliance, and fraud management. Most machine learning classification and modeling methods, such as binary logistic regression, multinomial logistic regression, linear and quadratic discriminant analysis, and decision trees, form the foundation of real-world modeling. Data availability and richness are crucial in data science applications.

9.15.2 PORTFOLIO MANAGEMENT

Return and risk are the most critical characteristics optimized by sophisticated algorithms for constructing portfolios. The algorithm allocates the invested amount into diverse asset classes to optimize portfolio return and risk based on user information such as retirement ages, investment amounts, and current ages and assets. After the initial allocation, the algorithm monitors the market and adjusts the allocation to maintain portfolio optimization. Robo-advisors, AI-enabled portfolio managers, are increasingly employed in real-world portfolio building due to their superior adaptability and optimization skills.

9.15.3 ALGORITHMIC TRADING

Algorithmic trading utilizes algorithms to trade stocks autonomously with minimal human interaction. Invented in 1970, algorithmic trading employs pre-programmed stock trading instructions to optimize trading returns and objectives at high frequency. Machine learning and artificial intelligence have revolutionized algorithmic trading by enabling fast, deep insights into stock prices and market movements.

9.15.4 FRAUD DETECTION AND ANALYSIS

Fraud identification and analysis represent a key application of financial machine learning. Due to widespread connectivity, high processing capacity in devices, and increased data stored and exchanged online, sensitive organizational and personal data are at risk. These challenges have transformed online fraud detection and analysis.

9.15.5 LOAN AND INSURANCE UNDERWRITINGS

Financial firms can leverage machine learning models to gain a competitive edge in loan, credit, and insurance underwriting. Historical consumer data, financial lending/borrowing data, insurance results, and debt default data can be utilized to train effective machine learning models at large banks and insurance organizations. For future lending and underwriting risks, learning algorithms can use learned patterns and trends to reduce defaults.

9.15.6 FINANCIAL CHATBOTS

Machine learning and AI have also automated finance. With appropriate data, machine learning models can analyze patterns to make better conclusions. These models often suggest future activities to facilitate corporate decision-making efficiently and effectively. AI-based financial applications can minimize errors by rapidly learning from past actions, saving time and money. Financial institution AI chatbots automate numerous routine processes and enhance client connections.

9.15.7 RISK MANAGEMENT

Machine learning is transforming how companies manage risks. Examples of risk management range from determining how much a bank should lend to a customer to enhancing process compliance or minimizing model risk.

9.15.8 ASSET PRICE PREDICTION

One of the most challenging problems financial professionals face is predicting asset prices. Speculation and various market conditions influence asset prices. The traditional technique relies on historical financial records and market performance to price an asset. Recently, machine learning-based models have been employed to accurately forecast asset prices using abundant data.

9.15.9 DERIVATIVE PRICING

Traditional derivative pricing models are based on several assumptions that do not hold in practice. These assumptions aim to establish an empirical relationship between predictor factors such as strike price, maturity period, and option type, and the target variable, derivative price. Machine learning models minimize error to fit the optimal function between predictors and targets, eliminating unnecessary assumptions. Machine learning represents the most effective derivative pricing paradigm due to its accuracy and speed of deployment.

9.15.10 MONEY LAUNDERING

According to a UN assessment, money laundering accounts for 2% to 5% of global GDP. Machine learning models can detect money laundering with few false positives.

9.16 EMERGING APPROACHES AND FRAMEWORKS OF MACHINE LEARNING IN FINANCE

Modelers and engineers in various fields, including finance and research, can now utilize new machine learning, data science, and AI skills and frameworks. Some are listed below:

1. **Virtual Agents:** The machine learning paradigm will increasingly employ agents for diverse tasks. These agents can conduct sophisticated data mining activities using a wide array of policy rules, procedures, and laws to automatically respond to inquiries.
2. **Cognitive Robotics:** These can automate many human tasks with more sophistication, speed, and precision.
3. **Text Analytics:** Utilizing advanced natural language processing techniques, frameworks, and models to analyze large and complex financial contracts and documents enhances decision-making speed and reduces risk.
4. **Video Analytics:** Advances in computer vision, image processing, speech processing, and speech recognition, combined with exponential hardware growth, have led to promising progress in compliance, audit, model validation, and automated financial report generation and presentation.

9.17 ARTIFICIAL INTELLIGENCE AND MACHINE LEARNING ARE TRANSFORMING INDIA'S FINANCIAL SECTOR

The next digital revolution is driven by AI. In the cognitive age, forward-thinking banks are leveraging AI to transform client interaction, research and development, cybersecurity, and back-office operations. These companies' innovative business models utilize AI to enhance strategic, operational, and financial performance.

AI will enhance manual and repetitive financial services processes. With digital-only transactions and numerous AI and ML use cases, most financial services will become automated. Banks can thrive by scaling original use cases to industrial size and managing their effects. Managing with algorithms instead of processes presents challenges. Customer journeys, staff tasks, supervision rules, and operational procedures evolve with technology.

The Reserve Bank of India (RBI) acknowledged the pandemic's effects on banking and non-banking institutions in its 2020 year-end "Report on Trend and Progress of Banking in India." FinTech, digital currencies, and others are transforming lending, investing, and payments. Therefore, traditional risk and compliance management solutions for regulated organizations may not suffice.

Like other firms, the pandemic and advances in AI/ML have accelerated digital transformation. In a Publicis Sapient Global Banking Benchmark Study of over 1,000 banking executives, incumbents and disruptors identified customer experience and operational transformation as pillars of digital transformation. How might AI/ML assist these institutions in transforming? Let us analyze how to employ these technologies.

9.18 IMPACT ON FINANCIAL SERVICES

Long-term AI may be more essential than short-term considerations. Future financial services institutions may be significantly influenced by AI:

1. **Operational Process Automation:** Banks are automating fundamental operations with AI and ML. Robotic process automation redesigns can identify improvements, exponentially accelerating automation growth.

2. **Customer Acquisition and Retention:** Banking companies are utilizing third-party data and marketing technology to identify new consumers and enhance their experiences through personalized interfaces. AI-enabled consumer-facing services facilitate smartphone-based document uploads and identification verification, greatly improving customer experience. This allows for tracking client engagement with the bank throughout their lifespan and leveraging this information to drive appropriate customer engagements via relevant channels.

3. **Workforce Management:** As customers explore new financial services, banks must effectively and profitably manage inquiries. This necessitates a sophisticated AI-based triage system that

prioritizes requests by importance and routes them to chatbots, web forms, or call centers, which cannot handle all demands.

4. **Credit Risk:** Credit scoring models are advancing with new technology. Cloud infrastructure can process enormous datasets and test new models at unprecedented speeds. Researchers may evaluate AI and ML models to obtain accurate credit scores through improved methods and testing.
5. **Regulatory Compliance:** New digital innovation laws will apply to banks undergoing significant transformations. Regulatory authorities recognize that AI and ML necessitate additional safeguards and standards. New methods can either enhance or exacerbate bank risk.
6. **Cybercrime Prevention:** AI algorithms can accurately detect money-laundering schemes using common criteria. MasterCard reduced fraud by 50% through this approach. Banks can protect the public in these unusual times.

9.19 OPTIMIZE USE OF AI/ML

Financial companies and regulators are innovating AI/data approaches rather than simply adopting them. Four actions financial institutions can take to optimize the use of AI/ML while digitally transforming include:

1. **Clarify Objectives, Identify Use Cases:** The first step in any successful data strategy is to set goals and identify smaller use cases to help achieve them. Maintaining an idea repository and discovering potential ideas through rapid proof-of-concepts and minimum viable products (MVPs) are key reasons to view AI/ML tracks as agile experiments. Before scaling solutions, banks could seek venture capital-style investments for experiments.
2. **Use the Right Data Effectively:** Most companies struggle to find and utilize the best data for analytics and AI/ML. Governance presents the next challenge. This structure must have the right scalable platform, people, and processes for data utilization.
3. **Hire the Right Talent and Capability:** Digital transformation requires hiring the right people (both technical and cultural) and upskilling technology and business users.

4. **Build the Right Partnerships:** Finding digital transformation experts for banks is crucial. Product companies, FinTech startups, and consulting organizations can provide significant insights into the competitive environment and evolving best practices.

9.20 RESULTS OF THE STUDY: ARTIFICIAL INTELLIGENCE AND MACHINE LEARNING IN FINANCE

Finance has adopted AI earlier than many other sectors. AI and ML have numerous applications in finance because of this early adoption. These applications may be familiar to traders, wealth managers, bankers, and insurers. Forward-thinking business owners and executives actively seek innovative uses of AI in finance and other sectors to gain a competitive edge.

9.21 HOW ARTIFICIAL INTELLIGENCE IS CHANGING THE FINANCIAL SERVICE INDUSTRY

In the 1980s, AI gained popularity in finance, with expert systems becoming commercialized. In the 1990s, fraud detection became a priority. Notable applications from 1993 included FinCEN's FAIS, which identified 400 potential money laundering cases worth 1 billion dollars over two years by examining over 200,000 transactions weekly. Although expert systems did not last in finance, they contributed to the evolution of AI as we know it today (International Robotics Federation, 2015).

Currently, financial institutions deploy artificial neural network technologies to flag unusual charges or claims for human review. In 1987, Security Pacific National Bank in the US established a Fraud Prevention Task Force to combat debit card fraud. Financial projects such as Kasisto and Moneystream utilize AI. Banks employ AI to organize, record, spend, and manage properties. An imitation financial trading tournament was won by robots in August 2001. AI has also reduced fraud and financial crimes by tracking user behavior patterns for irregularities. AI conducts regular financial statement audits, allowing many datasets to be evaluated swiftly, thereby reducing audit risk, boosting security, and shortening audit time (Buchanan, 2019).

Recently, professionals and stock market analysts have focused on AI breakthroughs. For stock movement prediction and analysis, artificial neural networks can selectively determine any nonlinear function with a sufficient number of hidden units, making them one of the most promising models (Fariya et al., 2024; Jiao, 2018).

9.22 APPLICATION OF ARTIFICIAL INTELLIGENCE IN THE FINANCIAL SERVICE INDUSTRY

AI is finally impacting our daily lives after decades of discussion. It is employed in numerous applications now, from language translators to facial recognition to virtual assistants, that we scarcely notice its presence. Additionally, other companies across various industries are integrating AI into their systems. Several factors have contributed to the rise of AI in finance. The banking sector uses AI for chatbots and instant messaging to resolve customer service issues, fraud detection through data analysis, underwriting, robo-advising, prediction, regulatory compliance, and more. Financial services can greatly benefit from AI, ML, and deep learning. The next sections will discuss transaction fraud prevention and the use of AI/machine learning.

1. **Fraud Detection and Risk Management:** AI screens and prevents misrepresentation, illegal tax avoidance, negligence, and other risks (Narrative Science, 2018). Companies utilize personal data and behavior to identify patterns and abnormal transactions. Mastercard also employs AI to identify fraudsters as part of its financial services network. Trade misconduct has been detected using similar methods (Goudarzi, Hickok, and Sinha, 2018).
2. **Credit Decisions:** AI evaluates prospective borrowers more quickly, accurately, and cost-effectively, reflecting a broader range of characteristics for better, data-backed decisions. Unlike traditional loan scoring, AI's credit scoring employs more complex rules. Lenders can distinguish high-default risk individuals from those who qualify but lack a credit history. Objectivity is another advantage of AI; machines are not biased like humans. Machine learning algorithms analyze credit status with optional information (e.g., smartphone data) to assess loan eligibility and provide customized options in digital banks and loan-issuing applications (Bachinskiy, 2019).
3. **Algorithmic Trading:** "Automated Trading Systems" dominate global financial markets. Algorithmic trading employs complex AI algorithms to execute millions of trades daily without

human intervention. High-frequency trading is one of the fastest-growing sectors in finance. Many banks, equity, and proprietary trading organizations utilize AI to manage their entire portfolios. Large corporate shareholders employ automated trading strategies, although larger proprietary corporations have traded with their own IT technology in recent years. Algorithmic trading utilizes high-speed and high-volume trading software based on inventory rates and market conditions (Motley Fool, 2019).

4. **Chatbots:** AI-based solutions are increasingly used in finance and banking. Major FinTech companies serve numerous customers and require chatbots for customer care. AI chatbots provide real-time responses, enhancing operational efficiency and safety (Buchanan, 2019). Nearly 64% of people find them beneficial. Banks have employed intelligent AI alternatives to improve user experience and accessibility to meet changing customer demands. These conversational interfaces facilitate low-cost, intelligent interactions with millions of customers. Juniper Research found that AI chatbots save banks four minutes per representative, potentially saving billions annually in the future. Thus, AI alternatives create substantial value for financial facilities (Chatbot News, 2019).

AI begins with chatbots for enterprises. Primarily, they serve as virtual assistants for customer service. Millennial customers prefer using AI to communicate with their banks, according to several research studies. Only 12% of this demographic uses the phone, while many prefer chatting, socializing, or messaging (Mubarak, 2019).

9.23 IMPACT OF ARTIFICIAL INTELLIGENCE ON THE FINANCIAL SECTOR

Initial economic growth is anticipated from increased labor productivity. Several factors will determine how AI will influence jobs in the future, including AI adoption and usage costs, workforce dynamics, labor supply, quality, and compensation.

AI and cloud computing rapidly process big data. This service saves time and money, boosts productivity, and enhances accuracy. Financial sector workers are technologically savvy and employ AI tools to streamline their tasks, allowing them to focus on checking accounts, speculating on outcomes, managing equipment, and addressing issues (MTI College, 2018). The speed, accuracy, and volume of computers compared to humans may drive AI implementation in corporate operations (O'Neill, 2016).

9.24 FINDINGS AND DISCUSSION

Technological change and AI in finance drive data collection. Table 9.1 illustrates fundamental steps to educate about technology-driven finance and AI in finance.

TABLE 9.1 AI in Finance: Stages of Technology Reform in the Financial Sector

SL. No.	Development Stages	Reform Technology	Mode or Services	Financial Performance	Impact of Technology in Finance (as Relationship)
1.	FinTech 1.0	Computer (IT in Finance)	Credit cards, ATMs, customer relationship management, and so on.	Low	Technology as a tool in finance.
2.	FinTech 2.0	Mobile Internet (Internet in Finance)	Third-party payments, e-insurance, e-banking, crowdfunding, e-commerce, and so on.	Medium	Technology reforms financial activities such as offers and services for ease and convenience.
3.	FinTech 3.0	AI, big data, blockchain, data science (AI in Finance)	Intelligent finance, data automation	High	Technology aids financial decision-making through machine intelligence.

Source: Authors' compilation.

AI in finance encompasses both classical and modern approaches. See Tables 9.2 and 9.3. These tables represent financial institutions and services, financial markets, e-financing, financial modeling, and financial systems, while also showcasing current financial appearances, intelligence perspectives, financial challenges, and AI techniques aimed at addressing financial issues through past and present performance.

9.25 AI AND ML STRATEGY RECOMMENDATION FOR FINANCIAL SECTOR

Leaders and early adopters face challenges with AI implementation. There are few AI use cases and managerial supports available for early adopters. The focus for leaders has shifted from "if" to "how." Leaders

TABLE 9.2 AI In Finance: A Modern Look

Financial Area	Traditional Finance Approach	AI in Finance Approach	Financial Problems	AI Techniques for Handling and Reform in Finance
Financial institutions and services	Insurance management, wealth and property management, foreign exchange market management, and energy management	AI as a smart alternative in finance	Property valuation and estimation, site selection and evaluation, property policy rules and governance, supply and demand forecasting, property optimization, insurance services and product selection, pricing and market positioning for insurance, risk management, and market personalization, recommendation, and customization	Text analysis, social media analysis, behavior analysis, simulation theory, profiling methods, statistical learning, numerical computation, knowledge discovery and evaluation, data mining, recommender systems, mathematical modeling, risk analytics, deep learning, artificial neural networks, and coupling learning
Financial markets	Cross-market analysis and micro- and macroeconomic market performance analysis	Global and cross-market performance and analysis	Micro- and macro-financial variables and modeling, testing, analyzing, and coupling interactions and relationships between economic influences, levels, and movements; cultural and political issues affecting financial variables; derivatives; regional and company performance; financial indicators in social, cultural, and economic contexts; and country-specific indicators	Machine learning, statistical modeling, mathematical modeling, multisource analysis, behavior analytics, event analysis, hybrid methods, relation learning methods, coupling learning, dependence modeling, interaction learning techniques, multivariate analysis, and sequence modeling
E-financing	Smart banking and e-payment, artificial intelligence (AI), e-commerce, internet banking, and finance	AI-driven online banking, mobile banking, Internet of Things (IoT)-based finance, and internet finance	Risk, fraud, and security issues; online market demand and supply; online financial products and services; estimation and prediction; online marketing, delivery, and storage; online mobile payment and support; secure funds; online insurance, automation, and banking; online fraud and credit; internet-based services; online investment and wealth management; and internet finance behavior analysis	Risk analytics, behavior analytics, user modeling, social media analysis, web analysis, profiling techniques, text analysis, predictive modeling, network analysis, deep learning, trajectory modeling, machine learning, data mining, online web analysis, security informatics, behavior informatics, and distributed learning techniques

TABLE 9.2 *(Continued)*

Financial Area	Traditional Finance Approach	AI in Finance Approach	Financial Problems	AI Techniques for Handling and Reform in Finance
Financial Modeling	Blockchain systems, security, and mechanisms	AI-driven blockchain	Blockchain modeling in financial systems; risk-averse and anti-attack blockchain strategies; portfolio optimization and product pricing	Blockchain mechanisms, bitcoin evaluation and usage, cryptographic contract models, secure smart contracts, supervised and unsupervised learning, fraud detection analysis, process analysis, event analysis techniques, agent-based learning, game theory, risk analysis, and representation learning

Source: Authors' compilation.

must address cultural resistance to AI and talent recruitment (MMC Ventures, 2019). Financial firms analyze data, make complex judgments, and advise executives. Modern financial functions leverage the collective brainpower and skills of many individuals. Managers must reengineer processes to effectively utilize AI (Seth et al., 2018).

A dynamic AI environment for the economy necessitates proper preparation and legislation. Investment in digital infrastructure enables organizations to compete across sectors and locations. The key business case method is AI (Ernst et al., 2018).

Organizational leaders should prioritize employee development rather than replacement. A culture of information and analytics is more crucial than AI itself. No prediction or explanation system can exist without results and consequences. Process data is essential for machine learning (ML). Employees must consider various factors to assist everyone. The AI project framework will aid executives in decision-making. An in-house startup culture will encourage employees to solve complex problems creatively. Maintaining a learning environment ensures everyone stays current. Transferring expertise is vital, as losing an AI representative could impact the organization (Lemay, 2019).

PwC advises financial institutions to adjust their IT working model to align with the new standard. Companies should invest in technology to enhance their understanding of customers. Institutions must prioritize cybersecurity before it becomes urgent. Organizations need the expertise and capabilities to implement and succeed (PwC, 2016).

AI can assist any company in making financial and accounting decisions. The benefits of AI will continue to grow, ensuring its longevity. Businesses and society must learn new technologies and adapt. Companies must embrace AI to remain competitive, and employees may need to update their skills to maintain employment.

9.26 FINDINGS OF THE STUDY

AI and ML are increasingly utilized in financial management, dominating financial modeling, data storage, and big data applications. AI has transformed digital banking and contactless transactions. It reduces costs and enhances efficiency, leading to improved consumer satisfaction, time management, and regulatory compliance. However, it also poses risks such as data breaches and cyberattacks. Strengthening security, hiring specialists, and increasing consumer awareness can help mitigate these risks.

9.27 SUGGESTIONS OF THE STUDY

- The widespread adoption of AI and its potential to limit human job opportunities necessitate deep learning. If computer and human personnel collaborate, the organization will thrive.
- Adopt AI based on industry demands, which requires skilled managers.
- Students seeking AI skills should receive comprehensive training in machine learning and algorithm development. Academic institutions should support such courses.

9.28 CONCLUSION

This paradigm encompasses several scholarly studies, including those of the authors. The benefits of investigative research include its ability to accurately define research domains. Reviewers can quickly select a topic based on the quantity, type, and quality of exploratory data rather than relying solely on systematic reviews. We selected the following articles from 110 leading banking AI and machine learning journals. The primary discourse analysis track includes papers with the highest citations, bibliometric scores, and recent publications. Without understanding the limitations of investigations, we would mislead ourselves. They do not assess evidence quality, as primary research articles provide an abundance of material. Smaller studies often oversimplify complexity. Investigative research emphasizes methodology and includes various study designs, unlike systematic assessments, which offer a narrative and descriptive account of past and present research.

This study addressed the following research questions to enhance understanding of the topic: How does AI alter opportunities and challenges? How is AI utilized in finance? How are Finland and the global community adopting AI? How will AI impact financial positions and functions? How will AI evolve? How can companies thrive in the competitive technological landscape? This concept suggests that AI could transform the global financial system. AI's capabilities in fraud detection, risk management, credit decision-making, algorithmic trading, and chatbots can enhance financial inclusion, operational efficiency, and personalization. AI is innovative, efficient, rapid, and scalable.

Despite these advantages, AI in finance faces numerous challenges, including a lack of trained personnel and data. Financial institutions are collaborating with startups and FinTech companies to develop AI solutions.

Companies in the Asia/Pacific region are proactive in adopting AI and ML. Due to government investment and AI education initiatives, Finland leads in AI adoption. The report indicates that AI and automation will influence job dynamics. Finance professionals will prioritize insights and actions over transactions. Future generations will increasingly rely on AI. Digital transformation will proliferate as finance shapes the new business model. This thesis suggests that financial sectors must adapt to transformative approaches, emphasizing the need for finance experts to embrace technology.

Any organization can leverage AI for financial and accounting decisions. The benefits of AI will expand, ensuring its permanence. Business and society must adapt to new technologies. Companies must adopt AI to remain competitive, and employees may need to acquire new skills to retain employment. I believe AI will enhance the efficiency of financial functions. AI and ML can improve communication between employees and clients, uncover patterns and connections in diverse data sets, and address real-time investment inquiries. As AI evolves, intelligent systems will replace many human decision-making tasks. I perceive data privacy as AI's most significant challenge. Ultimately, AI has the potential to enhance global prosperity.

KEYWORDS

- **algorithmic trading**
- **artificial intelligence**
- **blockchain**
- **cybersecurity**
- **finance**
- **FinTech**
- **machine learning**

REFERENCES

Antoncic, M. (2020). A paradigm shift in the board room: Incorporating sustainability into corporate governance and strategic decision-making using big data and artificial intelligence. *Journal of Risk Management in Financial Institutions, 13*(4), 290–294.

Babel, B., Buehler, K., Pivonka, A., Richardson, B., & Waldron, D. (2019). Derisking machine learning and artificial intelligence. McKinsey & Company. https://www.mckinsey.com/business-functions/risk/our-insights/derisking-machine-learning-and-artificial-intelligence (accessed on 17 January 2025).

Bahrammirzaee, A. (2010). A comparative survey of artificial intelligence in finance: Artificial neural networks, expert systems, and hybrid intelligence systems. *Neural Computing and Applications, 116*(1165–1195). Springer. https://doi.org/10.1007/s00542-010-0856-2.

Bharti Kumari, J. K. (2021). System dynamics approach for adoption of artificial intelligence in finance. In V. H. Saran & R. K. Misra (Eds.), *Advances in Systems Engineering* (pp. 555–575). Springer Nature Singapore.

Bhatia, A., Chandani, A., & Chhateja, J. (2020). Robo advisory and its potential in addressing the behavioral biases of investors: A qualitative study in the Indian context. *Journal of Behavioral and Experimental Finance, 25*(C). https://doi.org/10.1016/j.jbef.2020.100281.

Boyd, S., & Vandenberghe, L. (2013). *Convex Optimization*. Cambridge University Press. https://doi.org/10.1017/CBO9780511804441.

Bussmann, N., Giudici, P., Marnelli, D., & Papenbrock, J. (2019). Explainable AI in FinTech risk management. *Frontiers in Artificial Intelligence, 3*, 26. https://doi.org/10.3389/frai.2020.00026.

Cao, L. (2018). AI in finance: A review. *ACM Computing Surveys, 9*(4).

Cardoso, J. V. D. M., & Palomar, D. P. (2020). Learning undirected graphs in financial markets. In *Proceedings of the 54th Asilomar Conference on Signals, Systems, and Computers* (pp. 741–745). Pacific Grove, CA, USA. https://doi.org/10.1109/IEEECONF51394.2020.9443573.

Chan, C., Chow, C., Wong, J., Dimakis, N., Nayler, D., Bermudes, J., Raman, J., Lam, R., & Baker, M. (2019). Artificial intelligence applications in financial services: Asset management, banking, and insurance. Marsh & McLennan Companies.

Chawla, R. (2018). How AI supports financial institutions for deciding creditworthiness. *Entrepreneur*. https://www.entrepreneur.com/article/310262 (accessed on 17 January 2025).

Columbus, L. (2019). How AI is protecting against payments fraud. *Forbes*. https://www.forbes.com/sites/louiscolumbus/2019/09/05/how-ai-is-protecting-against-payments-fraud/#305acba44d29 (accessed on 17 January 2025).

Copeland, B. (2020). Artificial intelligence | Definition, examples, and applications. *Britannica*. https://www.britannica.com/technology/artificial-intelligence (accessed on 17 January 2025).

Deep, A. (2019). Six real-world applications of AI in retail. *HackerNoon*. https://hackernoon.com/6-real-world-applications-of-ai-in-retail-c50736028efd (accessed on 17 January 2025).

Dornadula, V. N., & Geetha, S. (2019). Credit card fraud detection using machine learning algorithms. *Procedia Computer Science, 165*, 631–641. https://doi.org/10.1016/j.procs.2020.01.057.

Dyzma, M. (2019). Fraud detection with machine learning: How banks and financial institutions leverage AI. *Netguru*. https://www.netguru.com/blog/fraud-detection-with-machine-learning-how-banks-and-financial-institutions-leverage-ai (accessed on 17 January 2025).

Eling, M., Nuessl, D., & Staubli, J. (2021). The impact of artificial intelligence along the insurance value chain and on the insurability of risks. *Geneva Papers on Risk and Insurance – Issues and Practices, 46*(2), 189–198. https://doi.org/10.1057/s41288-020-00201-7 (accessed on 17 January 2025).

Fariya, Saini, A., & Kashif, M. (2024). Exploring the influence of factors driving financial accessibility, financial activities, and financial education on sustainable development. In *Artificial Intelligence and Machine Learning-Powered Smart Finance* (pp. 23–49). IGI Global.

Fethi, M. D., & Pasiouras, F. (2009). Assessing bank efficiency and performance with operational research and artificial intelligence techniques: A survey. *European Journal of Operational Research, 204*(2), 189–198. https://doi.org/10.1016/j.ejor.2009.04.027.

Fountaine, T., McCarthy, B., & Saleh, T. (2019). Building the AI-powered organization. *Harvard Business Review*. https://hbr.org/2019/07/building-the-ai-powered-organization (accessed on 17 January 2025).

Fukui, T., Sato, S., & Takahashi, A. (2017). Style analysis with particle filtering and generalized simulated annealing. *International Journal of Financial Engineering, 4*(2, 3), 1750037. https://doi.org/10.1142/S2424786317500372.

Gu, S., Kelly, B., & Xiu, D. (2020). Empirical asset pricing via machine learning. *The Review of Financial Studies, 33*(5), 2233–2273. https://doi.org/10.1093/rfs/hhaa009.

Ho, G., Ip, W., Wu, C., & Tse, Y. (2012). Using a fuzzy association rule mining approach to identify the financial data association. *Expert Systems with Applications, 39*(10), 9054–9063. https://doi.org/10.1016/j.eswa.2012.01.144.

Huang, J., & Chai, J. (2020). Deep learning in finance and banking: A literature review and classification. *Frontiers of Business Research in China, 14*, 13. https://doi.org/10.1186/s11782-020-00082-6.

Kashif, M., David, A., Gupta, V. P., & Alam, S. (2024). Integration of artificial intelligence in the financial sector. In *Artificial Intelligence and Machine Learning-Powered Smart Finance* (pp. 96–108). IGI Global.

Kashif, M., Kumar, P., Ghai, S., & Kumar, S. (2023). Disruptive technologies in computational finance. In *Algorithmic Approaches to Financial Technology: Forecasting, Trading, and Optimization* (pp. 46–60). IGI Global.

Kashif, M., Shajar, S. N., Singhal, N., & Kumar, P. (2023). Achieving sustainable investment practices through green finance: Challenges and opportunities. In *Sustainable Investments in Green Finance* (pp. 234–244). IGI Global.

Kashif, M., Thiyagarajan, S., & Sridharan, P. (2017). Dynamics of Algeria's international reserves. *African Journal of Economic and Management Studies, 8*(4), 410–419. https://doi.org/10.1108/AJEMS-12-2016-0207.

Khandani, A. E., Kim, A. J., & Lo, A. W. (2010). Consumer credit-risk models via machine-learning algorithms. *Journal of Banking & Finance, 34*(11), 2767–2787. https://doi.org/10.1016/j.jbankfin.2010.06.012.

CHAPTER 10

Sustainable Finance in Focus: Assessing Customer Awareness and Engagement in Green Banking

KAPIL KUMAR AGGARWAL,[1,*] POONAM,[1] PAWAN KUMAR,[1] and RAJAT SHARMA[2]

[1] *University School of Business, Chandigarh University, Punjab, India*

[2] *Department of Management Studies (DOMS), Graphic Era (Deemed to be University), Dehradun, Uttarakhand, India*

**Corresponding author.*

ABSTRACT

This chapter explores the rising importance of sustainable finance and green banking, focusing on customer awareness and engagement with environmentally responsible financial practices. Using empirical data from 300 customers across key districts of Delhi, the study assesses the extent of consumer knowledge about Punjab National Bank's (PNB) green banking initiatives and the demographic factors influencing this awareness. The analysis highlights that gender, education, and income significantly impact awareness levels, while account tenure and residential status do not. It further reveals varied awareness of green banking services, with high familiarity around paper reduction and digital banking, and low awareness regarding green loans, mortgages, and solar-powered ATMs. The findings underscore the need for enhanced communication strategies to promote green finance adoption and suggest policy-level support for sustainable financial instruments like green loans, mutual funds, and insurance. The chapter concludes by emphasizing green banking's role in driving environmental stewardship within the financial sector and outlines future implications for promoting eco-conscious banking practices in India.

Transforming Business Finance in the Digital Era.
Sanjay Taneja, Mohammad Kashif, Ercan Özen, and Luan Vardari (Eds.)
© 2026 Apple Academic Press, Inc. Co-published with CRC Press (Taylor & Francis)

DOI: 10.1201/9781998511235-10

10.1 INTRODUCTION

In the pursuit of financial expansion, monetary development, and profit maximization, humans have compromised the environment's ability to support the survival of the human race. Growing environmental concern has prompted the development of new methods for assessing nations, industries, and organizations. In recent years, leaders of countries have been awarded the "Champion of the Earth Award" for their environmental achievements, economies have received the Golden Peacock Award for Environmental Management, and nations have been ranked according to the Green Economy Index for the World, among others (Poonam and Aggarwal, 2023). Monetary improvement could be unsustainable if climate concerns are ignored. Without effective support for proposals to finance such project initiatives, the exchange of environmental commodities and environmental protection, cross-national services would be insufficient (Singh, 2003). The financial community was also brought under its wing by the crucial need for environmental sustainability. These concerns spawned a new notion known as "green finance." Green finance refers to the funding of investments that have a positive impact on the environment as part of a long-term development strategy (Aggarwal et al., 2023).

Going Green is a key component of green finance, which is a broad term (Jin et al., 2021). Green banking encompasses efforts to mitigate climate change and safeguard the environment (Park and Kim, 2020), as well as investments in environmentally friendly goods and services (Lindenberg and Volz, 2016). The first aspect pertains to how banking is handled, such as whether it is digital or not, and the second is where the institution stores its money (Fabris, 2019). The goal of this research is to bring attention to the current state of Green Banking research (Sarma and Roy, 2021). This study identifies and analyzes significant research dimensions, such as research growth, geographical spread, relevant research venues for Green Banking, and main keywords. The study aims to determine the current state of Green Banking research. Given that Green Banking has received considerable attention from various sectors of the economy, this study is timely (Biswas, 2016; Lewis, 2001). The findings will assist a wide range of stakeholders, including academics and reviewers who will be able to use them to decide on future research themes in Green Banking, as well as policymakers who will be able to utilize them to introduce Green Banking research guidelines. A field study is therefore necessary to understand the actual circumstances surrounding customer awareness of green banking activities (Kashif et al., 2023a, b).

Evaluating client knowledge and involvement in environmentally friendly banking is crucial in the current environmentally conscious world. Green banking efforts strive to incorporate environmental sustainability into financial services, boosting investments in eco-friendly projects, delivering green products such as sustainable loans and investments, and lowering carbon footprints in banking operations. Assessing consumer awareness entails evaluating their understanding of green banking practices, including the ecological consequences of their financial choices and the accessibility of sustainable banking alternatives. Surveys, interviews, and focus groups can be utilized to evaluate clients' comprehension of green banking principles and their inclination to embrace eco-friendly financial products.

Analyzing customer participation delves into the extent to which clients actively engage in green banking initiatives. This involves examining their usage habits of eco-friendly banking products and services, such as renewable energy loans, green investment portfolios, or paperless banking options. By analyzing consumer behaviors and preferences, financial institutions may uncover trends, areas for improvement, and opportunities to expand their green banking solutions. Data analytics and consumer feedback systems are essential components of this process, as they provide valuable insights into customer satisfaction levels, obstacles encountered in implementing green banking practices, and opportunities for innovation.

It is crucial to employ effective communication tactics to increase knowledge and promote active participation in environmentally friendly banking practices. Banks need to educate clients about the environmental benefits of green banking, the relevance of their individual efforts, and the breadth of sustainable financial solutions available. This may be accomplished through various methods, including social media campaigns, educational seminars, and tailored marketing materials. Financial institutions may promote significant progress towards a more sustainable future by fostering a culture of environmental accountability and enabling consumers to make well-informed decisions. Consistently evaluating and adjusting strategies is essential for maintaining client awareness and involvement in green banking projects, ultimately leading to a more environmentally friendly and socially conscious banking industry.

Sustainable finance and green banking are now recognized as crucial foundations in global efforts to address environmental issues and promote sustainable development. Sustainable finance involves the integration of environmental, social, and governance (ESG) elements into financial decision-making processes (Kashif et al., 2017). This approach aims to allocate resources toward initiatives that yield positive environmental and social outcomes while also delivering financial returns. Green banking represents a banking strategy that explicitly seeks to foster environmentally friendly practices within the financial sector. This initiative includes offering sustainable financial products and services, reducing the environmental impact of banking operations, and supporting programs that promote environmental conservation and climate mitigation.

A key aspect of sustainable finance and green banking is the promotion and development of environmentally friendly financial solutions. The products offered include green loans, which provide funding for projects related to renewable energy, energy-efficient buildings, and sustainable agriculture initiatives. Additionally, green bonds are issued to generate financing for projects that are ecologically beneficial, such as renewable energy infrastructure or clean transportation systems. Banks play a vital role in channeling capital toward sustainable investments by providing these products, which aids in the transition to a low-carbon economy and fosters environmental sustainability.

Green banking encompasses various activities aimed at reducing the environmental impact of financial operations. This includes utilizing energy-efficient technology in bank branches and offices, adopting paperless banking practices, and minimizing waste through responsible resource management. By integrating sustainability principles into their daily operations, banks can effectively reduce their environmental footprint while serving as a model for other sectors. Furthermore, green banking programs often extend beyond internal operations to include collaboration with clients, suppliers, and stakeholders to promote sustainable practices throughout the value chain (Kashif et al., 2024).

Sustainable finance and green banking are essential components in the transition to a financial system that is both ecologically sustainable and socially responsible. By integrating ESG factors into financial decision-making and advocating for sustainable banking practices, banks can tackle pressing environmental challenges such as climate change and biodiversity loss. This approach not only benefits investors and society in the long run but also contributes to addressing significant environmental issues. As awareness of environmental concerns continues to grow, the role of sustainable finance and green banking in driving positive change is expected to become increasingly important.

10.2 PURPOSE OF THE STUDY

To determine the extent of consumer knowledge regarding PNB's green banking activities and identify how various factors influence customers' awareness of green banking.

10.3 REVIEW OF LITERATURE

Research on green banking has garnered significant attention. Below is a review of several studies. In her research paper titled "The Role of Green Banking in Sustainable Growth," Bahl Sarita (2012) outlined strategies to educate target groups and enhance awareness across internal and external subsystems to achieve sustainable growth through green banking. An empirical study on customer satisfaction toward the PNB Green Channel Counter in Coimbatore was conducted in 2014 by Moorthy D. and Mrs. V. Pradeepa. They employed the Likert five-point scale method to gauge client satisfaction. Their findings indicated that the GCC's transaction speed received the highest mean score of 4.47, followed by the GCC's user-friendliness, demonstrating that customers are inclined to complete certain tasks automatically rather than manually. According to Sharma Neetu et al. (2015) in their research article titled "A Study on Customers' Awareness of Green Banking Initiatives in Selected Public and Private Sector Banks with Special Reference to Mumbai," the banks have not implemented initiatives such as press outreach, an environmental policy, concessions for energy savings, solar ATMs, and green CDs, among others. In the South Canara district of Karnataka, Shobharani et al. (2016) investigated the perspectives of bank employees on green banking. The study focused on public opinion and awareness of green banking practices and strategies. The report revealed that the majority of bank staff are familiar with green banking; however, banks are not executing comprehensive green banking plans. Pal Naveen (2016) conducted an extensive investigation into customer perceptions of green banking efforts. This study aimed to address gaps concerning various green banking activities and client awareness of these programs. Based on primary data, the current study seeks to evaluate green banking practices and knowledge among stakeholders in Delhi, emphasizing the benefit of making green banking procedures even more environmentally friendly.

The influence of legislation and policy on the development and implementation of sustainable finance and green banking practices is significant. Regulatory frameworks, such as information disclosure requirements and sustainability criteria, are highlighted as critical factors for promoting transparency, accountability, and market integrity in the financial sector. The importance of green financial instruments, including green bonds, green loans, and sustainable investment funds, lies in their capacity to attract funding for projects that yield positive environmental impacts. Researchers analyze the demand for these products, their market growth, and their effects on sustainability outcomes.

Sustainable finance has emerged as a vital focus within the broader context of responsible investment and corporate social responsibility. It examines the incorporation of ESG considerations into investment decision-making processes. The evolution of sustainable finance is a prominent topic in the literature, indicating a shift from niche to widely adopted investment approaches. The origins of sustainable finance can be traced back to ethical investment movements and socially responsible investing, which have gradually integrated ESG criteria into their strategies. Researchers are exploring the factors that motivate and hinder investors, asset managers, and financial institutions from adopting sustainable finance practices as sustainability gains importance in financial decision-making.

Comparative analyses of the financial performance of sustainable investments versus conventional counterparts have been conducted. Empirical research attempts to assess whether the integration of ESG elements enhances or detracts from investment returns and risk management. While several studies suggest a positive correlation between sustainability and financial performance, results vary and depend on specific circumstances. Researchers investigate a range of factors influencing the relationship between sustainability and financial outcomes, including differences across sectors, geographic regions, and methodological approaches.

The landscape of sustainable finance is significantly shaped by regulatory frameworks and regulations. The effects of regulatory measures, such as mandates for information disclosure, sustainability reporting standards, and financial incentives for sustainability-promoting investments, are being examined. The effectiveness of these regulatory measures in fostering the adoption of sustainable finance practices and promoting transparency and accountability in financial markets is also a focal point. The role of voluntary initiatives, industry standards, and certification schemes in advancing sustainability within the finance sector is equally important.

In addition to legislative factors, the significance of investor preferences and market demand plays a crucial role in promoting sustainable finance. Research explores the motivations and actions of various investor categories, including institutional investors, retail investors, and impact investors (Fariya et al., 2024). Researchers analyze numerous factors influencing investment decisions, such as expectations of financial returns, perceptions of risk, ethical considerations, and methods for integrating ESG factors. Furthermore, the impact of financial intermediaries, such as asset managers and pension funds, on investment flows and the promotion of sustainability in the investment value chain is examined.

Sustainable finance underscores the growing importance of incorporating environmental, social, and governance factors into investment decision-making processes. Although research has made substantial progress in understanding the factors and implications of sustainable finance, challenges remain, including data availability, assessment methodologies, and the standardization of ESG criteria. Future research should prioritize addressing these challenges, exploring innovative funding mechanisms, and enhancing policy frameworks to accelerate the transition toward a more sustainable and inclusive financial system.

10.4 RESEARCH METHODOLOGY

The primary data provide the foundation for the current investigation. The study focuses solely on the Delhi region, particularly its four most significant districts: South, West, East, and North Delhi. In these four areas, Punjab National Bank has a total of 153 branches. Using the stratified random sampling method, the industrial and residential areas of these 153 branches were assigned appropriate weight. The researcher approached 300 clients, 10 from each branch, and collected the necessary primary data. During the years 2021–2022, data were gathered using a standardized questionnaire. Demographic segmentation, including age, gender, education, income, length of account history, and residential status, among other factors, was carefully considered when researching customer awareness.

10.4.1 PUNJAB NATIONAL BANK AND GREEN INITIATIVES

According to the Corporate Social Responsibility Report 2010–2011 (PNB, 2011), the Punjab National Bank (PNB) has implemented several actions to reduce emissions and energy use. PNB has a separate audit sheet for evaluating the effects of the green initiatives they have undertaken, and they are conducting electricity audits of their offices as part of an energy conservation initiative. More than 290 tree plantation drives have been planned by the bank. It began focusing on green building techniques, including the use of energy-efficient lighting, prompt repair of water leaks, double-sided printing, and the use of material sensors for fans, lights, and other appliances. In accordance with a "Green Pledge" made to the Ministry of New and Renewable Energy, the group established a butterfly park on the grounds of the Guruvayur Temple, which is home to 18 different varieties of medicinal plants.

For project loans, compliance with environmental and social safeguards, including the rehabilitation and resettlement of project-affected people, is to be ensured as a pre-disbursement condition. They have developed guidelines to ensure that all necessary approvals and permissions, including from the Pollution Control Board, are obtained before the disbursement of term loans. The bank is also considering taking steps toward sustainable development, particularly in light of the Equator Principles on project financing. The company received approval for nine wind energy projects with a combined funding cap of ₹185.81 crore, and Wind Power India 2011 also awarded them a second medal for "Best Wind Energy Power Financer."

10.4.2 BANK CUSTOMERS' GREEN BANKING AWARENESS

The researcher gathered information from 300 respondents regarding bank customers' awareness of green banking activities.

10.4.3 FACTORS AFFECTING BANK CUSTOMERS' AWARENESS OF GREEN BANKING

The public in general and bank clients in particular will benefit from the bank's efforts to green its banking operations. These initiatives are successful only when clients respond favorably to the introduction of these new financial services. In this regard, educating bank customers about the concept of green banking becomes a crucial prerequisite for success. The bank's clientele includes a variety of demographic characteristics that affect their awareness of the concept of green banking. The study aimed to examine all of these aspects. Conclusions based on Table 10.1 are explained below:

1. **Awareness and Gender:** It has been discovered that male customers are more aware than female customers. This suggests a considerable connection between gender and awareness of green finance.

TABLE 10.1 Results of a Consolidated Hypothesis Test on Bank Customers' Knowledge About Green Banking

Category	χ^2 Calculated Value	χ^2 Tabulated Value	P-Value	Result (χ^2 cal vs. χ^2 tab)	Decision
Gender wise	12.87885	3.84145	0.0003	χ^2 cal > χ^2 tab	Reject H_0
Education wise	31.39	9.48	0.0001	χ^2 cal > χ^2 tab	Reject H_0
Income-wise	17.76	7.81472	0.0005	χ^2 cal > χ^2 tab	Reject H_0
Period of account-wise	8.333	11.0705	0.1388	χ^2 cal < χ^2 tab	Accept H_0
Industrial and residential-wise	1.92	3.48	0.1371	χ^2 cal < χ^2 tab	Accept H_0

Source: Author's calculation.

2. **Awareness and Education:** Education is a prerequisite for bank customers' awareness of green banking. According to the survey, there is a correlation between customer knowledge of green banking and educational attainment.

3. **Awareness and Income:** The study indicates a strong correlation between income and individuals' awareness of green banking. Customers from the higher income category exhibit greater awareness than those from the lower income group.

4. **Awareness and Period of Account:** Table 10.1 shows that bank customers' knowledge about green banking is unrelated to the duration of their accounts with the bank. The length of the account does not significantly impact bank customers' awareness.

5. **Awareness and Location Status:** Regardless of whether one lives in an urban or rural area, awareness of green banking is attainable. This indicates the bank's efforts to provide green banking services and products in rural areas, as well as its initiatives to raise awareness among rural consumers.

10.4.4 BANK CLIENTS' KNOWLEDGE OF GREEN INITIATIVES

For its clients, the PNB has launched several green banking programs. Additionally, the PNB has undertaken various actions to inform bank customers about green banking activities. However, the bank's ability to implement these green banking initiatives depends on how well its customers can comprehend and attempt to use the new technology-based green banking products and services (Singh et al., 2023). In other words, the success of the bank's execution of green banking efforts relies on the degree of client knowledge regarding these initiatives. Consequently, the study aims to demonstrate the level of knowledge that bank customers possess concerning the various significant green banking efforts carried out by PNB in the study area. Table 10.2 presents this information.

TABLE 10.2 Bank Clients' Knowledge of Green Initiatives

Sl. No.	Green Initiatives	Aware	Neutral	Not Aware	Total
1.	Green checking	158	45	97	300
2.	Green loans	34	20	296	350
3.	Green mortgages	53	21	276	350
4.	Green CDs	61	23	266	350
5.	Facility of E-statement	116	39	195	350
6.	Facility of online banking	162	47	141	350
7.	Reduced use of paper	248	42	60	350
8.	Use of solar powered ATM	0	56	294	350
9.	Energy efficient branch	176	34	140	350
10.	Providing recyclable Debit and Credit Cards	88	40	222	350
11.	Online bill payment	158	26	166	350
12.	Controlled use of water and rainwater harvesting	98	12	240	350
13.	Bank environmental policy	70	23	257	350
14.	Mobile banking	165	35	150	350
	Total	1587	463	2800	4850

Source: Author's calculation.

According to a statistical investigation in Table 10.3, *H0* indicates that bank clients are notably unaware of PNB's green banking initiatives. *H1*: Bank clients are well-informed about PNB's efforts to promote green banking. Sample mean: 31.17; sample variance: 9.32; Z-score: 17.97, significance level: 5%; Z-table value: 1.64; P-value: 0.0001; Decision: Since $P = 0.005$, reject H_0.

Thus, it can be said that bank clients are largely aware of the green banking measures carried out by PNB. The table indicates that approximately 32% of bank customers in the research area are aware of all 14 PNB green banking programs. In instances where less paper is used, which directly contributes to environmental conservation, the highest awareness

TABLE 10.3 Statistical Results

Statistical Measure	Aware	Neutral	Not Aware	Total
Mean (M)	115.93	38.79	195.29	350
Standard deviation (SD)	68.22	11.35	77.12	0
Coefficient of variation (CV)	0.71	0.6	0.42	0

Source: Author's calculation.

rate of 76% is observed. Conversely, the solar-powered ATM remains unknown to customers. Despite the greater potential for utilizing solar electricity for ATMs, this highlights the lack of initiative in the research region regarding the adoption of solar-powered ATMs. The table's second significant finding reveals that more than 52% of bank customers are aware of green checking and energy-efficient branch options. Similarly, 48%, 47%, and 46% of bank clients are aware of mobile banking, internet banking, and online bill payment options, respectively. The statistics provided clearly demonstrate a substantial difference in customer awareness of these important green banking activities. Additionally, over 20% of bank clients recognize the importance of conserving water, collecting rainwater, and providing customers with recyclable debit and credit cards. The awareness level among bank consumers regarding green loans and green mortgages is below 5%. In the coming years, PNB needs to focus more on this issue and the utilization of solar-powered ATMs.

10.5 CONCLUSION

Initiatives in green finance have contributed to achieving sustainable development and maintaining ecological balance. PNB, India's largest public sector bank, has continued to be a pioneer in implementing green banking practices. PNB has begun efforts to educate bank clients about green banking. According to the study, PNB has made satisfactory progress in this area within the studied region. However, based on the findings of this study, it is recommended that PNB make significant efforts to inform clients about all green banking activities.

10.6 FUTURE IMPLICATIONS OF GREEN BANKING

Future times will witness a shift toward green banking. We also anticipate the introduction of several related green products, green services, and green legislation.

1. **Identify and Reward Environmentally Conscious Financial Institutions:** The Reserve Bank of India or another regulatory body will annually identify and reward environmentally conscious lenders of green loans.
2. **Environmentally Negligent Businesses:** Such businesses may face the risk of harming both their financial performance and market reputation.
3. **Green Rating Agencies:** Green Rating and Information Services of India Ltd. (GRISIL) will emerge.
4. **Green Mutual Funds:** These will be available in the markets to provide green analysis of lenders and consumers of green loans. Green mutual funds will allow environmentally conscious clients to invest in green initiatives, and investing in these will also yield tax breaks.
5. **Green Insurance:** The Insurance Regulatory and Development Authority (IRDA) is required to develop green insurance that offers coverage for various environmental risks.

KEYWORDS

- **customer awareness**
- **environmental development**
- **green banking**
- **green business practices**
- **green finance**
- **renewable energy**
- **sustainable finance**

REFERENCES

Aggarwal, K. K., Kaur, R., & Lakhera, G. (2023). Green finance: Addressing environmental challenges through sustainable investments. In *Sustainable Investments in Green Finance*. https://doi.org/10.4018/979-8-3693-1388-6.ch010.

Annadurai, A. (2014). Effectiveness of green banking technology of commercial banks in India. *International Journal of Research in Commerce and Management, 5*(12).

Bahl, S. (2012). The role of green banking in sustainable growth. *International Journal of Marketing Financial Services and Management, 2*. ISSN 2277–3622.

Biswas, D. (2016). A study of conceptual framework on green banking. *Journal of Commerce and Management Thought, 7*(1), 39.

Ch Sreesha. (2014). A study of green banking initiatives of selected private and public sector banks in India. *International Journal of Research, 1*(7), 807–815. ISSN 2348–6848.

Fabris, N. (2019). Cashless society – The future of money or a utopia? *Journal of Central Banking Theory and Practice, 8*(1), 53–66.

Fariya, Saini, A., & Kashif, M. (2024). Exploring the influence of factors driving financial accessibility, financial activities, and financial education on sustainable development. In *Artificial Intelligence and Machine Learning-Powered Smart Finance* (pp. 23–49). IGI Global.

Indian Banks Association. (2014). Green banking innovations. *The Indian Banker*. Retrieved from: http://www.theindianbanker.co.in/html/sto5.htm (accessed on 17 January 2025).

Jin, Y., Gao, X., & Wang, M. (2021). The financing efficiency of listed energy conservation and environmental protection firms: Evidence and implications for green finance in China. *Energy Policy, 153*, 112254. https://doi.org/10.1016/j.enpol.2021.112254.

Kashif, M., David, A., Gupta, V. P., & Alam, S. (2024). Integration of artificial intelligence in the financial sector. In *Artificial Intelligence and Machine Learning-Powered Smart Finance* (pp. 96–108). IGI Global.

Kashif, M., Kumar, P., Ghai, S., & Kumar, S. (2023). Disruptive technologies in computational finance. In *Algorithmic Approaches to Financial Technology: Forecasting, Trading, and Optimization* (pp. 46–60). IGI Global.

Kashif, M., Shajar, S. N., Singhal, N., & Kumar, P. (2023). Achieving sustainable investment practices through green finance: Challenges and opportunities. *Sustainable Investments in Green Finance*, 234–244. IGI Global.

Kashif, M., Thiyagarajan, S., & Sridharan, P. (2017). Dynamics of Algeria's international reserves. *African Journal of Economic and Management Studies, 8*(4), 410–419. https://doi.org/10.1108/AJEMS-12-2016-0207.

Lewis, A. (2001). A focus group study of the motivation to invest: 'ethical/green' and 'ordinary' investors compared. *The Journal of Socio-Economics, 30*(4), 331–341. https://doi.org/10.1016/S1053-5357(01)00072-3.

Lindenberg, N., & Volz, U. (2016). Green banking regulation: Setting out a framework. Report for the Practitioners' Dialogue on Climate Investments (PDCI). Deutsche Gesellschaft Für Internationale Zusammenarbeit (GIZ) GmbH.

Moorthy, D., & Pradeepa, V. (2014). Customer satisfaction towards PNB green channel counter – An empirical study. *International Journal of Informative and Futuristic Research, 12*(2), 319–325.

Pal, N. (2016). A systematic study of customer awareness towards green banking initiatives. *Proceedings*, 167–169.

Park, H., & Kim, J. D. (2020). Transition towards green banking: Role of financial regulators and financial institutions. *Asian Journal of Sustainability and Social Responsibility, 5*(1), 1–25. https://doi.org/10.1186/s41180-020-00028-2.

Poonam, & Aggarwal, K. K. (2023). Analysis of the impact of COVID-19 on the stock market and capability of investing strategies. *AIP Conference Proceedings, 2782*. https://doi.org/10.1063/5.0154174.

Punjab National Bank. (2018–2019). PNB's fourth sustainability report: Spearheading Digital India – Banking solutions for a sustainable tomorrow.

Punjab National Bank. (2019). *Quarterly Year 2019 Results: Digital Journey*.

Punjab National Bank. (2020). *Quarterly Year 2020 Results: Innovative Technology, Mobile App*.

Reserve Bank of India. (2009–2019). *Statistical Tables Relating to Banks in India*.

Reserve Bank of India. (2010–2019). Bank-wise debit cards and credit cards statistical report.

Reserve Bank of India. (2013). *RBI Report 2013 Booklet*.

Sarma, P., & Roy, A. (2021). A scientometric analysis of literature on green banking (1995-March 2019). *Journal of Sustainable Finance & Investment, 11*(2), 143–162. https://doi.org/10.1080/20430795.2020.1818320.

Sharma, G. (2017). Conceptual analysis of green banking in India and abroad. *National Journal of Arts, Commerce and Scientific Research Review, 4*(1), 75–81.

Sharma, N., K., S., & Gopal, R. (2015). A study on customers' awareness of green banking initiatives in selected public and private sector banks with special reference to Mumbai. *IOSR Journal of Economics and Finance (IOSR-JEF)*, e-ISSN: 2321–5933, p-ISSN: 2321–5925, 2835. Retrieved from: www.iosrjournals.org (accessed on 17 January 2025).

Shobha, C. K., & Sarala, K. S. (2016). Green banking initiatives: Problems and prospects in Punjab National Bank, Shivmoga City.

Shobharani, H., Deekshitha, V., & Sowmyashree, J. (2016). Green banking: The bank employees' perspective. *Proceedings*.

Singh, A., Taneja, S., & Kumar, P. (2023). Algorithmic approaches to financial technology: Forecasting, trading, and optimization. In *Algorithmic Approaches to Financial Technology: Forecasting, Trading, and Optimization*. https://doi.org/10.4018/9798369317464.

Singh, S. (2003). Green business prospects: Environmental goods and services at WTO. *Economic and Political Weekly*, 3240–3243.

Thomas, J., & Silby, L. (2018). Customers' awareness and adoption of green banking in Thrissur District. *ISSN: 2319–5770*, e-ISSN 2394–1138.

CHAPTER 11

Predictive Analytics in Finance: Harnessing AI and ML for Market Risk Management

RENU VIJ*

Department of AIT Management, Chandigarh University, Mohali, Punjab, India

**Corresponding author.*

ABSTRACT

This chapter explores the transformative impact of Artificial Intelligence (AI) and Machine Learning (ML) on predictive analytics for market risk management within the private insurance sector. As financial markets face growing complexity and volatility, the integration of AI and ML offers a proactive approach to risk identification, mitigation, and decision-making. The study investigates the application of predictive analytics in analyzing historical data, forecasting market trends, detecting fraud, managing portfolios, and enhancing personalized financial services. By leveraging algorithmic trading, credit scoring models, and natural language processing, the research demonstrates how AI and ML enable more accurate, real-time assessments of market conditions. Additionally, it examines ethical implications, data security challenges, and the need for responsible AI deployment. The chapter concludes that predictive analytics, empowered by AI and ML, is not merely a technological advancement but a strategic imperative for achieving financial resilience, operational efficiency, and sustainable growth in the rapidly evolving financial landscape.

Transforming Business Finance in the Digital Era.
Sanjay Taneja, Mohammad Kashif, Ercan Özen, and Luan Vardari (Eds.)
© 2026 Apple Academic Press, Inc. Co-published with CRC Press (Taylor & Francis)

DOI: 10.1201/9781998511235-11

11.1 INTRODUCTION

In the ever-evolving landscape of the financial industry, the private insurance sector stands at the forefront of transformative change, particularly in the realm of market risk assessment. This study embarks on a comprehensive analysis, delving into the untapped potential of Machine Learning (ML) and Artificial Intelligence (AI) within predictive analytics to navigate and understand market risks unique to the private insurance domain. As the financial sector contends with escalating uncertainties, it becomes increasingly imperative to harness advanced technologies to foresee and manage these risks effectively.

In the contemporary financial landscape, the private insurance sector is undergoing significant transformations, driven by the integration of advanced technologies. This study centers on the exploration of ML and AI within the domain of predictive analytics, specifically aimed at assessing market risks in private insurance. As uncertainties in the financial market continue to escalate, the imperative to leverage cutting-edge technologies for effective risk management becomes increasingly evident.

The growing complexity of market dynamics underscores the need for innovative approaches to understand and navigate potential risks. This research embarks on a journey to unravel the untapped potential of AI and ML in reshaping the private insurance sector's response to market uncertainties. The introduction of these technologies not only holds promise for enhancing risk assessment but also opens avenues for proactive risk mitigation.

The private insurance sector, a crucial component of the financial ecosystem, serves as a safety net for individuals and businesses, shielding them from various risks. However, this sector is not immune to the challenges posed by an ever-evolving market landscape, characterized by heightened uncertainties and complexities. In this context, understanding and effectively managing market risks have become paramount for sustaining a stable and thriving financial environment.

This analysis embarks on a comprehensive exploration of the potential of ML and AI in predictive analytics, specifically tailored to assess market risks within the private insurance sector (Kashif et al., 2023a, b). Recognizing the pivotal role of AI and ML in deciphering intricate market dynamics and anticipating risk patterns, the study delves into the intricate interplay between market volatility, customer behaviors, and the innovative capabilities of AI and ML methodologies.

Beginning with a critical overview of the current state of market risks within the private insurance sector, the analysis emphasizes the urgent need to address these challenges. It subsequently delves into the practical application of AI and ML in predicting potential market risks, with a keen focus on uncovering historical data patterns and conducting comprehensive analyses. Notably, the analysis sheds light on the efficacy of AI-driven models in the early detection of market risks, enabling proactive measures to mitigate their impact.

Furthermore, the research delves into pertinent considerations of data security, ethical implications, and potential biases that could arise within AI systems operating in the finance domain. By advocating for the strategic implementation of AI and ML in predictive analytics, the study underscores the transformative potential of these technologies in not only identifying high-risk market conditions but also in formulating targeted strategies to effectively manage market fluctuations. Ultimately, this analysis highlights the crucial role played by AI and ML in reshaping the private insurance sector, fostering stability, and enhancing overall market resilience and performance.

11.2 EXPERIMENTAL METHODS AND MATERIALS

11.2.1 SIGNIFICANCE

At the heart of this investigation lies the recognition of the critical role played by AI and ML in reshaping the private insurance sector. As market dynamics become more intricate, the need to assess and predict risks becomes paramount. This study not only addresses the urgency of this issue but also highlights the multifaceted approach taken to comprehend market risks encompassing elements such as market volatility and customer behaviors. By leveraging AI and ML methodologies, organizations can not only identify potential risks but also proactively mitigate their impact.

The significance of this research extends beyond the technological realm, touching upon ethical considerations, data security, and the potential biases that may permeate AI systems within the finance domain. This comprehensive examination aims to underscore how, by embracing predictive analytics, the private insurance sector can cultivate stable financial environments, fortify market resilience, and enhance overall performance, ultimately paving the way for a more robust and adaptive future in the financial landscape.

11.2.2 PREDICTIVE ANALYTICS AND MARKET

By embracing predictive analytics, the private insurance sector not only gains a strategic advantage but also positions itself to cultivate stable financial environments, fortify market resilience, and enhance overall performance. Predictive analytics serves as a powerful tool, enabling insurers to anticipate and respond effectively to dynamic market conditions, thereby fostering stability in their financial operations (Kashif et al., 2017). The cultivation of stable financial environments within the private insurance sector is intricately linked to the sector's ability to accurately predict and manage risks. Predictive analytics, powered by advanced technologies such as Machine Learning and Artificial Intelligence, facilitates a more nuanced understanding of market trends, customer behaviors, and emerging risks. This deeper comprehension allows insurers to proactively adjust their strategies, ensuring financial stability in the face of evolving market dynamics.

Fortifying market resilience becomes a natural outcome of incorporating predictive analytics into the operational fabric of private insurance entities. The predictive capabilities enable insurers to identify potential vulnerabilities and anticipate market shocks, empowering them to develop robust risk mitigation strategies. This proactive approach not only safeguards against unforeseen challenges but also instills confidence in stakeholders, contributing to the sector's resilience amidst economic uncertainties. Enhancing overall performance is a direct consequence of informed decision-making facilitated by predictive analytics. Insurers can optimize resource allocation, streamline operational processes, and tailor their products and services to meet evolving market demands. The data-driven insights derived from predictive analytics empower private insurance companies to make strategic, well-informed choices, ultimately leading to improved operational efficiency and financial performance.

11.3 DISCUSSION

11.3.1 MACHINE LEARNING REVOLUTIONARY IN FINANCE INDUSTRY

Machine learning has become increasingly prevalent in the finance industry, revolutionizing various aspects of financial services and operations. It has the potential to significantly improve decision-making, risk management, fraud detection, customer service, and many other key areas.

Some common applications of machine learning in finance are discussed in subsections.

11.3.1.1 ALGORITHMIC TRADING

Machine learning algorithms can analyze historical market data to identify patterns and make predictions about future market movements, helping traders make informed investment decisions. Algorithmic trading is a transformative force in financial markets, leveraging advanced algorithms to execute trades swiftly, implement complex strategies, and manage risks systematically. Its contribution to market liquidity and efficiency underscores its significance in the contemporary financial landscape.

Algo-trading is a sophisticated method of executing financial transactions that relies on automated algorithms to make trading decisions. This approach has gained significant prominence in financial markets due to its ability to analyze vast amounts of data at high speeds and execute trades with precision. Algo-trading is integral to modern financial systems, providing several advantages to market participants (Kashif et al., 2024). Its capacity to execute trades at speeds far beyond human capability allows algorithms to process market data, identify opportunities, and execute orders in fractions of a second, reducing latency and maximizing the chances of capturing favorable market conditions. This speed advantage is particularly crucial in markets where price movements occur rapidly.

Furthermore, algorithmic trading facilitates the implementation of complex trading strategies with precision and consistency. These algorithms can analyze historical data, identify patterns, and adapt to changing market conditions in real time. This adaptability allows for the swift adjustment of trading strategies based on market trends, news, or other relevant factors, contributing to more efficient and effective decision-making. Risk management is another key area where algorithmic trading excels. These algorithms can incorporate risk parameters, predefined limits, and stop-loss orders, enabling traders to mitigate risks systematically. Automated risk controls help prevent large losses and ensure that trading activities align with predetermined risk tolerance levels.

In addition to individual trade execution, algorithmic trading contributes to overall market liquidity. By providing continuous and automated trading, these algorithms enhance market efficiency and reduce bid-ask spreads, benefiting all market participants. The increased liquidity can lead to more accurate pricing and a reduction in transaction costs for traders. However, many issues, such as technological glitches, market manipulation risks, and the potential for unforeseen events impacting automated strategies, must be carefully considered and addressed. Additionally, the rapid evolution of technology and the competitive nature of algorithmic trading necessitate ongoing monitoring and adaptation of algorithms to maintain their effectiveness.

11.3.1.2 RISK MANAGEMENT

Machine learning models can be used to assess and manage risks by analyzing large datasets and identifying potential risks and anomalies in real-time, enabling financial institutions to make more accurate risk assessments and manage their portfolios more effectively.

Risk management in the financial sector, as noted by Arslanian (2019), has undergone a transformative evolution with the integration of machine learning models. This advanced technology offers unparalleled capabilities in assessing and managing risks by harnessing the analytical power of large datasets and identifying potential risks and anomalies in real-time. The utilization of machine learning in risk management empowers financial institutions to make more accurate risk assessments and enhances their ability to manage portfolios with heightened precision and effectiveness. One of the primary advantages of employing machine learning in risk management lies in its capacity to analyze vast amounts of data swiftly and comprehensively. Traditional risk management approaches often grapple with the limitations of processing large datasets in a timely manner. Machine learning models, on the other hand, excel in handling big data, enabling financial institutions to extract meaningful insights and identify potential risks with greater accuracy. Real-time risk assessment is a critical aspect facilitated by machine learning models. These models continuously analyze incoming data, swiftly detecting patterns or deviations that could signify potential risks. The real-time nature of this analysis allows financial institutions to respond promptly to emerging threats, making risk management a proactive and dynamic process rather than a reactive one.

Furthermore, machine learning models contribute to the identification of anomalies that might go unnoticed by traditional risk management methods. By learning from historical data patterns, these models can recognize deviations from the norm, signaling potential risks or irregularities in the financial landscape. This ability to discern anomalies enhances the overall risk detection capabilities of financial institutions, providing a more comprehensive risk management strategy. The accuracy of risk assessments is significantly elevated with the incorporation of machine learning. These models can adapt and learn from new data, continually refining their understanding of risk factors. This adaptability enhances the precision of risk predictions, allowing financial institutions to make informed decisions based on the most up-to-date information available.

11.3.1.3 MACHINE LEARNING AND MANAGING PORTFOLIO

Machine learning assists financial institutions in optimizing their asset allocations and making data-driven investment decisions. By considering a multitude of factors and potential risks, these models contribute to creating well-informed and balanced portfolios. This optimization is essential for maximizing returns while minimizing exposure to unnecessary risks.

The integration of machine learning models into risk management practices revolutionizes how financial institutions navigate the complexities of the market (Fariya et al., 2024). The ability to analyze large datasets in real-time, identify potential risks and anomalies, and continually adapt based on new information enhances the accuracy, efficiency, and proactiveness of risk management strategies. As the financial landscape continues to evolve, leveraging machine learning in risk management becomes increasingly indispensable for institutions seeking a competitive edge in today's dynamic markets.

11.3.1.4 FRAUD DETECTION

Machine learning algorithms can detect unusual patterns in financial transactions and flag potential cases of fraud, helping financial institutions identify and prevent fraudulent activities more effectively than traditional rule-based systems. These sophisticated algorithms excel in identifying unusual patterns within financial transactions, enabling them to efficiently flag potential cases of fraud. This capability empowers financial institutions to identify and prevent fraudulent activities with a level of effectiveness that surpasses traditional rule-based systems.

Machine learning algorithms bring a nuanced and dynamic approach to fraud detection by analyzing large datasets and recognizing patterns that might go unnoticed by conventional methods (M, 2022). Unlike rule-based systems that rely on predetermined criteria, machine learning models can adapt and evolve, learning from new data to continuously enhance their ability to identify emerging fraud patterns. Machine learning in fraud detection represents a paradigm shift from static rule-based systems to dynamic, adaptive models capable of handling the complexity and speed of modern financial transactions. The ability to detect unusual patterns, operate in real-time, and minimize false positives positions machine learning as a cornerstone in the ongoing battle against fraudulent activities within the financial sector. As financial threats continue to evolve, the role of machine learning in fraud detection becomes increasingly vital for institutions seeking robust and adaptive security measures.

11.3.1.5 CREDIT SCORING

Machine learning models can analyze customer data to assess creditworthiness more accurately, enabling financial institutions to make better lending decisions and offer more personalized financial products and services to their customers. Machine learning models, by virtue of their ability to process and interpret vast datasets, offer a more comprehensive evaluation of an individual's creditworthiness. Machine learning algorithms consider a diverse range of factors, such as transaction history, spending patterns, and even social and behavioral data. This holistic approach enables a more nuanced and accurate assessment of an individual's financial reliability. The utilization of machine learning in credit scoring facilitates the creation of personalized financial products and services. By understanding individual financial behaviors and preferences, institutions can tailor their offerings to meet the specific needs of customers. This personalization not only enhances customer satisfaction but also contributes to the overall financial well-being of individuals. The integration of machine learning in credit scoring revolutionizes the lending landscape by providing a more accurate and personalized approach to assessing creditworthiness.

11.3.1.6 PERSONALIZED BANKING SERVICES

Machine learning can analyze customer data to provide personalized recommendations and services tailored to individual needs and preferences, thereby enhancing customer experience and satisfaction. This utilization of advanced algorithms significantly improves the overall customer experience, leading to increased satisfaction. By analyzing vast datasets, machine learning models can identify patterns and trends in customer behavior, transaction history, and preferences. This enables financial institutions to gain valuable insights into individual customer needs, allowing them to customize their services accordingly (Stolin, 2018). Personalized banking services powered by machine learning surpass traditional one-size-fits-all approaches. These algorithms can identify specific financial habits, anticipate needs, and offer timely and relevant recommendations. For instance, machine learning can provide personalized investment advice, suggest suitable savings plans, or propose optimized credit options based on individual financial behaviors. Moreover, machine learning facilitates continuous learning and adaptation. As customer preferences evolve, these algorithms can adjust their recommendations and services in real-time, ensuring that personalized banking experiences remain relevant and valuable.

11.3.1.7 ROBO-ADVISORS

Machine learning-powered robo-advisors can deliver automated, algorithm-driven financial planning services with minimal human intervention, assisting individuals in making investment decisions and managing their portfolios more efficiently and cost-effectively. Utilizing advanced algorithms, robo-advisors analyze extensive financial data, market trends, and individual risk profiles to provide tailored investment recommendations. This data-driven approach enables them to offer personalized advice suited to the unique financial goals and risk tolerances of each user. This automation streamlines the investment process, making it more accessible to a broader range of users. Investors can leverage robo-advisors to create and manage portfolios, execute trades, and rebalance assets without the need for constant oversight or active decision-making.

11.3.1.8 NATURAL LANGUAGE PROCESSING (NLP) IN TRADING

NLP techniques can analyze news, social media, and other textual data to assess market sentiment and predict market trends, helping traders and investors make more informed decisions. This understanding of prevailing sentiments enables traders and investors to anticipate trends and react strategically to market dynamics.

11.3.2 MARKET ANALYSIS AND FORECASTING

Machine learning models can analyze large datasets to identify market trends and predict future market movements, enabling investors and financial analysts to make more accurate forecasts and better-informed investment decisions (Singh et al., 2023). The swift processing of large datasets allows these models to uncover patterns that traditional analysis methods may overlook, contributing to a more data-driven and precise approach to understanding and predicting financial market dynamics.

11.4 CONCLUSION

The incorporation of predictive analytics into finance, specifically leveraging AI and machine learning for market risk management, marks a significant advancement in the financial sector. The profound impact of AI and machine learning on evaluating and mitigating market risks is evident in their capacity to sift through extensive datasets, discern patterns, and provide real-time insights.

The integration of predictive analytics not only enhances the precision of risk assessments but also empowers financial institutions to proactively address emerging challenges. The predictive capabilities of AI and machine learning models contribute to more resilient risk mitigation strategies, allowing for timely responses and adaptive decision-making in the face of dynamic market conditions.

Furthermore, the thorough exploration of market volatility, customer behaviors, and other risk factors through predictive analytics facilitates a comprehensive understanding of the financial landscape. This, in turn, enables the development of targeted strategies and optimized resource allocation, fostering more robust and efficient financial operations.

As the financial sector undergoes continual transformation, adopting predictive analytics becomes essential for maintaining competitiveness and resilience. The ongoing refinement of models based on real-time data ensures that financial institutions remain agile in navigating market uncertainties. Additionally, the incorporation of ethical considerations, robust data security measures, and transparent practices in predictive analytics frameworks underscores a commitment to responsible and sustainable financial practices.

In essence, predictive analytics, fueled by AI and machine learning, transcends being merely a technological advancement; it becomes a strategic imperative for financial institutions striving to thrive in an ever-evolving landscape. By harnessing the predictive prowess of these technologies, the finance sector can anticipate, adapt, and ultimately redefine the future of risk management, fostering stability, resilience, and enduring success.

KEYWORDS

- **artificial intelligence**
- **decision-making**
- **financial environments**
- **machine learning**
- **private insurance sector**
- **risk assessments**

REFERENCES

Arslanian, H., & Fischer, F. (2019). *The Future of Finance: The Impact of FinTech, AI, and Crypto on Financial Services*. Springer.

Ashtiani, M. N., & Raahemi, B. (2022). Intelligent fraud detection in financial statements using machine learning and data mining: A systematic literature review. *IEEE Access, 10*, 72504–72525. https://doi.org/10.1109/ACCESS.2021.3096799.

Bunea, S., Kogan, B., & Stolin, D. (2018). FinTech and the banking bandwagon. *Journal of Financial Transformation, 47*, 25–33.

Cao, L. (2021). AI in finance: Challenges, techniques, and opportunities. *ACM Computing Surveys (CSUR), 55*, 1–38.

Chopra, R., & Sharma, G. (2021). Application of artificial intelligence in stock market forecasting: A critique, review, and research agenda. *Journal of Risk and Financial Management, 14*, 526.

De Sá, A. G., Pereira, A. C., & Pappa, G. L. (2018). A customized classification algorithm for credit card fraud detection. *Engineering Applications of Artificial Intelligence, 72*, 21–29.

Fariya, S., Saini, A., & Kashif, M. (2024). Exploring the influence of factors driving financial accessibility, financial activities, and financial education on sustainable development. In *Artificial Intelligence and Machine Learning-Powered Smart Finance* (pp. 23–49). IGI Global.

Hang, X., & Chen, Y. (2017). An artificial intelligence application in portfolio management. *Advances in Economics, Business and Management Research, 37*, 86–100.

Iwari, S., Ramampiaro, H., & Langseth, H. (2021). Machine learning in financial market surveillance: A survey. *IEEE Access, 9*, 159734–159754.

Kashif, M., David, A., Gupta, V. P., & Alam, S. (2024). Integration of artificial intelligence in the financial sector. In *Artificial Intelligence and Machine Learning-Powered Smart Finance* (pp. 96–108). IGI Global.

Kashif, M., Kumar, P., Ghai, S., & Kumar, S. (2023). Disruptive technologies in computational finance. In *Algorithmic Approaches to Financial Technology: Forecasting, Trading, and Optimization* (pp. 46–60). IGI Global.

Kashif, M., Shajar, S. N., Singhal, N., & Kumar, P. (2023). Achieving sustainable investment practices through green finance: Challenges and opportunities. In *Sustainable Investments in Green Finance* (pp. 234–244). IGI Global.

Kashif, M., Thiyagarajan, S., & Sridharan, P. (2017). Dynamics of Algeria's international reserves. *African Journal of Economic and Management Studies, 8*(4), 410–419.

Mullainathan, S., & Obermeyer, Z. (2017). Does machine learning automate moral hazard and error? *American Economic Review, 107*, 476–480.

Singh, A., Taneja, S., & Kumar, P. (2023). Algorithmic approaches to financial technology: Forecasting, trading, and optimization. In *Algorithmic Approaches to Financial Technology: Forecasting, Trading, and Optimization*. https://doi.org/10.4018/9798369317464.

Sirignano, J., & Cont, R. (2019). Universal features of price formation in financial markets: Perspectives from deep learning. *Quantitative Finance, 19*, 1449–1459.

CHAPTER 12

Revolutionizing Finance: A Primer on Machine Learning Applications

GUNJAN BHATIA and R. V. PALANIVEL

Berlin School of Business and Innovation, Belin, Germany

ABSTRACT

This chapter provides an in-depth overview of how machine learning (ML) is revolutionizing the financial services industry by enhancing efficiency, security, and decision-making processes. It explores the foundational concepts of ML and showcases a wide range of real-world applications, including robo-advisors, algorithmic trading, fraud detection, credit scoring, and automated underwriting. Emphasizing the use of ML for process automation, predictive analytics, and customer personalization, the chapter illustrates how financial institutions can leverage vast datasets to improve outcomes and streamline operations. Despite challenges such as high implementation costs, infrastructure limitations, and talent shortages, the benefits—ranging from cost reduction and risk mitigation to improved compliance and financial inclusion—underscore ML's transformative potential. The discussion also touches on ethical and operational considerations, ultimately advocating for the strategic adoption of ML to remain competitive in an increasingly digital and data-driven financial landscape.

12.1 INTRODUCTION

Have you ever wondered how the financial services industry has expanded to account for approximately 25% of the global economy? Artificial intelligence (AI) is utilized in the core business processes of both Renaissance

Transforming Business Finance in the Digital Era.
Sanjay Taneja, Mohammad Kashif, Ercan Özen, and Luan Vardari (Eds.)
© 2026 Apple Academic Press, Inc. Co-published with CRC Press (Taylor & Francis)

DOI: 10.1201/9781998511235-12

Technologies, the top-performing investment fund, and JPMorgan, the most valuable bank in the world. The finance sector extensively employs machine learning to streamline processes and save time. It is reported that machine learning is being utilized by 70% of financial services companies. This technology can significantly optimize operations in finance departments and enterprises, presenting various applications in the finance industry.

12.2 MEANING

In classical programming, a computer performs tasks by following a predetermined set of instructions. Conversely, in machine learning, the computer is assigned a task along with a set of examples (data), and its role is to determine how to complete the task based on the provided examples. Machine learning is a crucial component of the expanding field of data science. Algorithms are trained to generate predictions or classifications and to extract valuable insights from data mining projects using statistical techniques. These insights subsequently inform business and application decisions, ideally influencing key growth metrics. Although no magic is involved (well, perhaps a little), machine learning in finance may seem magical. However, building effective infrastructure, gathering relevant datasets, and employing the appropriate algorithms are more critical to the success of machine learning projects. The financial services sector is currently experiencing a notable increase in the adoption of machine learning.

12.3 A FEW EXAMPLES OF MACHINE LEARNING APPLICATIONS IN THE FINANCE SECTOR

12.3.1 AUTOMATION OF CORPORATE FINANCE PROCESSES

Financial companies benefit from the ability to automate and streamline business processes in numerous ways. For instance, organizations can utilize these technologies to automate repetitive tasks such as data entry and financial monitoring. This allows employee focus to shift towards projects that genuinely require human intervention.

12.3.2 IMPROVED RELATIONS WITH CUSTOMERS

Customer relations represent one of the most beneficial areas where machine learning is applied in finance. Financial companies leverage machine learning (ML) technologies, such as chatbots, to enhance customer experiences by providing real-time recommendations and on-demand assistance. In insurance firms, customer acquisition and onboarding processes are often automated to streamline and expedite operations.

12.3.3 ROBO-ADVISORS FOR SECURITY ANALYSIS AND PORTFOLIO MANAGEMENT

A prominent example of a machine learning application in finance is robo-advisors. Depending on the financial institution providing the service, these may vary slightly. However, the term "robo-advisor" generally refers to online services that assist users in creating and managing investment portfolios while offering investment advice. This process relies on a multitude of user-specified input parameters. For example, risk preferences gather data on the choices users would make in unforeseen circumstances to assess their needs.

12.3.4 PROJECTING THE STOCK MARKET

In the finance sector, ML technology is frequently employed to forecast stock prices and influence trading decisions. It makes predictions about the future by utilizing extensive historical datasets. The following two forms of trading are enabled by machine learning technology:

1. **Algorithmic Trading:** Rapidly and accurately identifying patterns and developing trading strategies; and
2. **High-Frequency Trading (HFT):** The process of detecting trading opportunities and executing trades quickly.

12.3.5 IDENTIFYING FRAUD

Machine learning models learn by identifying patterns. These patterns help them comprehend typical behavior and simplify the identification of suspicious practices, such as insider trading or money laundering.

12.3.6 CREDIT SCORING AND ONLINE LENDING PLATFORMS

The finance sector employs machine learning tools to evaluate loan applications and determine credit scores. Based on a user's financial history, online lending platforms recommend loans and generate real-time reports.

12.3.7 PREVENTIVE AND MANAGEMENT OF RISKS

By identifying risks based on historical data and probability statistics, ML technology is frequently used in finance to support investment decisions. It can also be applied to develop risk management strategies and assess potential outcomes.

12.3.8 BIG DATA AND UNSTRUCTURED ANALYSIS

In finance, machine learning has simplified the extraction and analysis of unstructured data from documents such as financial reports or contracts.

12.3.9 AUTOMATION OF THE TRADE SETTLEMENT PROCESS

The trade settlement process can be labor-intensive and prone to errors. Occasionally, trades can go awry. Before the implementation of machine learning in finance, office workers at financial institutions had to process trade failures, determine their causes, and rectify the issues. The use of ML tools that automatically identify problems and provide suggestions for solutions has streamlined this labor-intensive process.

12.3.10 VALUING AND MANAGING ASSETS

Asset managers utilize ML and AI to value and manage assets such as bonds and stocks. Data-driven decisions reduce human error caused by loss aversion or confirmation bias.

Machine learning solutions are remarkable because they do not require explicit programming; instead, they learn from experience. In essence, one must select the models and provide them with data. The model then automatically adjusts its parameters to yield better results.

Data scientists train machine learning models using pre-existing datasets, which they subsequently apply to real-world scenarios.

Based on its training data, the model autonomously produces results while operating in the background. To maintain models' relevance and functionality, data scientists can retrain them as frequently as necessary.

Generally, results become more accurate with the inclusion of more data. Coincidentally, the financial services sector often handles massive datasets. Petabytes of information are available regarding payments, clients, bills, money transfers, and more. Machine learning is ideally suited for this purpose.

With the rapid advancement of technology and the availability of open-source algorithms, it is challenging to envision a financial services industry devoid of machine learning.

12.4 CHALLENGES OF USING MACHINE LEARNING IN THE FINANCIAL SERVICES INDUSTRY

- Companies frequently have utterly irrational expectations regarding machine learning and its potential benefits for their enterprises.
- Research and development (R&D) in machine learning is expensive.
- Another significant issue is the lack of data science (DS) and machine learning (ML) engineers. The graph below shows how quickly the demand for machine learning and artificial intelligence skills is rising.
- Financial incumbents lack the necessary agility concerning updates to their data infrastructure.

12.5 ADVANTAGES OF USING MACHINE LEARNING IN THE FINANCIAL SERVICES INDUSTRY

Despite the obstacles, numerous financial firms are already leveraging this technology. The following illustrates how executives in the financial services sector view machine learning with great seriousness, and they have several valid reasons for doing so:

- Reduced operational costs due to process automation.
- Increased revenues resulting from improved productivity and enhanced user experiences.
- Better compliance and reinforced security.

Numerous open-source machine learning tools and algorithms are well-suited for use with financial data. Furthermore, well-established financial services firms have sizable budgets that allow them to purchase cutting-edge computer hardware.

Machine learning has the potential to improve many facets of the financial ecosystem because of the quantitative nature of the financial sector and the abundance of historical data.

This explains why so many financial companies are making significant R&D investments in machine learning. It can be costly for laggards to ignore artificial intelligence (AI) and machine learning (ML).

12.6 WHICH FINANCIAL APPLICATIONS EXIST FOR MACHINE LEARNING?

Let us examine a few intriguing uses of machine learning in the financial industry.

12.6.1 AUTOMATION OF PROCESSES

One of the most popular uses of machine learning in finance is process automation. Technology enables increased productivity, the automation of monotonous tasks, and the replacement of manual labor.

Machine learning thus allows businesses to scale up services, enhance customer experiences, and optimize costs. The following are some examples of machine learning automation in finance:

- Chatbots;
- Automating call centers;
- Automating documentation;
- Gamification of staff development, among other things.

Here are a few instances of automated banking processes. JPMorgan Chase introduced the Contract Intelligence (COIN) platform, which employs machine learning techniques such as natural language processing. The program scans legal documents and extracts pertinent information. Approximately 360,000 labor hours would be required for the manual review of 12,000 annual commercial credit agreements. In contrast, the same number of contracts can be reviewed in a matter of hours thanks to machine learning (Kashif et al., 2023a).

12.6.2 SECURITY

As transactions, users, and third-party integrations increase in the finance industry, so do security threats. Furthermore, machine learning algorithms excel at identifying fraud. Banks, for example, can use this technology to track thousands of transaction parameters in real-time for each account. Every action a cardholder takes is scrutinized by the algorithm, which determines whether the attempted activity is typical for that specific user. Such a model is highly accurate in identifying fraudulent behavior.

To verify the transaction, the system may request additional identification from the user if it detects questionable account activity. If at least 95% of the transaction appears to be fraudulent, the system can even choose to block it entirely. Machine learning algorithms require only a few seconds, or even fractions of a second, to evaluate a transaction. The speed enables the prevention of fraud before it occurs, as opposed to merely identifying it after the crime has already been committed.

Another security application of machine learning in finance is financial monitoring. Data scientists can train the system to identify numerous micropayments and detect money laundering tactics such as smurfing.

Additionally, machine learning algorithms can significantly enhance network security. Given that machine learning is the best tool available for analyzing thousands of parameters in real-time, data scientists train systems to identify and isolate cyber threats. It is likely that soon, this technology will drive the most sophisticated cybersecurity networks. Notable FinTech companies that make significant investments in security machine learning include Adyen, Payoneer, PayPal, Stripe, and Skrill (Kashif et al., 2023b).

12.6.3 CREDIT SCORING AND UNDERWRITING

The underwriting duties that are prevalent in the insurance and financial industries are a perfect fit for machine learning algorithms. With hundreds of data entries for every customer, data scientists use thousands of customer profiles to train their models. Then, in real-world settings, a trained system can perform the same underwriting and credit-scoring tasks. These scoring engines greatly increase the speed and accuracy of work done by human workers.

Because they have access to extensive historical customer data, banks and insurance companies can use these entries to train machine learning models. Alternatively, they can utilize datasets produced by large utility or telecom firms. For instance, BBVA Bancomer has partnered with Destacame, a different credit-scoring platform. The bank aims to provide more Latin American consumers with limited credit histories access to credit. Destacame uses open APIs to obtain bill payment information from utility companies. Destacame generates a credit score for a customer based on their bill-paying habits and forwards the information to the bank.

12.6.4 AUTOMATED TRADING

Machine learning aids in improving trading decisions in algorithmic trading. A mathematical model tracks news and trade data in real-time, looking for trends that could drive up or down movements in stock prices. Based on its forecasts, it can then take proactive action and sell, hold, or purchase stocks.

Human traders cannot analyze thousands of data sources simultaneously as machine learning algorithms can. Machine learning algorithms assist human traders in gaining a slight edge over the market average. Additionally, that slight advantage frequently translates into substantial profits given the enormous volumes of trading activities (Bhatnagar et al., 2024).

12.6.5 ROBOTIC ADVISING

These days, robo-advisors are widely used in the financial industry. There are currently two main ways that machine learning is utilized in the advisory space.

Portfolio management is an online wealth management service that optimizes, manages, and distributes clients' assets using statistics and algorithms. Users input their current financial information and objectives, such as saving $1 million by the age of 50. The current assets are then allocated among investment options by a robo-advisor based on the goals and risk preferences.

12.7 WHAT ARE SOME APPLICATIONS OF MACHINE LEARNING IN FINANCE?

Despite all of AI's and machine learning's benefits, even well-funded businesses frequently struggle to realize the full potential of these technologies. The incumbents in the financial services industry want to take advantage of the unique opportunities presented by machine learning, but, in all honesty, they do not understand data science or how to apply it.

They continually encounter the same issues, such as the absence of business KPIs. Budgets are then depleted, leading to inflated estimates. Having an appropriate software infrastructure in place is not sufficient, though it is a good starting point. To deliver a valuable machine learning development project, a clear vision, strong technical talent, and determination are required.

Idea validation should begin as soon as you have a firm grasp on how this technology will support the achievement of organizational goals. Data scientists should handle this task. They investigate the concept, assist organizations in creating workable KPIs, and help you arrive at reasonable estimates.

12.8 CONCLUSION

Machine learning has streamlined operations in the financial sector, making them easier and less time-consuming. There are many challenges to its implementation, such as high costs, a lack of skilled employees in this field, and others, as described earlier in this chapter. Still, it remains a crucial component of the financial sector, as many machine learning tools reduce operational costs associated with process automation and provide enhanced productivity and compliance.

It is advisable to implement machine learning in the financial sector, as it aids in process automation, provides security against online fraud, facilitates automated trading, and offers numerous other services to financial institutions. Therefore, considering the advantages of machine learning, it is beneficial for financial institutions to leverage it, as it represents the future of the financial sector.

KEYWORDS

- **algorithms**
- **artificial intelligence**
- **data science**
- **financial sector**
- **machine learning**
- **renaissance technologies**
- **trading**

REFERENCES

Bailey, M. D., & Wilmott, P. (2020). *Machine Learning in Finance: From Theory to Practice*. Wiley.

Bhatnagar, M., Kumar, P., Taneja, S., Sood, K., & Grima, S. (2024). From digital overload to trading zen: The role of digital detox in enhancing intraday trading performance. In *Business Drivers in Promoting Digital Detoxification* (pp. 148–176). IGI Global.

Johnson, B. (2010). *Algorithmic Trading and DMA: An Introduction to Direct Access Trading Strategies*. Wiley.

Kashif, M., Kumar, P., Ghai, S., & Kumar, S. (2023b). Disruptive technologies in computational finance. In *Algorithmic Approaches to Financial Technology: Forecasting, Trading, and Optimization* (pp. 46–60). IGI Global.

Kashif, M., Shajar, S. N., Singhal, N., & Kumar, P. (2023a). Achieving sustainable investment practices through green finance: Challenges and opportunities. In *Sustainable Investments in Green Finance* (pp. 234–244). IGI Global.

Lopez de Prado, M. (2018). *Advances in Financial Learning*. Wiley.

Lopez de Prado, M. (2020). *Machine Learning for Financial Markets*. University Press.

Pavliv, A., et al. (2019). Machine learning in finance: Why, what & how. *N-iX Insights*. Retrieved from: https://www.n-ix.com/machine-learning-in-finance-why-what-how/ (accessed on 17 January 2025).

Zuhair, M. G., McGinnity, T. M., & Prasad, G. (2020). Deep learning for time series forecasting in finance: A survey. *IEEE Transactions on Neural Networks and Learning Systems*.

CHAPTER 13

A Machine Learning Algorithm for Forecasting Customer Churn in the Motor Insurance Industry

REEPU,[1] SANJAY TANEJA,[2,*] MANDEEP SINGH,[3,*] AND ERCAN OZEN[4]

[1]*University School of Business, Chandigarh University, Mohali, Punjab, India*

[2]*Graphic Era (Deemed to be University), Dehradun, Uttarakhand, India*

[3]*AIT-APEX, Chandigarh University, Mohali, Punjab, India*

[4]*Department of Banking and Finance, University of Uşak, Türkiye*

**Corresponding author.*

ABSTRACT

This chapter presents a comprehensive study on forecasting customer churn in the motor insurance industry using a hybrid machine learning approach. Recognizing the high cost of customer acquisition and the strategic importance of retention, the study proposes a predictive model combining Grey Wolf Optimization (GWO) with Kernel Extreme Learning Machine (KELM) to enhance churn prediction accuracy. Drawing on real-world motor insurance datasets, the model identifies key behavioral and policy-related factors contributing to customer attrition, such as policy claims, premium changes, policy benefits, and servicing consistency. The methodology includes robust data preprocessing using Expectation Maximization, model training, and evaluation through confusion matrices and ROC curve analysis. The study demonstrates that the hybrid GWO-KELM model significantly outperforms

Transforming Business Finance in the Digital Era.
Sanjay Taneja, Mohammad Kashif, Ercan Özen, and Luan Vardari (Eds.)
© 2026 Apple Academic Press, Inc. Co-published with CRC Press (Taylor & Francis)

DOI: 10.1201/9781998511235-13

traditional classifiers in forecasting churn and offers actionable insights for customer segmentation and targeted retention strategies. The findings support the strategic application of machine learning to mitigate churn risk and drive sustainable growth in the insurance sector.

13.1 INTRODUCTION

In the realm of motor insurance, companies often dedicate a significant portion of their resources, time, and energy toward acquiring new business. While it is crucial to replace lost clients and expand into new markets, the primary objective remains maintaining relationships with existing or past customers. In today's landscape, where consumers are more discerning and competition is fierce, retaining customers has become paramount for motor insurance organizations. Through literature review, it has been found that the cost of acquiring new customers can be up to five times greater than that of retaining current ones. Furthermore, even a small increase in customer retention can have a positive impact on an organization's revenue. Therefore, while seeking new business opportunities is important, it should not come at the expense of neglecting existing customer relationships.

Having multiple insurance policies with the same organization increases the chances of renewing policies. When a customer cancels their policies, it is called "churning." Predicting when customers might churn can help motor insurance companies take steps to keep them as customers. It's important for companies to retain their existing customers because acquiring new ones is difficult and expensive. Losing customers means losing revenue, which harms the company's reputation and growth. The study proposes using churn prediction to help with retention efforts.

With the intensifying competition in the motor insurance market, insurance companies have become increasingly aware of the need to put forth more effort into retaining existing clients and preventing them from switching to other competitors. Acquiring new customers is a complex process, making it essential for motor insurance organizations to maintain a low churn rate by keeping their old clients satisfied. This has prompted researchers to develop methods for predicting customer churn in order to improve company performance. The consistent decline in retention rates within the motor insurance industry has been identified as a key factor motivating research on customer churn prediction. By identifying users who are likely to switch providers beforehand, motor insurance companies can focus their resources on retaining these individuals rather than contacting every policyholder indiscriminately. It is this motivation that drives our proposed research project.

13.2 RESEARCH CHALLENGES

Insurance companies, specifically vehicle insurance, struggle with retaining customers due to policies being renewed annually and competition from other providers. Predicting customer churn is important for improving service quality and gaining new users. However, it is difficult to predict unless customers directly contact the organization with complaints. The attrition of customers, or the rate at which they switch to competitors, is a major issue that results in declining revenue. To address this, organizations use various methods for forecasting attrition and building better customer relationships. Retaining existing high-risk customers is a vital issue in insurance segments and requires identifying risk parameters and analyzing the time until a churn event.

Motor insurance providers face increasing competition and struggle to retain customers due to factors like service quality and benefits offered. High churn rates make it difficult to keep customers, who often switch for better offers from other providers. Developing effective methods to overcome these challenges is a difficult task as customer behaviors and intentions vary greatly.

13.3 RESEARCH AIM

Our work aims to create a machine learning model to predict customer churn for motor insurance companies. We designed an accurate prediction model using an optimization strategy. This study highlights the importance of machine learning in real-time applications for organizational growth.

13.4 OBJECTIVES OF THE STUDY

- To develop a model with high accuracy in prediction when compared to the existing data mining algorithms.
- To apply the developed machine learning model to determine the most significant factors for customer attrition in the motor insurance sector.
- To develop customer segments using the developed model by applying the machine learning algorithm for the prediction of the attrition rate of customers in the vehicle insurance sector.

13.5 REVIEW OF LITERATURE

Research focuses on framework structure and uses multiple datasets to investigate potential expansions in findings. The under-sampling method accidentally selects a record set suitable for predicting attrition. Neural network models show high scores, prompting exploration of hyperparameter tuning to improve prediction accuracy (Scriney, Nie et al., 2020).

OCSVM under-sampling improves classifier performance by extracting support vectors from the majority class and combining them with the minority class. Multiple kernels were used to test their impact on unstable datasets. Projected under-sampling simplified system construction and produced significant results when compared to other works (Sunderkumar, Ravi et al., 2015).

Educated customers churn due to insurer attitude, industry workers care about brand names, and low-importance customers prioritize policy timeframes. The insurer-customer relationship affects churn. Dropping churn customers is possible. Results help managers prevent client attrition and switching to competitors (Soeini and Rodpysh, 2012).

Reducing churn customers is a major concern in client relationship management and advertising, especially in fields like telecommunications, finance, and insurance. Researchers are studying how to create an index formula to understand why customers leave. They developed a formula using six classification methods (Decision tree QUEST, Decision tree C5.0, Decision tree CHAID, Decision trees CART, Bayesian network, Neural network) (Rodpysh, 2013).

A new system called BaYcP has been developed to address customer churn behavior. It uses a two-phase approach: first, data is collected, and a risk profiling score is generated based on decision trees and associated with a threshold value. Then, a prediction model is created using the Bayesian classifier method on suitable topographies based on scores above the threshold. The model has an accuracy of 97.89%, outpacing other models and frameworks (Bhattacharya, Ladha et al., 2020).

13.6 DATA REPROCESSING

Transparency of data is one of the vital qualities of the collected data. It explores the perceptible rate of the data acquisition process. It also assists in making a better decision process. Moreover, it looks for obtaining similar decision outcomes. The preprocessing of the data brings drastic changes in deriving decisions about the data perceptibly.

In this study, the researchers have come up with a way to sample data using something called the Expectation Maximization technique, Figure 13.1. This process has two stages: the E-Step and M-Step. It helps us figure out how likely it is that certain data points belong to certain groups by exploring their probability distributions and learning parameters. This approach works well with different machine learning algorithms, but sometimes it can be difficult if there are variables that we don't know about (called latent variables). By estimating values for these latent variables, we can improve our estimates of maximum likelihood estimation until we get an accurate answer. The researchers also used this approach to estimate missing data in a dataset where some of the information was not observable. They did this by assuming that each process relied on the Gaussian probability distribution and then estimated parameters for those distributions so they could combine and distribute the given points effectively.

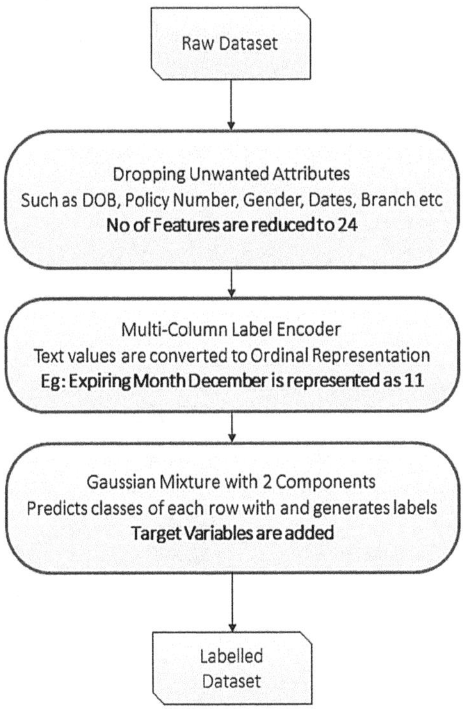

FIGURE 13.1 Data processing.

13.7 DATASET DESCRIPTION

An insurance dataset is collected from a motor insurance company. This is used for experimental purposes. The dataset has the details of each customer recorded throughout the one-and-a-half-month period. It consists of 37 columns and 1,000 rows, in which only relevant features are taken to create the training classifier, shown in Figures 13.2(a) and (b).

13.8 RESULTS AND DISCUSSION

The hybrid classifier is evaluated for its ability to characterize test data sources using various optimal constraints. The accuracy of the algorithm in characterizing test data is also demonstrated. Parameters are set for GWO-KELM to mine similar patterns, utilizing iterative methods such as penalty function, reward function, and feasibility to derive an optimal solution among other complex methods available. A population size of 40 grey wolves is used, with 150 iterations performed on all constrained benchmark functions. Additionally, 30 Monte Carlo runs are executed on each constrained benchmark function for effective validation of the

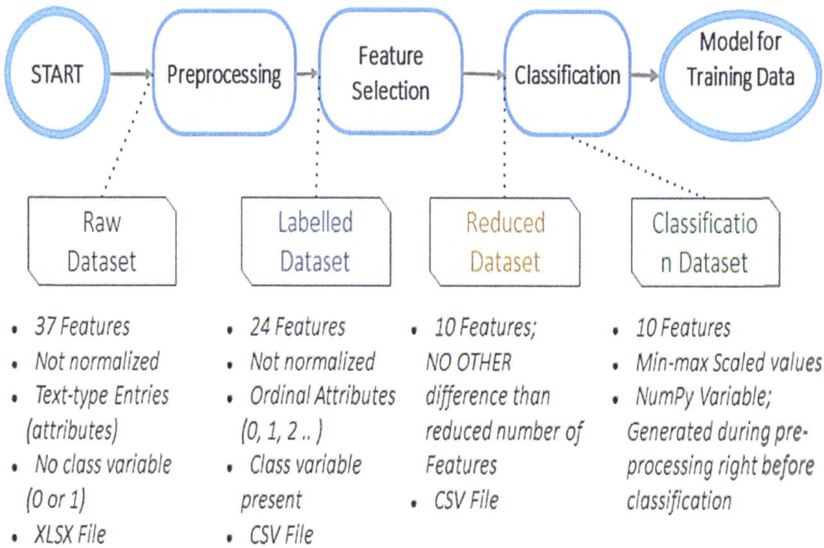

(a)

(Continued...)

1. **Start**
2. **Preprocessing** - Basic Transformations on Dataset before applying any ML algorithm
    a. **Import** Raw Dataset
    b. **Remove Obvious Irrelevant Features** (manual process) present in the Dataset
    c. Apply **Data transformation** to applicable features (Text to Nominal Conversion)
    d. If Dataset has Target Variables, go to step e
        i. As the Data present is assumed to be in Gaussian Distribution, Apply Gaussian Mixture to generate probabilistic model
        ii. Classify and Label the dataset
    e. **Save** Transformed dataset as **Labelled Dataset**
3. **Feature Selection**
    a. Create a Feed Forward Neural Network **(Extreme Learning Machine)** with initial params
    b. Import Labelled Dataset
    c. Use the **Grey Wolf Optimization Algorithm** to identify features and train network s.t -
        i. **Least Entropy** in Softmax, KNN, and K Means algorithms
        ii. **Best** of Multiple **Argument Partitions** are selected
        iii. **Cross-validation** score is the highest for the chosen argument partition
    d. Generate weights of ELM Kernel and save it as a NumPy file
    e. From the results of step (2c), get the names of Features; remove other features
    f. Save dataset as **Reduced Dataset**
4. **Classification**
    a. **Pre-processing:** Do min-max scaling to all variables; Perform train-test split on the DS
    b. **Import** Labelled Dataset and Weights of network generated in previous step
    c. **Train Network** using the Train-Split of Labelled Dataset and **Test Network** using Test-DS
    d. **Replace** the original target variables with predicted labels
    e. Save Dataset as **Classification Dataset**
5. **Model Generation**
   LR_Model = **LogisticRegression**(reduced_dataset, target_variables = predicted_labels)
6. **End**

(b)

FIGURE 13.2 (a) Dataset description; and (b) overall view of algorithm.

proposed GWO algorithm compared to existing machine learning classifiers. An impartial comparison between these algorithms requires parameter settings, which can be a challenging task during execution. For GWO and KELM algorithms, two random vectors r_1 and r_2 are taken from a range of (0,1) while controlling parameters α have linearly decreasing values ranging from 2–0 over the course of iterations; chaotic function variables a=0.5 and b=0.2 are utilized as well. The study objected to detecting the two classes, namely, churners and non-churners. Thus, a confusion matrix is displayed as follows.

Figure 13.3 presents the confusion matrix for hybrid GWO-KELM techniques. It contains two dimensions, wherein the X-dimension relates to the predicted label and the Y-dimension relates to the true label.

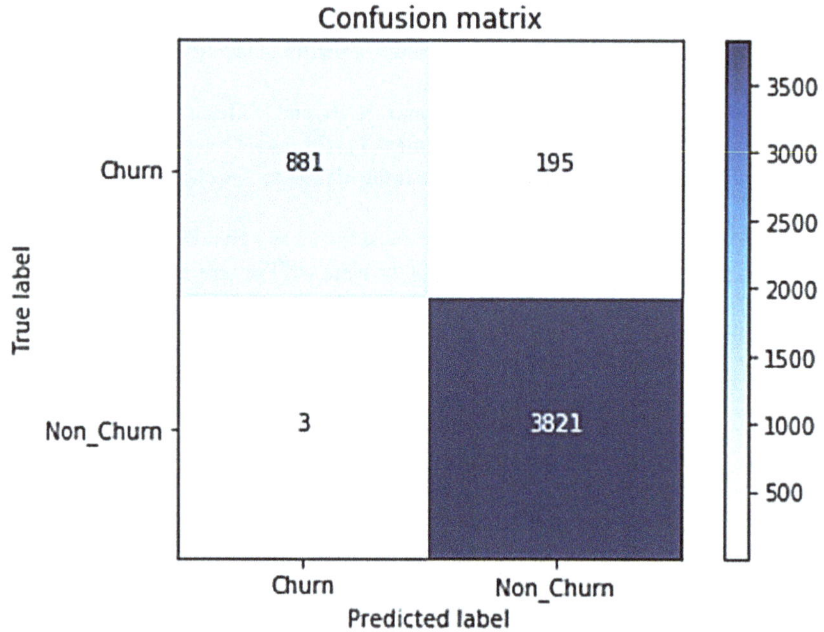

FIGURE 13.3 Confusion matrix for hybrid GWO-KELM.

Figure 13.4 presents the confusion matrix for hybrid GWO-KELM techniques. It contains two dimensions wherein the X-dimension relates to the predicted label and the Y-dimension relates to the true label.

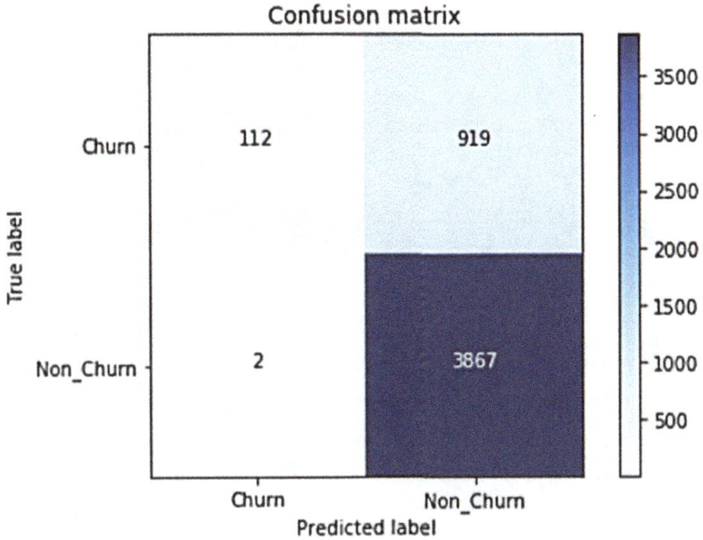

FIGURE 13.4 Confusion matrix for existing, KELM.

Receiver operating characteristics (ROC) is a performance measure investigated in this study. ROC graphs are useful tools for organizing classifiers and visualizing their performance. These graphs have traditionally been used in medical decision-making, but more recently, they have become increasingly popular in machine learning and data mining research. Although seemingly straightforward, there are several common misconceptions and pitfalls that can arise when using ROC graphs.

The classification problems addressed in this study involve two classes: positive and negative labels assigned to each instance I. A classifier maps instances to these labels by predicting the appropriate class membership based on continuous output values associated with different thresholds.

ROC graphs are 2D plots that depict the tradeoff between true positive rates (TP rate) plotted along the y-axis and false positive rates (FP rate) plotted along the x-axis. Each classifier generates an FP rate-TP rate pair that corresponds to a single point on the graph representing its overall accuracy or error rates.

The lower left point of the graph represents perfect classification where no errors occur, whereas the upper right point depicts inequality constraints for positive classifications only. Finally, the arrival rate of perfect classification is represented at point (0,1) in Figure 13.5.

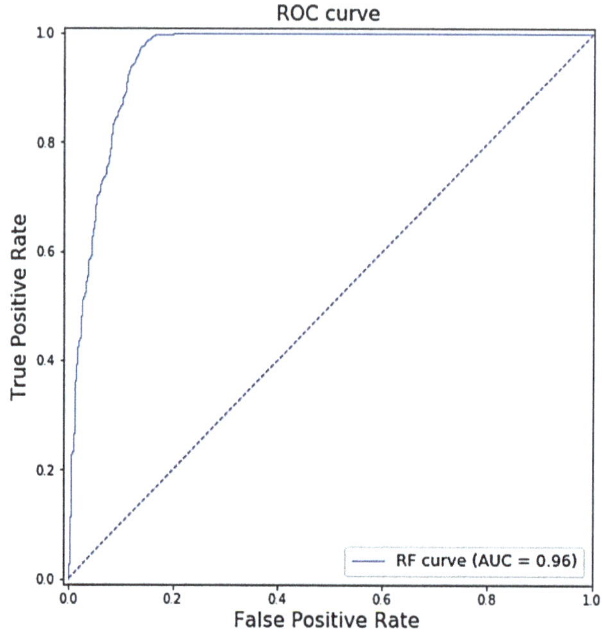

FIGURE 13.5 ROC curve analysis for the hybrid GWO-KELM model.

The concept of an optimal solution is more straightforward in single-objective optimization. The majority of solutions lie in Pareto optimality, where a point is considered Pareto optimal only if it cannot be moved while reducing at least one objective function without increasing any other. Typically, several Pareto optimal points are used to balance objectives and articulate preferences.

There are two types of preference articulation methods: prioritization of preferences and a posteriori articulation of preferences. Prioritization helps users specify the relative importance of objectives or optimization algorithm runs. Scalarization methods merge multiple objectives into a single scalar function by incorporating parameters such as components, weights, or exponential functions with a priori articulation of preferences.

The business interpretation of this can be detailed as follows. In a dataset initially containing XX influencing parameters, the selection has been refined to the nine most influential parameters:

1. **Customer Type:** Individual customers tend to renew policies more than corporate customers.

2. **Policy Add-Ons:** Policies without the benefit of Nil Depreciation tend to renew more frequently compared to policies with other add-on benefits. Typically, in the market, this coverage is available only for the first three years of the policy, making it non-existent for policies older than three years.
3. **Claims History:** Policies without claims in the previous year are more likely to be renewed compared to policies with claims. The higher churn rate among claim-holders may indicate dissatisfaction with the claims process.
4. **Branch Consistency:** Customers who continue with the same servicing branch are more likely to renew their policy compared to those whose servicing branch was changed during the policy tenure.
5. **Renewal Premium:** Churn is lower when the renewal premium is lower than the current premium. Customers tend to leave when the premium increases due to factors such as the loss of a No-Claim Bonus (NCB), policy break-in, rate revisions, or location changes.
6. **Car Type:** Small car owners are more likely to renew their policies compared to customers with high-engine-capacity cars.
7. **Sum Insured:** Churn is lower for policies where the sum insured falls within the lower bands (typically for smaller or older cars with lower insured declared values [IDVs]) compared to policies with higher sum insured amounts.
8. **Policy Expiry Timing:** Policies due for renewal in the last quarter of the financial year (January–March) tend to have lower churn rates compared to those expiring in other months.
9. **Policy Count per Customer:** Customers with up to two policies with the same insurer exhibit lower churn rates. A few examples of additional customer retention initiatives that can be taken up by the insurance companies based on the results observed are listed below:

   i. Increase efforts to retain good and profitable corporate customer policies.
   ii. Improve "customer experience" during claims.

iii. Keep the customer servicing branch the same as far as possible.
iv. On a case-by-case basis, look at additional offers to good customers for whom the renewal premium has gone up compared to the expiring policy premium.
v. Increase efforts to retain good customers with cars that have higher engine sizes or where the sum insured falls in higher sum insured bands.
vi. Can increase efforts to retain good and profitable customer policies in the period from Q1 to Q3 of the financial year. Another challenge in Customer Churn Prediction (CCP) is the unavailability of relevant information. Undoubtedly, for CCP, a vast amount of information is being gathered, but sometimes the actual or desired data required for analysis will be unavailable.

In our study, the collected data samples for the preprocessing stage have optimal constraints. After the model is prepared with astounding accuracy, it must have the capacity to anticipate the list of churners from the genuine dataset, which does not include irrelevant information. In common terms, identifying which types of churn patterns occur or the reasons for churns is tedious to determine. This results in a loss of profit for the company. Sometimes, for predicting customer actions, information from multiple sources is explored and integrated to derive a specific result. As this information is multifarious in nature, during information transfer, a vast amount of noisy information might get added, thus creating problems. Therefore, the information gathered must be reprocessed by discarding the noisy information. The preprocessing step usually consumes a significant amount of time. In CCP, customers' privacy is also at risk. Customers get into trouble while providing their details to companies. As companies use customers' personal details for their own interests, customers' privacy will be at greater risk. This refrains customers from giving their strategic data and thus poses a big hindrance to the CCP procedure. While studying or understanding customer actions, generally, the transactional or purchasing actions are considered, whereas the deep analysis of customers/users and their situations is greatly ignored. The transactional activities of customers are dependent on their attitudinal, social, physiological, and many other unjustifiable factors. However, the consideration of all possible factors affecting CCP is explored. Many prediction frameworks employ customers' transactional data alone for CCP. However, the information captured while performing numerous transactions by customers is inadequate for CCP, as it does not provide sufficient proof for predicting the churn action of customers. Thus, the available raw information must be converted into optimal knowledge for acquiring the required inferences.

KEYWORDS

- **algorithms**
- **churning**
- **customer churn**
- **data mining**
- **machine learning**
- **motor insurance**
- **neural network**
- **real-time applications**

REFERENCES

Abdelhadi, S., Elbahnasy, K., & Abdelsalam, M. (2020). A proposed model to predict auto insurance claims using machine learning techniques. *Journal of Theoretical and Applied Information Technology, 98*, 3428–3437.

Anil Kumar, D., & Ravi, V. (2008). Predicting credit card customer churn in banks using data mining. *International Journal of Data Analysis Techniques and Strategies, 1*(1), 4–28.

Bagheri, M., Valipour, M., & Amin, V. (2012). The bankruptcy prediction in Tehran shareholding using neural network and its comparison with logistic regression. *TJMCS, 5*(3), 219–228.

Baicker, K., & Chandra, A. (2006). The labour market effects of rising health insurance premiums. *Journal of Labour Economics, 24*(3), 443–474.

Bhattacharya, P., Ladha, A., Kumar, A., Verma, A., & Bodkhe, U. (2020). BaY cP: A novel Bayesian customer churn prediction scheme for Telecom sector. In *2020 Sixth International Conference on Parallel, Distributed and Grid Computing (PDGC)* (pp. 260–265). IEEE.

Coussement, K., & Van den Poel, D. (2008). Integrating the voice of customers through call center emails into a decision support system for churn prediction. *Information & Management, 45*(3), 164–174.

Dasgupta, K., Singh, R., Viswanathan, B., Chakraborty, D., Mukherjea, S., Nanavati, A. A., & Joshi, A. (2008). Social ties and their relevance to churn in mobile telecom networks. In *Proceedings of the 11th International Conference on Extending Database Technology: Advances in Database Technology (EDBT 08)*, Nantes, France (pp. 668–677).

General Insurance Council (GIC). (2019–2020). *Yearbook 2019–20.*

Insurance Regulatory and Development Authority of India (IRDAI). (2019–2020). *Annual Report 2019–20.*

Kaur, M., & Kang, S. (2016). Market basket analysis: Identify the changing trends of market data using association rule mining. *Procedia Computer Science, 85*, 78–85.

Lalwani, P., Mishra, M. K., Chadha, J. S., & Sethi, P. (2021). Customer churn prediction system: A machine learning approach. *Computing*, 1–24.

Larivière, B., & Van den Poel, D. (2005). Predicting customer retention and profitability by using random forest and regression techniques. *Expert Systems with Applications, 29*(2), 472–484.

Rodpysh, K. V. (2013). Providing a method for determining the index of customer churn in industry. *International Journal of Information Technology, Control and Automation (IJITCA), 3*, 45–53.

Soeini, R. A., & Rodpysh, K. V. (2012). Applying data mining to insurance customer churn management. *International Proceedings of Computer Science and Information Technology, 30*, 82–92.

CHAPTER 14

The Utilization of Machine Learning Techniques in the Prediction and Manipulation of Consumer Purchase Intentions

SNEHA SINGH,* DEEPAK KAUSHAL, and MUSKAN SINGH

Department of Management Studies, Graphic Era (Deemed to be University), Dehradun, Uttarakhand, India

*Corresponding author.

ABSTRACT

This chapter explores the transformative role of machine learning (ML) in analyzing and predicting consumer purchase intentions within the evolving landscape of digital commerce. As traditional models of consumer behavior, such as the Theory of Planned Behavior and the Fishbein Model, fall short in addressing the complexities of modern data-rich environments, ML emerges as a powerful tool to decode patterns and personalize marketing strategies. The study discusses key ML applications, including predictive modeling, sentiment analysis, and recommendation systems, all of which contribute to a nuanced understanding of consumer decision-making processes. It also examines the strategic impact of these technologies on marketing—enabling targeted advertising, dynamic pricing, and personalized user experiences. Alongside the benefits, the chapter critically addresses ethical concerns, including data privacy, algorithmic bias, and consumer manipulation. Future directions emphasize the need for transparent AI practices, explainability, interdisciplinary collaboration, and responsible data governance. By integrating ML with consumer analytics, businesses can achieve deeper engagement and more ethically grounded marketing strategies in the digital age.

Transforming Business Finance in the Digital Era.
Sanjay Taneja, Mohammad Kashif, Ercan Özen, and Luan Vardari (Eds.)
© 2026 Apple Academic Press, Inc. Co-published with CRC Press (Taylor & Francis)

DOI: 10.1201/9781998511235-14

14.1 INTRODUCTION

In recent times, organizations have been escalating through a more powerful, vague, composite, and economic context in which socioeconomic, environmental, and technical aspects of the current competitive advantage are frequently called into question by changes, which makes it ephemeral and fleeting (Mariani and Wamba, 2020). Enormous technology transformations are about to occur, and among the biggest disruptors will be immersive technologies, which will change how consumers behave (Ambika et al., 2023; Vlačić et al., 2021). In the contemporary landscape of commerce, understanding consumer behavior is paramount for businesses seeking to thrive in an increasingly competitive market. The traditional methods of market research and consumer studies, while foundational, often fall short in capturing the intricacies of modern purchasing decisions, and as a result, the availability of web-based data sources emerged as an extension to traditional surveillance systems (Gupta and Katarya, 2020). Customer analytics and other business analytics technologies provide businesses with a competitive advantage that can investigate consumer behavior patterns through the application of big data analytics (BDA) and data mining (Khade, 2016; Prasad and Ghosal, 2022;). Within this data deluge lies a wealth of information that, if properly harnessed, can offer profound insights into consumer preferences, motivations, and ultimately, their purchase intentions. Consumer purchase intention, the inclination of an individual to make a purchase, serves as a pivotal precursor to actual buying behavior. Recognizing the complexity and multidimensionality of this phenomenon, businesses are turning to advanced analytical tools to decipher the patterns hidden within the vast datasets at their disposal. Machine learning, a subset of artificial intelligence, has emerged as a powerful ally in this pursuit, offering the ability to process, analyze, and derive meaningful conclusions from immense datasets at a speed and scale beyond the capabilities of traditional methodologies. According to Kunz et al. (2019), emerging service technologies such as artificial intelligence, robotics, and augmented reality are dramatically altering the customer experience in sectors that provide services.

This research aims to delve into the symbiotic relationship between machine learning and consumer purchase intention. By amalgamating insights from psychology, marketing, and computer science, we seek to unravel the nuanced dynamics that influence consumer decision-making in an era where digital interactions play a central role in shaping preferences. The integration of machine learning into the analysis of consumer behavior represents a paradigm shift, allowing businesses to move beyond conventional demographic profiling and embrace a more personalized and adaptive approach to marketing. As we embark on this exploration, it is essential to recognize the transformative potential of machine learning in revolutionizing not only how businesses understand consumer behavior but also in shaping strategies to influence and predict purchase intentions. The subsequent sections of this chapter will delve into the existing literature on consumer behavior, examine the various applications of machine learning in this domain, and critically evaluate the impact of these technologies on marketing strategies. Additionally, we will navigate the ethical considerations and challenges associated with the adoption of machine learning in consumer behavior analysis, providing a holistic perspective on the implications of this evolving intersection of technology and commerce. Through this comprehensive analysis, we endeavor to contribute to a nuanced understanding of the role machine learning plays in decoding the intricacies of consumer purchase intention in the digital age.

14.2 LITERATURE REVIEW

Consumer behavior has long been a focal point in marketing research, aiming to unravel the intricacies of decision-making processes that precede a purchase. Traditional models, rooted in psychological and sociological theories, have laid the groundwork for understanding the factors influencing consumer intentions. Ajzen (1991) introduced and elucidated the theory of planned behavior (TPB), expanding on Fishbein and Ajzen's (1977) original idea of reasoned action. The theory of reasoned action emphasizes that attitude and subjective norms have an impact on a person's intention to engage in a given behavior (Fishbein and Ajzen, 1975). The idea of reasoned action concentrated on forecasting human intentions with regard to making decisions, making purchases, and so forth. Perceived behavioral control is an additional latent variable that is included in TPB (Sharma and Foropon, 2019). TPB examines three factors—attitude, subjective norms, and perceived behavioral control—in an effort to determine how consumers want to behave in a particular way (Giampietri et al., 2018). Additionally, TPB emphasizes that the best indicator of consumer behavior is intention (Nahapetyan et al., 2019). Similarly, the Fishbein Model emphasizes the role of beliefs and attitudes in shaping behavioral intentions. While these models provide valuable theoretical frameworks, they often face challenges in adapting to the dynamic and data-rich environment of the digital age. The advent of machine learning has revolutionized the study of consumer behavior, offering a new paradigm for researchers and marketers alike. The literature on this intersection has expanded rapidly, reflecting the urgency of adapting to a landscape where online interactions and transactions generate massive amounts of data.

14.2.1 TRADITIONAL MODELS OF CONSUMER BEHAVIOR

The theory of planned behavior and the Fishbein Model, though influential, exhibit limitations in the context of contemporary data analytics. These models rely heavily on self-reported data and may struggle to accommodate the multifaceted nature of digital interactions. The dichotomy between traditional and digital consumer behavior necessitates a more adaptive and data-driven approach.

14.2.2 MACHINE LEARNING APPROACHES

1. **Supervised Machine Learning:** When the guided machine learning algorithms use the labeled training data, they learn from their mistakes. They look at the training data and suggest a tool that can be used to map new data sets. There are two main types of supervised learning: classification and regression. This type of information is limited and can be either binary (e.g., in anomaly detection) or multitudinous (e.g., in speech and face recognition). The regression method finds the link between a dependent variable and one or more independent factors. This is often used to predict what will happen in the future (Abbas et al., 2022).
2. **Unsupervised Learning:** In unsupervised learning, all incoming data and samples are not labeled. In this kind of learning, the learned model won't use input-output classes. Dimensionality reduction, clustering, and density estimates can be used to describe the learning process. In math and statistics problems, the clustering method is used to group data. If you need to use this method for something unexpected, like getting unclassified data from anywhere (Lugmayr et al., 2019), you can.

3. **Reinforcement Learning:** Between supervised learning and unsupervised learning, which does not involve label information, reinforcement learning (RL) is regarded as an intermediate form of learning. There is a correlation between RL and the value of incentives for making sound decisions and maximizing benefits. According to Mnih et al. (2015), you can accomplish this by using either policy search or value function approximation.

As the literature suggests, the evolution from traditional models to machine learning approaches signifies a paradigm shift in the study of consumer behavior. Machine learning's ability to uncover latent patterns, predict consumer behavior, and facilitate personalized marketing strategies holds immense promise for businesses navigating the complexities of the modern market. The subsequent sections of this chapter will delve deeper into specific applications of machine learning, exploring how these techniques are practically employed to predict and influence consumer purchase intentions and shape the landscape of contemporary marketing research.

14.3 MACHINE LEARNING APPLICATIONS IN CONSUMER PURCHASE INTENTION

The integration of machine learning in analyzing and predicting consumer purchase intention brings forth a multitude of applications, each contributing to a more nuanced understanding of the complex decision-making processes that precede a purchase. These applications are:

1. **Predictive Modeling:** Machine learning, particularly supervised learning, has proven to be a powerful tool in predictive modeling for consumer purchase intention. By leveraging historical data, these models can identify patterns and relationships between various factors and the likelihood of a consumer making a purchase. Regression analysis, for instance, allows researchers to model the quantitative relationship between predictor variables (such as online behavior, demographics, and historical purchase data) and the target variable of purchase intention. Classification algorithms, on the other hand, can categorize consumers into groups based on their likelihood to make a purchase, enabling businesses to tailor marketing strategies to specific segments. Predictive modeling not only aids in understanding current consumer behavior but

also provides a forward-looking perspective, allowing businesses to anticipate future trends and preferences. This application is particularly valuable in dynamic and competitive markets where staying ahead of consumer preferences is crucial for success.

2. **Sentiment Analysis:** The process of automatically extracting sentiments, emotions, and views from written language is known as sentiment analysis (Lombardo et al., 2019). The primary benefit of sentiment analysis is its capacity to precisely detect and categorize users' attitudes and sentiments (whether positive, negative, or neutral) in communications to gauge their feelings over specific goods, topics, or services (Agüero-Torales et al., 2019). Natural language processing (NLP) techniques, a subset of machine learning, enable sentiment analysis, a critical tool for understanding the emotional underpinnings of consumer behavior. By analyzing textual data from sources such as customer reviews, social media comments, and product feedback, machine learning algorithms can discern sentiment and identify positive or negative attitudes toward a product or brand. As a result of the widespread use of social media platforms, the quantity of data generated by users is continuously expanding at an exponential rate. This has resulted in the requirement for an increase in the number of people, the length of time, and the amount of work required to manage the growing volume and variety of data. On the other hand, monitoring the emotions of the public in a timely manner is of utmost importance for businesses and government organizations at the present moment (Xu et al., 2022). Sentiment analysis contributes to the comprehension of the emotional factors influencing purchase intention. Positive sentiment may indicate a strong affinity for a product, while negative sentiment can reveal areas for improvement. Additionally, sentiment analysis can capture nuances such as sarcasm or irony, providing a more accurate representation of consumer opinions. Businesses can use these insights to tailor marketing strategies, address customer concerns, and enhance overall customer satisfaction.

3. **Recommendation Systems:** A hallmark application of machine learning, play a pivotal role in influencing consumer purchase intentions. These systems leverage collaborative filtering and

content-based filtering algorithms to analyze user behavior and preferences, generating personalized recommendations for products or services. Collaborative filtering considers the preferences of similar users, recommending items that users with similar tastes have liked. Content-based filtering, on the other hand, recommends items based on the characteristics of the items and the user's preferences. Hybrid approaches, combining both collaborative and content-based methods, further enhance the accuracy and relevance of recommendations. By providing personalized suggestions, recommendation systems not only enhance the user experience but also influence purchase decisions. The more accurately a system understands and predicts a consumer's preferences, the more likely it is to guide them toward relevant products, ultimately increasing the likelihood of a purchase.

These machine learning applications collectively contribute to a comprehensive understanding of consumer purchase intentions. By harnessing the power of predictive modeling, sentiment analysis, and recommendation systems, businesses can tailor their strategies to align with individual preferences, emotions, and behaviors, fostering a more personalized and effective approach to marketing in the digital age. The subsequent sections of this chapter will delve into the impact of these applications on marketing strategies and explore the challenges and ethical considerations associated with their implementation in consumer behavior analysis. Figure 14.1 represents the machine learning approaches.

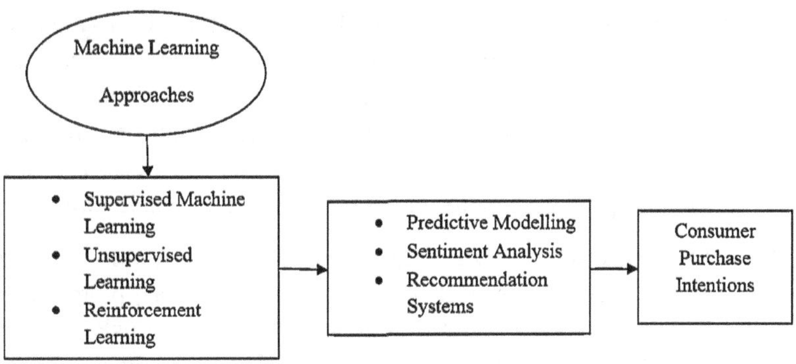

FIGURE 14.1 The conceptual framework.

Source: Compiled by Author.

14.4 IMPACT ON MARKETING STRATEGIES

The integration of machine learning applications in understanding and predicting consumer purchase intention has a profound impact on shaping and optimizing marketing strategies. These technologies empower businesses to move beyond generic, mass-market approaches, enabling a more personalized, targeted, and effective engagement with consumers such as:

1. **Targeted Advertising:** Machine learning algorithms, through predictive modeling, enable businesses to craft highly targeted advertising campaigns. By analyzing historical data and identifying patterns in consumer behavior, these algorithms can predict which individuals are more likely to respond positively to specific advertisements. This enables businesses to allocate advertising budgets more efficiently, reaching the audiences most likely to convert into customers. Targeted advertising minimizes wasted resources on irrelevant audiences, and based on their predicted purchase intentions, businesses can create a more resonant connection with potential customers.
2. **Personalized Marketing Campaigns:** The insights derived from sentiment analysis and recommendation systems contribute to the development of personalized marketing campaigns. Sentiment analysis allows businesses to understand the emotional context surrounding their products or services, helping them tailor marketing messages to resonate with consumer sentiments. Positive sentiments can be amplified, while concerns expressed in negative sentiments can be addressed proactively. Recommendation systems, by providing personalized product or service suggestions, contribute to creating a more individualized customer experience. Whether through email marketing, website recommendations, or other channels, businesses can leverage these systems to offer relevant and appealing products, increasing the likelihood of conversion.
3. **Optimization of Product Recommendations:** Machine-learning-driven recommendation systems play a pivotal role in optimizing product recommendations. By continuously analyzing user behavior and preferences, these systems adapt to changing consumer tastes and trends. Businesses can dynamically adjust their product recommendations based on real-time data, ensuring

that suggestions remain relevant and enticing. Optimized product recommendations not only enhance the customer experience but also drive sales. As consumers are presented with items that align closely with their preferences and purchase history, the likelihood of making a purchase increases. This level of personalization contributes to building customer loyalty and satisfaction.

4. **Dynamic Pricing Strategies:** Machine learning applications also impact pricing strategies through dynamic pricing models. By analyzing market conditions, competitor pricing, and consumer behavior, machine learning algorithms can recommend optimal pricing strategies. Variable pricing enables companies to instantly modify their prices, responding to changes in demand, the competitive landscape, or other external factors. Dynamic pricing strategies can enhance competitiveness, maximize revenue, and improve overall market positioning. By aligning prices with consumer expectations and market dynamics, businesses can optimize pricing strategies to attract price-sensitive consumers and maximize profitability.

In summary, the impact of machine learning on marketing strategies is transformative. From targeted advertising to personalized campaigns and optimized product recommendations, these technologies empower businesses to navigate the complexities of consumer behavior with unprecedented precision. The next sections of this chapter will delve into the challenges and ethical considerations associated with the adoption of machine learning in consumer behavior analysis, providing a balanced perspective on the implications of these technologies.

14.5 CHALLENGES AND ETHICAL CONSIDERATIONS

As businesses increasingly leverage machine learning applications to understand and influence consumer purchase intentions, a range of challenges and ethical considerations emerge. Navigating these issues is critical to ensuring responsible and transparent use of these technologies including:

1. **Privacy Concerns:** Privacy is often a problem. To share data and information in IoT settings, smart devices like sensors and wearable technology are used. Users don't always know where and how their personal data is shared through these devices. Smart IoT devices

store private and sensitive information about their users and clients, which could be used in a bad way. For IoT devices to talk to each other, they all need security standards like encryption and authentication. Privacy breaches, leaks, and dangers are major problems that keep people from using these technologies (Ferrag and Shu, 2021).

2. **Data Security and Integrity:** To make a machine learning method work correctly, it is very important to use accurate data for both datasets and training data. If you have a training dataset with bad data, it might stop you from using a certain learning method. To keep the IoT network safe, ML methods must use authenticated training datasets (Musonda et al., 2019). Also, any hacker can easily learn the type of attack and the weak spots in the device, as well as change the dataset that is used in the ML method.
3. **Backup Security Mechanisms:** It is usually hard to correctly describe and guess a cyber-attack on an IoT setting if the defense policy is "bad" during the learning process. This can sometimes go wrong and cause IoT networks to lose a lot of data. Backup security techniques might also be able to solve this issue of preventing the exploration of IoT systems during the learning process. ML-based security methods need to be used in more systems to deal with this problem and make IoT services more reliable, resilient, and safe by lowering the chances of choosing bad policies.
4. **Computational Cost:** It is necessary to have a significant quantity of datasets for training along with an intricate method for feature extraction in order to use many machine learning-based techniques. This results in high processing costs and an increase in the complexity of the system. On account of this, it is difficult to discover novel machine learning approaches that have minimal costs associated with communication and processing (Ferrag et al., 2021).
5. **Infrastructure Issues:** Attackers can always get through the software more easily if the system is not strong. This is also called a "zero-day attack," and it is very hard to spot with normal security measures and plans. To make an IoT system that is safe, it is necessary to build a strong and smart infrastructure (Hussain et al., 2019). Safety and security features must be thought about and built into the IoT system at all stages.

6. **Bias in Algorithms:** It is possible for machine learning algorithms to maintain and even exacerbate preexisting biases if they are trained on flawed historical data. This is because the algorithms are trained on historical data. It is possible for this to lead to discriminatory outcomes, in which particular groups of customers are treated unfairly or are not given opportunities.
7. **Lack of Interpretability:** Machine learning models, especially complex ones like neural networks, are often considered "black boxes" that provide predictions without clear explanations. This lack of interpretability raises challenges in understanding how and why a particular prediction was made. Interpretable machine learning models and explainability tools are essential to addressing this challenge. Ensuring that stakeholders, including consumers, can comprehend the decision-making processes of these models enhances trust and accountability in the use of machine learning for consumer behavior analysis.
8. **Manipulation of Consumer Behavior:** While the goal of machine learning applications is often to predict and understand consumer behavior, there is potential for these technologies to be used to manipulate consumer choices. Personalized recommendations and targeted advertising, if not ethically managed, can exploit vulnerabilities in consumer decision-making. Ethical considerations should be embedded in the design and deployment of machine learning systems. Businesses must prioritize transparency, honesty, and consumer welfare to avoid unintended consequences and potential harm resulting from manipulative practices.

In conclusion, addressing the challenges and ethical considerations associated with machine learning in consumer behavior analysis is crucial for fostering trust, safeguarding privacy, and ensuring the responsible use of these technologies. The next section of this chapter will explore future directions and offer recommendations for businesses and researchers to navigate these challenges effectively.

14.6 FUTURE DIRECTIONS AND RECOMMENDATIONS

As the field of machine learning in consumer behavior analysis continues to evolve, several future directions and recommendations emerge.

These considerations aim to guide businesses, researchers, and policy-makers toward responsible and innovative practices in the creation and application of machine learning applications.

1. **Transparent and Ethical AI Practices:** Transparency and ethical considerations should be at the forefront of AI development. Businesses must adopt clear and transparent AI practices, ensuring that consumers are informed about how their data is used, what algorithms are employed, and the potential implications for their privacy. Ethical guidelines, such as those developed by industry associations and regulatory bodies, can serve as a foundation for responsible AI practices.
2. **Interdisciplinary Collaboration:** The complex nature of consumer behavior requires interdisciplinary collaboration between experts in psychology, marketing, computer science, and ethics. Future research should focus on fostering collaboration to develop holistic approaches that integrate insights from diverse disciplines. This interdisciplinary approach can lead to a more comprehensive understanding of consumer behavior, resulting in more effective and ethical machine learning applications.
3. **Explainable AI and Interpretability:** Magnifying the ability and the machine learning models' accessibility is a critical area for outlook research. As consumers and regulatory bodies demand transparency in algorithmic decision-making, the development of explainable AI models and interpretability tools becomes paramount. This ensures that stakeholders can understand and trust the outcomes of machine learning applications.
4. **Continuous Monitoring and Bias Mitigation:** Continuous monitoring of machine learning models is essential to identify and mitigate biases that may emerge over time. Researchers and practitioners should prioritize ongoing assessments of models to ensure fairness and prevent unintended consequences. Implementing bias detection and mitigation strategies should be a standard practice in the creation and application of artificial intelligence (AI) applications.
5. **Privacy-Preserving Techniques:** To address privacy concerns, future research should focus on advancing privacy-preserving techniques. This includes developing methods such as federated

learning, homomorphic encryption, and differential privacy, which allow the analysis of data without exposing sensitive information. Privacy-preserving techniques can strike a balance between extracting valuable insights and safeguarding individual privacy.

6. **Responsible Data Governance:** Putting strong information oversight procedures in place is crucial to ensuring the dependable use of consumer data. This involves clearly defining data ownership, implementing secure data storage and transmission practices, and adhering to relevant data protection regulations. A commitment to responsible data governance builds trust with consumers and regulatory authorities.
7. **Collaboration with Regulatory Bodies:** Collaboration between businesses and regulatory bodies is essential to developing and enforcing standards for the ethical use of machine learning in consumer behavior analysis. Proactive engagement with regulators can contribute to the creation of guidelines that balance innovation with consumer protection. Businesses should stay informed about evolving regulations and work collaboratively to ensure compliance.
8. **Ethical Guidelines for Advertising and Marketing:** Given the potential for machine learning applications to influence consumer behavior through advertising and marketing, the development and adherence to ethical guidelines in this domain are crucial. Industry associations and stakeholders should work together to establish ethical standards that prioritize consumer welfare, prevent manipulation, and ensure transparent practices in advertising and marketing strategies.

To sum up, the aforementioned suggestions and future directions are meant to serve as a roadmap for the ethical creation and implementation of machine learning applications for the study of consumer behavior. By prioritizing transparency, ethical considerations, and collaboration, businesses, and researchers can contribute to the advancement of technology while ensuring that it aligns with societal values and consumer expectations. The comprehensive integration of these recommendations can lead to a more ethical, transparent, and effective use of machine learning in understanding and influencing consumer purchase intention.

14.7 CONCLUSION

In the rapidly evolving landscape of consumer behavior analysis, the integration of machine learning applications has brought about an exciting period of opportunities and difficulties. This chapter has explored the complex effects of machine learning on understanding and predicting consumer purchase intention, delving into applications, challenges, ethical considerations, and recommendations for the future. The advancements in predictive modeling, sentiment analysis, and recommendation systems driven by machine learning have reshaped the way businesses understand and interact with consumers. Predictive models empower businesses to anticipate trends and tailor their strategies to specific consumer segments, while sentiment analysis provides a nuanced understanding of emotional factors influencing purchase decisions. Recommendation systems, through personalized suggestions, enhance user experiences and significantly impact purchase intention.

However, there are difficulties and ethical issues that come with machine learning's transformative power. Privacy concerns, bias in algorithms, the lack of interpretability, the potential for manipulation, and security risks demand careful navigation. Future research and industry practices must address these issues to ensure the responsible development and deployment of machine learning applications. The recommendations put forth in this chapter advocate for transparent and ethical AI practices, interdisciplinary collaboration, explainable AI, continuous monitoring and bias mitigation, privacy-preserving techniques, responsible data governance, collaboration with regulatory bodies, and ethical guidelines for advertising and marketing. These recommendations serve as a roadmap for businesses, researchers, and policymakers to navigate the complexities of machine learning in consumer behavior analysis while prioritizing consumer welfare and societal values. As we move forward, the responsible use of machine learning in consumer behavior analysis will play a pivotal role in shaping not only the future of marketing strategies but also the ethical foundations of how businesses engage with their audiences. By embracing these recommendations and addressing the challenges head-on, stakeholders can contribute to a future where technology and consumer interests harmoniously coexist, fostering a digital landscape that is both innovative and ethical.

KEYWORDS

- **artificial intelligence**
- **consumer purchase intention**
- **datasets**
- **digital interactions**
- **machine learning**
- **sentiment analysis**

REFERENCES

Abbas, G., Mehmood, A., Carsten, M., Epiphaniou, G., & Lloret, J. (2022). Safety, security and privacy in machine learning based Internet of Things. *Journal of Sensor and Actuator Networks, 11*(3), 38. Available at: https://www.mdpi.com/2224-2708/11/3/38 (accessed on 17 January 2025).

Agüero-Torales, M. M., Cobo, M. J., Herrera-Viedma, E., & López-Herrera, A. G. (2019). A cloud-based tool for sentiment analysis in reviews about restaurants on TripAdvisor. *Procedia Computer Science, 162*, 392–399. Available at https://www.sciencedirect.com/science/article/pii/S1877050919320125 (accessed on 17 January 2025).

Ajzen, I. (1991). The theory of planned behavior. *Organizational Behavior and Human Decision Processes, 50*(2), 179–211.

Ambika, A., Shin, H., & Jain, V. (2023). Immersive technologies and consumer behavior: A systematic review of two decades of research. *Australian Journal of Management*, 1–25. Available at: https://journals.sagepub.com/doi/abs/10.1177/03128962231181429?journalCode=auma (accessed on 17 January 2025).

Ferrag, M. A., & Shu, L. (2021). The performance evaluation of blockchain-based security and privacy systems for the Internet of Things: A tutorial. *IEEE Internet of Things Journal, 8*(24), 17236–17260.

Ferrag, M. A., Shu, L., Friha, O., & Yang, X. (2021). Cyber security intrusion detection for agriculture 4.0: Machine learning-based solutions, datasets, and future directions. *IEEE/CAA Journal of Automatica Sinica, 9*(3), 407–436.

Fishbein, M., & Ajzen, I. (1977). Belief, attitude, intention, and behavior: An introduction to theory and research. *Philosophy and Rhetoric, 10*(2), 130–132.

Giampietri, E., Verneau, F., Del Giudice, T., Carfora, V., & Finco, A. (2018). A theory of planned behavior perspective for investigating the role of trust in consumer purchasing decisions related to short food supply chains. *Food Quality and Preference, 64*, 160–166. Available at: https://www.sciencedirect.com/science/article/abs/pii/S0950329317302161 (accessed on 17 January 2025).

Gupta, A., & Katarya, R. (2020). Social media-based surveillance systems for healthcare using machine learning: A systematic review. *Journal of Biomedical Informatics, 108*, 103500. Available at: https://www.sciencedirect.com/science/article/pii/S1532046420301283 (accessed on 17 January 2025).

Hussain, M., Mehmood, A., Khan, S., Khan, M. A., & Iqbal, Z. (2019). Authentication techniques and methodologies used in wireless body area networks. *Journal of Systems Architecture, 101*, 101655. Available at: https://www.sciencedirect.com/science/article/abs/pii/S138376211930462X (accessed on 17 January 2025).

Khade, A. A. (2016). Performing customer behavior analysis using big data analytics. *Procedia Computer Science, 79*, 986–992. Available at: https://www.sciencedirect.com/science/article/pii/S1877050916002568 (accessed on 17 January 2025).

Kunz, W. H., Heinonen, K., & Lemmink, J. G. (2019). Future service technologies: Is service research on track with business reality? *Journal of Services Marketing, 33*(4), 479–487.

Lombardo, G., Fornacciari, P., Mordonini, M., Sani, L., & Tomaiuolo, M. (2019). A combined approach for the analysis of support groups on Facebook—the case of patients of hidradenitis suppurativa. *Multimedia Tools and Applications, 78*, 3321–3339. Available at https://link.springer.com/article/10.1007/s11042-018-6512-5 (accessed on 17 January 2025).

Lugmayr, A., Danelljan, M., & Timofte, R. (2019). Unsupervised learning for real-world super-resolution. In *2019 IEEE/CVF International Conference on Computer Vision Workshop (ICCVW)* (pp. 3408–3416). IEEE. Available at https://arxiv.org/abs/1909.09629 (accessed on 17 January 2025).

Mariani, M. M., & Wamba, S. F. (2020). Exploring how consumer goods companies innovate in the digital age: The role of big data analytics companies. *Journal of Business Research, 121*, 338–352. Available at: https://www.sciencedirect.com/science/article/abs/pii/S0148296320305956 (accessed on 17 January 2025).

Mnih, V., Kavukcuoglu, K., Silver, D., Rusu, A. A., Veness, J., Bellemare, M. G., & Hassabis, D. (2015). Human-level control through deep reinforcement learning. *Nature, 518*(7540), 529–533.

Musonda, C., Monica, M. K., Nyirenda, M., & Phiri, J. (2019). Security, privacy and integrity in Internet of Things—A review. In *Proceedings of the ICTSZ International Conference in ICTs* (pp. 148–152). Available at: https://www.researchgate.net/publication/332571675_Security_Privacy_and_Integrity_in_Internet_Of_Things_-_A_Review (accessed on 17 January 2025).

Nahapetyan, L., Orpinas, P., Glass, A., & Song, X. (2019). Planning ahead: Using the theory of planned behavior to predict older adults' intentions to use hospice if faced with terminal illness. *Journal of Applied Gerontology, 38*(4), 572–591.

Prasad, B., & Ghosal, I. (2022). Forecasting buying intention through artificial neural network: An algorithmic solution on direct-to-consumer brands. *FIIB Business Review, 11*(4), 405–421.

Sharma, A., & Foropon, C. (2019). Green product attributes and green purchase behavior: A theory of planned behavior perspective with implications for circular economy. *Management Decision, 57*(4), 1018–1042.

Vlačić, B., Corbo, L., e Silva, S. C., & Dabić, M. (2021). The evolving role of artificial intelligence in marketing: A review and research agenda. *Journal of Business Research, 128*, 187–203. Available at: https://www.sciencedirect.com/science/article/abs/pii/S0148296321000643 (accessed on 17 January 2025).

Xu, Q. A., Chang, V., & Jayne, C. (2022). A systematic review of social media-based sentiment analysis: Emerging trends and challenges. *Decision Analytics Journal, 3*, 100073. Available at: https://www.sciencedirect.com/science/article/pii/S2772662222000273 (accessed on 17 January 2025).

CHAPTER 15

Equitable Horizons: Navigating Gender Bias in Investment Behavior Through Machine Learning

VIVEK VERMA* and PRAVEEN SINGH

Department of Management Studies, Graphic Era (Deemed to be University), Dehradun, Uttarakhand, India

*Corresponding author.

ABSTRACT

This chapter explores the intricate intersection of gender bias and machine learning within the domain of investment behavior. As machine learning becomes a cornerstone of financial decision-making—fueling algorithmic trading, portfolio optimization, and risk assessment—it simultaneously raises concerns about the perpetuation of systemic gender biases embedded in historical data and decision-making frameworks. The chapter examines how machine learning models, often trained on biased datasets and lacking interpretability, can inadvertently reinforce gender disparities in the investment landscape. It also delves into the complexities of data-driven decision-making, the challenges posed by algorithmic opacity, and the broader societal and psychological dimensions influencing gendered investment behaviors. Furthermore, the chapter outlines key opportunities for addressing these biases through ethical AI practices, diverse stakeholder engagement, and inclusive data strategies. By integrating technological innovation with a commitment to fairness and equity, this chapter advocates for a reimagined financial ecosystem that upholds inclusivity while harnessing the power of machine learning.

Transforming Business Finance in the Digital Era.
Sanjay Taneja, Mohammad Kashif, Ercan Özen, and Luan Vardari (Eds.)
© 2026 Apple Academic Press, Inc. Co-published with CRC Press (Taylor & Francis)

DOI: 10.1201/9781998511235-15

15.1 INTRODUCTION

In the dynamic landscape of finance, the integration of machine learning (ML) has ushered in a new era of data-driven decision-making and algorithmic trading. While the transformative potential of ML in optimizing investment strategies is evident, an emerging concern looms over the inadvertent perpetuation or exacerbation of gender biases in investment behavior. Gender bias, according to the European Institute for gender equality (2023), refers to "prejudiced actions or thoughts based on the gender-based perception that women are not equal to men in rights and dignity." This chapter delves into the intricate relationship between machine learning and gender bias, exploring the nuanced challenges and opportunities that arise at the intersection of these two domains. Traditionally, investment decisions have been shaped by historical data, human intuition, and established industry practices. However, the advent of ML technologies has introduced algorithms that can analyze massive datasets, identify patterns, and execute trades at speeds beyond human capability. In the pursuit of optimizing investment portfolios, it becomes imperative to scrutinize how these algorithms interact with and potentially perpetuate gender biases prevalent in the financial landscape (Mahapatra et al., 2015). The concept of gender bias in investment behavior extends beyond the unequal representation of men and women in the financial sector. Based on various cognitive psychological research, overconfidence has been described as the overestimation of one's own abilities in different areas or contexts (Shah and Malik, 2021). It encompasses the complex interplay of societal stereotypes, historical disparities, and systemic biases that may manifest in machine learning models. As algorithms rely on historical data for training, they risk inheriting and even amplifying biases present in that data. Consequently, understanding the challenges posed by gender bias in ML-driven investment becomes paramount for developing ethical and inclusive financial systems.

This chapter aims to unravel the multifaceted dimensions of this issue by examining the pivotal role of machine learning in shaping investment behavior. From the mechanics of algorithmic trading to the underlying challenges of data bias and model interpretability, we navigate the evolving landscape where technological innovation intersects with social dynamics. Moreover, we explore opportunities to mitigate gender biases, emphasizing the importance of ethical AI practices and fostering diversity and inclusion within the financial and technological spheres. As we embark on this exploration, it is crucial to recognize that the intersection of machine learning and gender bias is not only an academic pursuit but a societal imperative. By unraveling the complexities of this relationship, we hope to contribute to the ongoing dialogue on creating financial systems that are not only efficient and profitable but also equitable and inclusive for all.

15.2 UNDERSTANDING GENDER BIAS IN INVESTMENT BEHAVIOR

Investment behavior, a complex interplay of individual decision-making, market dynamics, and historical trends, has long been influenced by societal factors, including gender biases (Alrabadi et al., 2018). Historically, women have been underrepresented in the financial sector, a phenomenon that has contributed to the perpetuation of stereotypes and biases. Investees may be wary of female fund managers for two major reasons: (irrational) prejudice against female fund managers as a result of gender bias (e.g., Becker, 1971) and (rational) statistical discrimination (e.g., Phelps, 1972). As ML algorithms increasingly take center stage in investment strategies, it becomes imperative to scrutinize the ways in which these technologies may interact with and potentially exacerbate gender biases ingrained in financial decision-making. There are visible differences in risk aversion and overconfidence based on gender differences, but such differences do not show any statistically significant results (Shaikh et al., 2019).

15.2.1 DATA-DRIVEN DECISION MAKING

Machine learning algorithms thrive on data, particularly historical datasets that encapsulate the intricacies of financial markets over time. However, these datasets may carry the imprints of historical biases and gender disparities. If women are historically underrepresented in investment decisions or subjected to biased evaluations, the algorithms trained on such data may inadvertently perpetuate these biases. This raises questions about the fairness and inclusivity of the investment models being developed.

15.2.2 ALGORITHMIC TRADING AND MARKET DYNAMICS

Algorithmic trading, a paradigm increasingly powered by machine learning, introduces a new dimension to market dynamics. These algorithms operate at speeds that surpass human capabilities, executing trades in microseconds based on real-time market information. The concern arises when considering the impact of algorithmic trading on existing gender biases. Does the speed and efficiency of these algorithms amplify existing inequalities, or can they be harnessed to promote fairness in market transactions? Understanding the intricate relationship between algorithmic trading and gender bias is crucial for developing a financial ecosystem that is both efficient and equitable.

15.3 CHALLENGES OF GENDER BIAS IN MACHINE LEARNING MODELS

15.3.1 DATA BIAS

The foundation of machine learning models lies in the data used for training. If this data reflects biased investment decisions, it can perpetuate and even amplify gender biases. For instance, if historical investment data undervalues women-led businesses or disproportionately favors male investors, the resulting models may unknowingly perpetuate these imbalances. Addressing data bias requires a meticulous examination of datasets to ensure they are diverse, representative, and free from systemic biases.

15.3.2 MODEL INTERPRETABILITY

Many machine learning models, especially complex ones like neural networks, operate as "black boxes" that lack transparency in their decision-making processes. Understanding how these models arrive at certain predictions, particularly in relation to gender bias, is essential. The opacity of these models can pose challenges in identifying and rectifying biases, necessitating the development of interpretable models that allow for scrutiny and accountability.

In unraveling the challenges posed by gender bias in machine learning models, it becomes evident that a nuanced understanding of both financial dynamics and societal influences is essential. By addressing data biases and enhancing model interpretability, the financial industry can pave the way for investment strategies that are not only profitable but also just and inclusive. The journey toward mitigating gender bias in investment behavior is a multifaceted one that requires collaboration between technologists, financiers, and advocates for diversity and inclusion.

15.4 THE ROLE OF MACHINE LEARNING IN INVESTMENT

The integration of ML into the investment landscape has transformed traditional approaches, ushering in an era of data-driven decision-making, predictive analytics, and algorithmic trading. As financial institutions increasingly rely on advanced technologies, understanding the profound impact of machine learning on investment strategies becomes paramount. Few studies have focused on how to reduce gender bias during the resume screening process (Deshpande et al., 2020), in machine learning models (Feldman and Peake, 2021), and in facial recognition systems (Dhar, 2020).

15.4.1 DATA-DRIVEN DECISION MAKING

15.4.1.1 HARNESSING HISTORICAL DATA

Machine learning algorithms thrive on large datasets, particularly historical financial data. These datasets encapsulate a wealth of information, including market trends, asset performances, and economic indicators. ML algorithms leverage this historical data to identify patterns, correlations, and anomalies, enabling them to make predictions and inform investment decisions. This shift towards data-driven decision-making has the potential to enhance the accuracy and efficiency of investment strategies.

15.4.1.2 RISK ASSESSMENT AND PORTFOLIO OPTIMIZATION

ML algorithms excel in assessing risks associated with various investment opportunities. By analyzing historical market behaviors, these algorithms can identify potential risks and formulate strategies to mitigate them. Additionally, machine learning contributes to portfolio optimization by dynamically adjusting asset allocations based on real-time market conditions (Kashif et al., 2017). This adaptive approach enhances the resilience of investment portfolios against market fluctuations. Mutual fund investors direct significantly less money to female-managed funds (Niessen-Ruenzi and Ruenzi, 2019).

15.4.2 ALGORITHMIC TRADING AND MARKET DYNAMICS

15.4.2.1 REAL-TIME DECISION MAKING

Algorithmic trading, a subset of machine learning applications in finance, involves the use of pre-defined algorithms to execute trades automatically.

These algorithms operate at speeds far exceeding human capacity, allowing for real-time decision-making in response to market changes. The speed and efficiency of algorithmic trading contribute to increased liquidity and reduced transaction costs, revolutionizing the dynamics of financial markets.

15.4.2.2 MARKET EFFICIENCY AND LIQUIDITY

Machine learning in investment contributes to market efficiency by processing vast amounts of information quickly and accurately. This efficiency enhances liquidity as algorithmic traders provide continuous buying and selling, narrowing bid-ask spreads and facilitating smoother market transactions. However, it also raises questions about whether these algorithms unintentionally contribute to market volatility or exacerbate existing inequalities.

15.4.3 CHALLENGES OF MACHINE LEARNING IN INVESTMENT

15.4.3.1 DATA QUALITY AND BIAS

The success of machine learning models relies heavily on the quality of the data used for training. Issues such as incomplete data, inaccuracies, or inherent biases in historical datasets can lead to suboptimal predictions and investment strategies (Mittal, 2022). Recognizing and addressing these challenges is essential to ensure the reliability and fairness of machine learning applications in finance.

15.4.3.2 MODEL COMPLEXITY AND INTERPRETABILITY

As machine learning models, especially deep neural networks, become more complex, their decision-making processes often become opaque or difficult to interpret. The lack of model interpretability raises concerns about accountability, ethical considerations, and the potential for unintentional biases. Striking a balance between model complexity and interpretability is a critical challenge in the development and deployment of machine learning in investment.

In conclusion, the role of machine learning in investment is transformative, offering unprecedented opportunities for data-driven decision-making and algorithmic efficiency. However, as financial institutions navigate this technological frontier, addressing challenges related to data quality, bias, and model interpretability is paramount. A thoughtful and ethical integration of machine learning in investment practices has the potential to revolutionize financial markets while ensuring fairness, transparency, and accountability.

15.5 CHALLENGES OF GENDER BIAS IN MACHINE LEARNING MODELS

As ML models play an increasingly pivotal role in shaping decision-making processes, concerns about the perpetuation of gender biases have come to the forefront. The challenges associated with gender bias in ML models are multifaceted, spanning issues related to biased training data, model complexity, and interpretability. Addressing these challenges is crucial to ensuring that machine learning technologies contribute to fair and equitable outcomes rather than reinforcing existing societal inequalities.

15.5.1 DATA BIAS

15.5.1.1 HISTORICAL DISPARITIES

One of the primary challenges in mitigating gender bias in ML models lies in the historical disparities present in training data. If historical data reflects gender-based stereotypes, discriminatory practices, or skewed representations, the resulting models may inadvertently perpetuate these biases. For instance, if training data predominantly features male-led businesses or reflects traditional gender roles in financial transactions, the ML model may not generalize well to diverse and inclusive scenarios.

15.5.1.2 REPRESENTATION AND DIVERSITY

Ensuring representation and diversity in training data is essential for combating gender bias. Inadequate representation of women, non-binary individuals, or diverse gender identities can lead to skewed outcomes. A lack of diversity in the data hampers the model's ability to generalize across different demographic groups, reinforcing existing biases rather than adapting to a more inclusive understanding of gender dynamics in financial contexts.

15.5.2 MODEL COMPLEXITY AND INTERPRETABILITY

15.5.2.1 BLACK BOX MODELS

Many advanced ML models, especially deep learning models, operate as "black boxes" whose internal workings are challenging to interpret. The lack of transparency in decision-making processes makes it difficult to discern how and why a model arrived at a particular prediction. In the context of gender bias, this opacity raises concerns about the unintentional encoding and propagation of biases within the model.

15.5.2.2 EXPLAINABILITY AND ACCOUNTABILITY

The interpretability of ML models is essential for ensuring accountability and understanding the factors contributing to a model's decisions. Establishing explainability mechanisms allows stakeholders to trace back the decision-making process and identify potential biases. Lack of explainability can hinder efforts to recognize, rectify, and prevent gender bias, making it crucial to strike a balance between model complexity and interpretability (Kashif et al., 2023).

15.5.3 INTERSECTIONALITY AND CONTEXT SENSITIVITY

15.5.3.1 INTERSECTIONAL BIASES

Addressing gender bias in ML models requires an understanding of intersectionality—the interconnected nature of social categorizations such as gender, race, and socioeconomic status. Failing to account for intersectional biases can lead to a narrow view of gender dynamics, overlooking the unique challenges faced by individuals with intersecting identities. Ensuring models are sensitive to the complexity of human experiences is essential for creating inclusive and fair predictions.

15.5.3.2 CONTEXT SENSITIVITY

ML models must be context-sensitive to adapt to diverse social and cultural contexts. Gender norms and expectations can vary significantly across different regions and communities. Models that lack sensitivity to these contextual variations may inadvertently perpetuate biases or fail to recognize the unique factors influencing gender dynamics in specific environments.

In conclusion, the challenges of gender bias in ML models require a comprehensive and interdisciplinary approach. From addressing data bias and ensuring diversity in training datasets to enhancing model interpretability and considering intersectionality, researchers, developers, and policymakers must collaborate to create machine learning systems that contribute to a more equitable and inclusive society. Recognizing and actively mitigating gender bias in ML models is not only a technological imperative but a step towards building a fair and just future for all.

15.6 OPPORTUNITIES FOR ADDRESSING GENDER BIAS IN INVESTMENT BEHAVIOR

As concerns about gender bias in investment behavior grow, there are significant opportunities to address these issues through proactive measures and ethical considerations. Tackling gender bias in the context of machine learning and investment involves a combination of technological, organizational, and societal approaches (Olsen, 2001).

15.6.1 ETHICAL AI PRACTICES

15.6.1.1 FAIRNESS METRICS AND EVALUATION

Incorporating fairness metrics during the development and evaluation of machine learning models is a crucial step in addressing gender bias. By quantifying and assessing the fairness of predictions across different gender groups, developers can identify and rectify biases that may be present in the models (Singh et al., 2023). Regularly updating and refining these metrics ensures ongoing efforts to mitigate bias in investment-related predictions.

15.6.1.2 BIAS DETECTION AND MITIGATION

Implementing robust mechanisms for detecting and mitigating biases within machine learning models is essential. These mechanisms can include pre-processing techniques to balance dataset representations, in-processing algorithms to adjust model predictions, and post-processing methods to rectify biased outcomes. Continuous monitoring and improvement of these processes contribute to creating more equitable investment models.

15.6.2 DIVERSITY AND INCLUSION IN FINANCE AND TECHNOLOGY

15.6.2.1 FOSTERING A CULTURE OF INCLUSIVITY

Promoting diversity and inclusion within the finance and technology sectors is a fundamental opportunity for addressing gender bias. By creating an inclusive workplace culture, organizations can ensure that diverse perspectives, including those related to gender, are integrated into the development and deployment of machine learning models. A diverse workforce can bring a range of experiences that help in identifying and rectifying biases.

15.6.2.2 DIVERSE STAKEHOLDER ENGAGEMENT

Engaging diverse stakeholders, including investors, users, and experts, in the development and assessment of machine learning models enhances the chances of identifying and addressing gender bias. Creating forums for open discussions and feedback loops involving individuals from different backgrounds and experiences contributes to a more comprehensive understanding of potential biases and their impact.

15.6.3 EDUCATION AND AWARENESS

15.6.3.1 TRAINING ON GENDER BIAS

Providing education and training on gender bias is essential for professionals working in the fields of finance and technology. Ensuring that developers, data scientists, and decision-makers are aware of the potential biases and their consequences enables them to make informed decisions during the development and deployment of machine learning models.

15.6.3.2 RAISING AWARENESS AMONG USERS

Investors and end-users of machine learning applications should be made aware of the potential biases inherent in these models. Transparent communication about the limitations and potential impact of gender bias in investment predictions empowers users to critically assess and contextualize the information provided by these models.

15.6.4 REGULATORY FRAMEWORKS

15.6.4.1 INCENTIVES FOR FAIRNESS AND INCLUSION

Establishing regulatory frameworks that incentivize fairness and inclusion in machine learning models can be a powerful tool. Governments and regulatory bodies can encourage organizations to prioritize ethical considerations in their algorithms by providing benefits or imposing penalties based on the fairness and inclusivity of their models.

15.6.4.2 AUDITING AND ACCOUNTABILITY

Implementing auditing processes for machine learning models can ensure ongoing compliance with ethical standards. Organizations can be held accountable for the impact of their models, and audits can serve as a mechanism for identifying and rectifying biases. Transparent reporting on the steps taken to address gender bias enhances accountability and trust.

In conclusion, the opportunities for addressing gender bias in investment behavior are manifold, requiring a holistic approach that combines technological advancements, organizational initiatives, educational efforts, and regulatory frameworks. By embracing these opportunities, stakeholders can work collaboratively towards creating a financial landscape that is not only technologically advanced but also fair, inclusive, and respectful of diverse gender perspectives.

15.7 CONCLUSION

In the evolving intersection of machine learning and investment behavior, the recognition and mitigation of gender bias emerge as imperative facets of building a fair and inclusive financial landscape. As explored throughout this chapter, the challenges posed by gender bias in machine learning models necessitate a comprehensive and proactive approach. However, the opportunities to address these challenges present a roadmap towards creating a more equitable financial ecosystem.

The infusion of ethical AI practices stands out as a pivotal opportunity. By incorporating fairness metrics, bias detection, and mitigation techniques into the development and deployment of machine learning models, stakeholders can systematically work towards minimizing gender biases. Regular assessments, adjustments, and transparency in the evaluation process contribute to fostering trust and accountability.

Diversity and inclusion serve as powerful catalysts in this journey. Fostering a culture of inclusivity within the finance and technology sectors not only ensures a broader range of perspectives in the development process but also creates an environment where potential biases can be identified and rectified collaboratively. Engaging diverse stakeholders, including investors and experts, reinforces the commitment to addressing gender bias comprehensively.

Education and awareness play a crucial role in empowering professionals and end-users alike. Providing training on gender bias to those involved in the development of machine learning models enables informed decision-making. Simultaneously, raising awareness among investors and users about the limitations and potential biases in these models encourages critical evaluation and interpretation of their predictions.

Regulatory frameworks emerge as a regulatory opportunity to drive change. Governments and regulatory bodies can incentivize organizations to prioritize fairness and inclusion in their algorithms. Implementing auditing processes ensures ongoing compliance, and transparent reporting fosters accountability, making organizations responsible for the impact of their models on gender bias.

In conclusion, the journey towards addressing gender bias in investment behavior through machine learning is a multifaceted one. It requires collaboration among researchers, practitioners, policymakers, and advocates for diversity and inclusion. By embracing the outlined opportunities, stakeholders can not only harness the power of machine learning for optimal investment strategies but also contribute to the creation of a financial landscape that upholds principles of fairness, transparency, and inclusivity for all individuals, regardless of gender. As the financial industry continues to evolve, the commitment to mitigating gender bias remains essential for building a future where technology serves as an enabler of equity and justice.

15.8 FUTURE PROSPECTS

The future prospects of addressing gender bias in machine learning-driven investment behavior hold promising opportunities for transformative change. As technology continues to advance and societal awareness grows, several key trends and directions emerge that pave the way for a more inclusive and equitable financial landscape.

15.8.1 ADVANCED FAIRNESS MEASURES

The ongoing refinement of fairness measures within machine learning models offers a promising avenue. Future developments may include more sophisticated algorithms for detecting and mitigating gender biases, ensuring a nuanced understanding of diverse contexts and intersections of identity. These advanced measures will contribute to the continual improvement of models, making them more attuned to the complexities of gender dynamics.

15.8.2 EXPLAINABLE AI AND INTERPRETABILITY

Advancements in explainable AI (XAI) represent a crucial trajectory for the future. As machine learning models become more complex, efforts to enhance interpretability will be essential. Future models are likely to integrate interpretable features, enabling stakeholders to understand the decision-making processes and identify potential biases more effectively. This transparency will be instrumental in building trust and ensuring accountability.

15.8.3 INCLUSIVE DATA COLLECTION

The future holds promise in terms of more inclusive data collection practices. Efforts to address data bias may involve intentional strategies to diversify datasets, ensuring adequate representation of various gender identities and experiences. Collaborative initiatives between the financial sector, tech industry, and advocacy groups may lead to the creation of comprehensive, unbiased datasets that form the foundation for fair and inclusive machine learning models.

15.8.4 AUGMENTED HUMAN DECISION-MAKING

While machine learning augments decision-making processes, the future may witness a more synergistic approach between machines and human expertise. Combining the analytical capabilities of machine learning with human judgment and ethical considerations could lead to more balanced, informed, and socially responsible investment decisions. This collaborative approach has the potential to mitigate biases and create a more holistic investment strategy.

15.8.5 ETHICAL AI REGULATION

Anticipating the importance of ethical AI, future regulatory frameworks are likely to become more sophisticated. Governments and regulatory bodies may institute stricter guidelines for fairness, transparency, and accountability in machine learning applications, including those within the financial sector. The establishment of clear ethical standards will incentivize organizations to prioritize gender-inclusive practices.

15.8.6 GLOBAL COLLABORATIONS AND STANDARDS

Given the global nature of finance and technology, future prospects involve increased international collaborations to establish standardized practices for mitigating gender bias. Collaborative efforts between countries, organizations, and research institutions can facilitate the development of shared best practices, ensuring a consistent and inclusive approach to machine learning in investment on a global scale.

15.8.7 CONTINUOUS EDUCATION AND AWARENESS

The future will likely see a continued emphasis on education and awareness programs. Integrating courses on ethics and bias mitigation in machine learning into educational curricula for data scientists, developers, and financial professionals will be essential. These programs will cultivate a generation of professionals equipped with the knowledge and skills to navigate and address gender bias in technology.

15.8.8 TECH-ENABLED FINANCIAL INCLUSION

As machine learning becomes more adept at understanding and addressing biases, it has the potential to drive financial inclusion. Future prospects involve leveraging technology to create personalized and accessible financial services that cater to diverse needs, thus reducing disparities in investment opportunities and outcomes across gender lines.

In conclusion, the future prospects of addressing gender bias in machine learning-driven investment behavior offer a hopeful vision of progress and inclusivity. By combining technological advancements, regulatory frameworks, global collaborations, and ongoing education, stakeholders can shape a future where machine learning not only optimizes investment strategies but also actively contributes to a financial landscape that is fair, transparent, and respectful of diverse gender perspectives. As these trends unfold, the finance and technology sectors have the opportunity to pioneer positive change, setting the stage for a more equitable and inclusive future.

KEYWORDS

- **algorithmic trading**
- **artificial intelligence**
- **data bias**
- **financial systems**
- **gender bias**
- **investment behavior**
- **machine learning**

REFERENCES

Alrabadi, D. W. H., Al-Abdallah, S. Y., & Aljarayesh, N. I. A. (2018). Behavioral biases and investment performance: Does gender matter? Evidence from Amman Stock Exchange. *Jordan Journal of Economic Sciences, 5*(1), 77–92.

Deshpande, K. V., Pan, S., & Foulds, J. R. (2020). Mitigating demographic bias in AI-based resume filtering. In *Adjunct Publication of the 28th ACM Conference on User Modeling, Adaptation and Personalization* (pp. 268–275). July 2020. https://doi.org/10.1145/3386392.3399569. Available at: https://dl.acm.org/doi/10.1145/3386392.3399569 (accessed on 17 January 2025).

Kashif, M., Kumar, P., Ghai, S., & Kumar, S. (2023). Disruptive technologies in computational finance. In *Algorithmic Approaches to Financial Technology: Forecasting, Trading, and Optimization* (pp. 46–60). IGI Global.

Kashif, M., Thiyagarajan, S., & Sridharan, P. (2017). Dynamics of Algeria's international reserves. *African Journal of Economic and Management Studies, 8*(4), 410–419.

Mahapatra, M. S., & Mehta, S. (2015). Behavioral finance: A study on gender-based dilemma in making investment decisions. *Sumedha Journal of Management, 4*(1), 4–16.

Mittal, S. K. (2022). Behavior biases and investment decisions: Theoretical and research framework. *Qualitative Research in Financial Markets, 14*(2), 213–228.

Niessen-Ruenzi, A., & Ruenzi, S. (2019). Sex matters: Gender bias in the mutual fund industry. *Management Science, 65*(7), 3001–3025.

Olsen, R. A., & Cox, C. M. (2001). The influence of gender on the perception and response to investment risk: The case of professional investors. *The Journal of Psychology and Financial Markets, 2*(1), 29–36.

Phelps, E. S. (1972). The statistical theory of racism and sexism. *The American Economic Review, 62*(4), 659–661.

Shah, I., & Malik, I. R. (2021). The impact of overconfidence, loss aversion, and regret aversion on investors' trading frequency: Empirical evidence of Pakistan Stock Exchange. *Journal of Managerial Sciences, 15*(1), Jan-Mar 2021. Available at SSRN: https://ssrn.com/abstract=3802443 (accessed on 17 January 2025).

Shaikh, G. M., Karim Katpar, N., Kalhoro, M., Abro, Y. K., & Phanwar, G. A. (2019). Do behavioral biases in gender differences affect investment decisions? *Sociology International Journal, 3*(4), 326–336.

Singh, A., Taneja, S., & Kumar, P. (2023). Algorithmic approaches to financial technology: Forecasting, trading, and optimization. In *Algorithmic Approaches to Financial Technology: Forecasting, Trading, and Optimization.* https://doi.org/10.4018/9798369317464. Available at: https://www.igi-global.com/book/algorithmic-approaches-financial-technology/329966#:~:text=of%20computational%20finance.-,Algorithmic%20Approaches%20to%20Financial%20Technology%3A%20Forecasting%2C%20Trading%2C%20and%20Optimization,and%20algorithms%20in%20financial%20operations (accessed on 17 January 2025).

Index

D

H

I

N

For Product Safety Concerns and Information please contact our EU representative GPSR@taylorandfrancis.com
Taylor & Francis Verlag GmbH, Kaufingerstraße 24, 80331 München, Germany

www.ingramcontent.com/pod-product-compliance
Lightning Source LLC
LaVergne TN
LVHW020627300926
849161LV00004B/629

* 9 7 8 1 9 9 8 5 1 1 2 2 8 *